T0279491

Advance F

"Any clinician or educator working with sincere, confused men left bewildered and concerned needs this book. Anyone working with the myriads of women who have been harassed or molested needs this book. Anyone looking at the impact of inappropriate behavior on families and on the culture—in a word, anyone who takes the #MeToo groundswell seriously should read this engaging, well thought-out guide to today's sexually perplexed. An essential addition to the field."

—**Terry Real**, LICSW, author of *The New Rules of Marriage*

"David Wexler and Holly Sweet courageously explore the severity continuum (less harmful/noncriminal to very harmful/criminal) that underlies sexual misconduct, drawing implications for counseling women and men. They skillfully describe the sociocultural contexts (e.g., gender role norms, societal power structures) that create and impact the perpetrators and victims whose experiences fall on the noncriminal end of the continuum. Grounded in this sociocultural analysis, their case studies impart important insights for connecting with these men and for helping them challenge their internalized gender role norms and associated behaviors. This book also examines how men's and women's lives intersect around sexual misconduct issues and how they can work together to reduce societal sexism. Wexler and Sweet apply their combined decades of counseling to create a must-read resource for all therapists who work with men and men's issues."

—**Pam Remer, Ph. D.**, Counseling Psychology, Emerita Faculty, University of Kentucky, Licensed Counseling Psychologist, Commonwealth of Kentucky, author of *Feminist Perspectives in Therapy: Empowering Diverse Women*

"In the rapidly growing culture of the #MeToo environment, the nuances and complexities of the issues on both sides of #MeToo circumstances, genders, and treatment issues have never been more critical than they are right now. Our society is at an apex with this issue that education can help correct patterns of behavior that have harmed so many and help heal survivors and uninformed offenders as well. But to do that, we have to understand the differentiation in offenders—their typologies and motivations, the insidious ways that this malady has hidden in our spoken and unspoken beliefs. Change IS here, and as brave victims step forward with more disclosures, we have to steer this climate towards education and healing in which this book is our template and guide."

—**Sandra L. Brown, M.A.**, author of *Women Who Love Psychopaths: Inside the Relationships of Inevitable Harm with Psychopaths, Sociopaths, and Narcissists*; *Counseling Victims of Violence: A Handbook for Helping Professionals*; and *How to Spot a Dangerous Man Before You Get Involved*

"This timely resource informs psychotherapists that #youtoo are responsible to learn the continuum of sexual misconduct that has been too often avoided within our clinical settings. A plethora of diverse clinical examples along with many specific suggestions provide a solid foundation for improving the mental, physical, gender and sexual health of our clients."

—**Douglas Braun-Harvey, MFT, CST**, The Harvey Institute, coauthor of *Treating Out of Control Sexual Behavior: Rethinking Sex Addiction*

#METOO-INFORMED THERAPY

A Norton Professional Book

#METOO-INFORMED THERAPY

Counseling Approaches for Men, Women, and Couples

DAVID B. WEXLER
HOLLY B. SWEET

W. W. NORTON & COMPANY
Independent Publishers Since 1923

This book is intended as a general information resource for professionals practicing in the field of psychotherapy and mental health. It is not a substitute for appropriate training, peer review, and/or clinical supervision. Standards of clinical practice and protocol vary in different practice settings and change over time. No technique or recommendation is guaranteed to be safe or effective in all circumstances, and neither the publisher nor the author(s) can guarantee the complete accuracy, efficacy, or appropriateness of any particular recommendation in every respect or in all settings or circumstances.

All case subjects described in this book are composites. Any URLs displayed in this book link or refer to websites that existed as of press time. The publisher is not responsible for, and should not be deemed to endorse or recommend, any website other than its own or any content that it did not create. The author, also, is not responsible for any third-party material.

Copyright © 2021 by David B. Wexler and Holly B. Sweet
"Two Truths: The Need for Intersectional Awareness"
copyright © 2021 by Leona Smith Di Faustino

All rights reserved
Printed in the United States of America
First Edition

For information about permission to reproduce selections from this book, write to Permissions, W. W. Norton & Company, Inc., 500 Fifth Avenue, New York, NY 10110

For information about special discounts for bulk purchases, please contact W. W. Norton Special Sales at specialsales@wwnorton.com or 800-233-4830

Manufacturing by Sheridan Books
Production manager: Katelyn MacKenzie

ISBN: 978-0-393-71466-1 (pbk.)

W. W. Norton & Company, Inc., 500 Fifth Avenue, New York, N.Y. 10110
www.wwnorton.com

W. W. Norton & Company Ltd., 15 Carlisle Street, London W1D 3BS

1 2 3 4 5 6 7 8 9 0

To all the brave survivors who have spoken up,
and to all the women and men who care.

Contents

Part II: FINDING SOLUTIONS: POSITIVE STRATEGIES FOR CLINICIANS AND EDUCATORS

Acknowledgments

Many thanks to Deborah Malmud of Norton Professional Books, who first approached us with the idea about a book to help all of us understand the impact of #MeToo issues on our clinical work with women, men, and couples, and to Sara McBride Tuohy, Mariah Eppes, and Marne Evans, who shaped and edited this project. It has been a pleasure to work with this team.

Special, special thanks to Leona Smith Di Faustino, LCSW, who contributed such valuable perspectives to our understanding of how #MeToo offenses are especially complex for people of color and the LGBTQ+ population (see Chapter 5).

Many of our trusted colleagues have given their time and wisdom generously to reviewing early drafts of our work and contributed their ideas and encouragement: Alan Berkowitz, Doug Braun-Harvey, Sandra Brown, Cori Colkins, Michele Harway, Elyssa Klann, Judith Logue, Ryan McKelley, Fredric Rabinowitz, Terry Real, Sara Schapiro, Marianne Tamulevich, and Joel Wong.

Other colleagues graciously contributed their clinical experiences dealing with #MeToo issues and helped us shape our thoughts and clinical applications—thank you to Connie Brunig, Bill Eddy, Jonathan Gale, Karen Hyland, and Joel Lazar.

Thanks to our many colleagues at the Society for the Psychological Study of Men and Masculinities, Division 51 of the American Psychological Association, who helped us think through male gender roles as they apply to #MeToo behavior.

A special shout-out goes to the many women and men who have participated over the years in MIT classes, seminars, and workshops directed at understanding how gender roles might contribute to #MeToo behavior. Some of them have gone on to conduct workshops for undergraduates on how to reduce #MeToo behavior on campus through experiential education.

And, finally, thank you to all the women and men who have spoken out over the last few years and those who have spoken out before—especially Tarana Burke, who coined the term "Me Too" in 2006 and has worked so hard for many years to help victims become survivors and raise the consciousness of all. It takes a village.

Preface

As the #MeToo movement exploded into national consciousness in 2017, we saw and heard more and more stories of men being forced to self-examine, women speaking up, and couples tackling issues that had never quite emerged before. A book needed to be written to help counselors find ways to constructively address #MeToo behavior in their therapy sessions.

Some of our colleagues have told us that we would get into trouble for trying to write a book on the #MeToo movement in these volatile times. Everybody knew that, no matter how respectful, nuanced, and careful we were, we were bound to alienate some readers: those who would believe we were apologists for male predators, or that we were not calling out women who remained silent, or that we were "blaming the victim" by asking women to take a more assertive stance wherever possible, or that we believed too easily that there were women who unfairly accused men, or that we were putting too much of a burden on women to help educate men about how to act. Because of the importance of the issues raised, however, we were willing to write a book that might stir up controversy, believing it is better to engage in difficult dialogues than shy away from them.

DAVID: *As a man, I feel a sense of collective responsibility. Like many other men I knew, the #MeToo stories started me scouring though my past for incidents where I might have made a woman uncomfortable, crossed a line that I didn't realize was there, or didn't care because I was young, male, and stupid. And, like many other men, I became determined to utilize everything I knew about how men think, feel, and act to help wake myself and other men up.*

> **HOLLY:** *As the #MeToo movement began to gain traction, I found myself remembering the experiences I have had, as a woman, where I accepted the status quo that men were more valuable than women, that men had a right to put down women or take advantage of them sexually. I remembered all the stories I heard for many years from students, clients, and friends about the sexual misconduct they suffered at the hands of men, from clumsy contact to near rape. Most of all, I remembered the value of helping women to be more assertive, to become survivors and not victims, to be in control and not controlled, and to harness personal and collective power. I wasn't always on the front line of feminist political action, but I did what I could to help women speak up.*

The two of us have collectively spent decades as clinicians in the trenches confronting men and helping them heal, and helping women recover from sexual misconduct and become more empowered. We have navigated the fine line between addressing clearly unacceptable behavior by men and expressing compassion (most of the time) for the better person within a man who has violated a woman's sexual boundaries. We have worked with women who have been victims of sexual misconduct, encouraging and supporting them in their efforts to deal successfully with the consequences of "men behaving badly."

We offer you the benefit of what we have both learned from clinical experience, from the research we have been influenced by, and from what we continue to struggle with in the path towards full equality and respect between the sexes. We know that we don't know it all. We are white, straight, and privileged. We can only see what we see from our own perspectives. We are therefore grateful that we have been able to benefit from the wisdom of many colleagues who have offered their valuable perspectives about issues we may not fully understand. And we are grateful that we have been able to include at least one chapter specifically addressing the uniquely challenging #MeToo experiences for people of color or other marginalized groups, especially the LGBTQ+ population. Thank you to Leona Smith Di Faustino for her valuable contributions (see Chapter 5).

Please join us on our journey to understand and constructively work with clients who have been offenders or victims, as our culture continues to hear women's voices too long suppressed.

David B. Wexler, Ph.D.
Holly B. Sweet, Ph.D.
November 2020

Introduction

The rapid rise of the #MeToo movement has created a seismic shift in how we perceive relationships between men and women. But the scope of behaviors that fall within this category is full of gray areas for many clients, supervisors, professors, employees, and students—and for all of us counselors, therapists, and educators who are trying to guide people through this. We will look at the range of #MeToo behaviors and motivations and consequences in the gray areas that comprise sexual misconduct. It is important to note that we will not be covering criminal behavior such as rape, domestic violence or child molestation which is outside the scope of this book. These are issues that we leave to other books. They are beyond the gray areas with which we will be dealing: stupid and juvenile actions as well as more serious offenses such as noncriminal sexual assault. Still, the psychological and social conditions that generate the range of sexual misconduct that we actually are addressing permeate the environment in which criminals feel empowered to act.

We want to help men who offend or are just confused, guide women who need help recovering from or stopping harassment and finding a voice, explore ways for men to be allies in the #MeToo movement, and help couples whose relationships can be enhanced by understanding #MeToo issues.

All of us working in the roles of counselors, therapists, and educators need as much information and perspective as possible to explore the complex issues in this particular realm of gender relations in a way that empowers women and helps men be more respectful of women's boundaries.

The behaviors we are addressing under the umbrella of #MeToo include those of authority figures in power over subordinates as well as peer-to-peer sexual misconduct. They include people who might be in a position to advance (or sabotage) someone's career. While we will not be addressing every single one of these situations in our case studies, we recognize that #MeToo violations include actions by a wide variety of men not covered in our book, including military personnel, coaches, therapists, priests, ministers, rabbis, and important political figures. Most of the situations we are addressing involve actions by people who are well known to the victimized party. The situations we explore involve complex interactions and politics between the two individuals that are rarely as simple as one terrible person simply forcing himself on another.

It is important to note what we are focusing on in this book, since we cannot address all the circumstances and nuances raised by sexual misconduct. We have therefore chosen ones that we believe might appear often in a clinician's office or in any setting where counseling is taking place. These include exploring the gray areas of sexual misconduct by men towards women (not focusing on women towards women or men, or men towards men). We also chose to include female-identified people under the term "women" and male-identified people under the term "men" for the sake of simplicity (although there are certainly unique issues of sexual misconduct towards transpeople).

In this very complex field, it is tempting to adopt simplistic, black-and-white narratives about #MeToo behaviors, like the following:

- Men who harass women are all sexual predators
- Women shouldn't have to make any changes in their behavior
- Men who harass or assault women are only and always driven by needs for power
- A woman who feels traumatized has always been the victim of assault or harassment
- There are no gray areas when it comes to sexual misconduct
- Women are always powerless against men who mistreat them sexually
- Men don't have any role in the #MeToo movement
- It's irrelevant to care about WHY men are doing this—they just need to STOP!

Of course, our work would be much easier if these beliefs were actually true. But, unfortunately for all of us who prefer simplicity and clarity, these statements are not true. Or, at least, they are only partially true, and they do not apply to all situations that fall under the umbrella of #MeToo.

Our book is focused both on finding ways to empower women in confronting sexual misconduct, and on understanding and addressing the core problems of men committing sexual misconduct and its impact on women who are the recipients of that behavior. However, we are opposed to declaring a gender war. Men certainly need to be held accountable. But seeing men only as predators and women only as prey is not the way to build the better world of relationships that we all envision. The missions of holding men accountable *and* trying to engage men in a non-shaming fashion are not incompatible. They're just complicated. And they are easily misunderstood by people in many camps who will insist that the problems are simpler than they really are.

The only simple truth is that there is (and always has been) a high frequency of men engaging in sexual behaviors that are damaging to women. And, as a society and as people in the helping professions, we need to find ways for these to stop.

#METOO-INFORMED
THERAPY

Part I

UNDERSTANDING THE IMPACT OF THE #METOO MOVEMENT

Chapter 1

The Big Picture
Sexual Misconduct in Our Culture

Tarana Burke started the "Me Too" movement over 10 years ago when she encouraged girls and women of color to tell their stories of being victims of sexual assault and harassment, including rape. These stories were important not only as a form of social support from others; they also helped reveal the widespread problem of sexual harassment and assault in American culture. The movement was relatively small until October 2017, when Alyssa Milano created the hashtag #MeToo on social media. That hashtag quickly went viral and has now spread to all forms of media.

With the advent of the #MeToo movement, girls and women finally had a platform and the community support to speak out against men's harassing, abusive, and often criminal behavior. Women were activated to take power individually and collectively, insisting that a woman's voice be equal to that of a man, and that the assault on a women's psyche and body be made visible and believed. The #MeToo movement has given women the chance to speak up, be heard and supported, and to hold their offenders accountable for their actions.

The Impact of the #MeToo Movement on Our Culture

The #MeToo movement has had a powerful and positive impact on American culture, finally revealing the widespread incidents of sexual misconduct. There has been much (and long overdue) soul searching about how to prevent additional #MeToo behaviors in academia and in the workplace. Because of the #MeToo movement, the attitudes of the American public toward the sexual mistreatment of women by men have undergone a sea change. The #MeToo movement provides survivors a context to expose assaults ranging from low-level sexual misconduct by a peer (for example, making a sexually inappropriate comment) to rape by an authority figure (such as a doctor or supervisor) against whom one often has little recourse, especially if the perpetrator is well known and powerful.

In recent years, the power of the movement to topple public figures accused of sexual misconduct has risen. These men (such as Al Franken and Charlie Rose) were respected in their careers until it became clear they violated the personal boundaries of women who worked for them in demeaning ways. Questions have been raised about how power plays into sexual misconduct and how men in authority may feel they have license to take advantage of women subordinates in disrespectful and coercive ways. In egregious cases of sexual assault, such as Larry Nassar with the women's gymnastics team, Harvey Weinstein with aspiring actresses, and Jeffrey Epstein with underage girls, their sense of entitlement and power associated with their positions was used to intimidate and silence women who were, or felt, powerless to confront the perpetrator.

Sexual misconduct is not limited to positional power in the workplace. Adolescent male bonding that takes place in fraternities or high school clubs can lead to sexual disrespect and degradation of women. This disrespect is not only allowed but often ignored by authorities, prevailing in a climate where men often assume the right to treat women as sexual objects and women don't often feel like they have the right to speak out against this treatment. This attitude was seen publicly during the confirmation hearings of Supreme Court Justice Brett Kavanaugh. As a high school student, Kavanaugh belonged to a prep school culture that encouraged men to sexually harass women and assume that women deserved it or wanted it. Even if women made it clear they didn't want it, their wishes were ignored, sometimes with physical force. Worse, male students in such a culture are often encouraged by their peers to act like a "stud," having non-relational sex with women who didn't want it but who felt pressured or unable to say no.

Like Clarence Thomas before him (accused by Anita Hill of sexual harassment during his Senate hearings for the Supreme Court), Kavanaugh went on to become a Supreme Court judge, while the testimony of their accusers (Anita Hill and Christine Blasey Ford) was not seen as credible or important by the senators involved in the hearings, the large majority of them men. These senators rejected their compelling testimonies of sexual misconduct in favor of what might be considered the "old boys' network" to allow Kavanaugh and Thomas to become Supreme Court justices.

What Exactly Is Sexual Misconduct?

Determining and agreeing on what exactly qualifies as "sexual misconduct" is complicated. We do not claim to have the last word on the exact definition of the term, The term "sexual misconduct" does not have a legal meaning and covers a range of attitudes and actions that society does not universally agree upon. The ill-defined situations and nuances associated with the term can unfortunately lead to gray areas when discussing certain behaviors. Joanne Laucius, a journalist for the *Ottowa Citizen*,[1] says, "What is sexual misconduct exactly? Depends on whom you ask." Elizabeth Sheehy, the Shirley Greenberg Chair for Women and the Legal Profession, University of Ottawa, is quoted as saying "sexual misconduct is a social issue and not a fixed line . . . it's not found under criminal law, in human rights codes, or collective agreements".[2] Ally Crockford, a public educator at the Ottawa Rape Crisis Center, is quoted as saying that "sexual misconduct is a term we're seeing a lot more often. We're seeing it as a catch-all phrase for sexual behavior that we find unacceptable but we are still unclear how it should be classified. It could be any number of things—someone is made to feel uncomfortable, or they feel they are being watched or looked at in a certain way. To be honest, women know it from day-to-day life. But they can't look at it and say there's a legal definition."[3] Michelle Cottle, former contributing editor at *The Atlantic*, goes further to say, "there are almost infinite shades of creepy behavior . . . it's hard to tell where the new lines will be drawn since it is uncharted territory."[4]

This landscape is confusing and varies considerably. For example, on the university level, definitions are quite different. A few examples show how varied and sometimes vague these definitions can be. Massachusetts Institute of Technology guidelines define sexual misconduct as "a broad range of behaviors including sexual harassment, non-consensual sexual contact, non-consensual sexual penetration, rape, and sexual exploitation."[5] Duke University's definition focuses more on violence, defining sexual misconduct as "sex/gender-based harassment, sex/gender violence, sexual exploitation, relationship violence (domestic violence) and dating violence, and stalking."[6]

For the purposes of our book, we have limited our definition of #MeToo behaviors to "any misconduct of a sexual nature that is of lesser offense than a felony sexual assault (such as rape and molestation), particularly where the situation is normally non-sexual and therefore unusual for sexual behavior, or where there is some aspect of personal power or authority that makes sexual behavior inappropriate. A common theme, and the reason for the term *misconduct*, is that these violations occur during work or in a situation of power imbalance. It frames offenses which are noncriminal but nevertheless violating of another person's personal boundary in the area of sexuality and intimate personal relationships."[7] This definition includes behavior both by peers and by authority figures.

Throughout the book, we will be using the terms "sexual misconduct" and "#MeToo behaviors" interchangeably as broad categories encompassing other descriptions like "sexual boundary violations" and "sexual harassment" and "inappropriate sexual behavior." We struggled with the fact that there is no clear consensus about what "sexual misconduct" covers, and can be conflated with physically abusive or criminal behavior such as rape. Given this lack of clarity, we chose to concentrate primarily on the gray area: the many different and confusing aspects of inappropriate sexual boundary violations committed by men towards women in both personal and professional settings. It is our hope that we can help elucidate the nuances of sexual misconduct that will help both men and women better understand and change unwanted sexual behavior that is widespread in our culture.

Sexual Misconduct:
A Spectrum of Behaviors and Contexts

The many definitions of sexual misconduct make it hard to understand what we consider important distinctions: Was the boundary violation verbal or physical? If physical, was it a touch or was it penetration? Where did this misconduct take place? Who was involved? And to add to the complexity, one woman's experience of a sexual boundary violation, inappropriate behavior, or sexual harassment may be another woman's experience of friendly flirting. Every woman and every story is different. Past experience of any kind of sexual trauma or harm can be a determining variable how severely a woman is affected.

The idea that sexual misconduct is on a spectrum of behaviors is not always popular. Matt Damon found this out through reactions to his statements in an interview with Peter Travers. In the interview Damon said, "I do believe that there's a spectrum of behavior, right ? And we're going to have to figure—you know—there's a difference between patting someone on the butt and rape or child molestation, right? Both of these behaviors need to be confronted and eradicated without question, but they shouldn't be conflated, right?"[8]

In swift reaction to his comments, a tweet by Alyssa Milano on December 15, 2017 confronted this concept when she said "I have been a victim of each component of the sexual assault spectrum of which you speak. They all hurt. And they are all connected to a patriarchy intertwined with normalized, accepted, even welcome misogyny."[9] In an interview with Edward Helmore, Minnie Driver echoed this attitude in her reaction to Damon's comments saying, "I realized that most men, good men, men I love, there is a cut-off in their ability to understand . . . it's all fucking wrong and it's all bad, and until you start seeing it under one umbrella it's not your job to compartmentalize or judge what is worse and what is not."[10]

However, we *do* believe that #MeToo sexual misconduct involves a spectrum of behaviors, much as one looks at the autism spectrum disorder gradation of malfunction, from high functioning Asperger's disorder to low functioning autism, or the domestic violence continuum of verbal put-downs to massive beatings. It therefore is imperative that we categorize and contextualize these behaviors according to a rubric of factors that allow for the complexity of sexual misconduct. Treatments of victims and offenders will necessarily be different depending on some of the following factors.

1. People involved: Is it peer-to-peer (such as two students at a party) or is there a power differential (such as professor–student or supervisor–supervisee), where resisting sexual misconduct could result in a failing grade or being fired or demoted?
2. Type of behavior: Is it verbal misconduct or physical misconduct? If verbal, what does it look like? If physical, how is this defined? Is it inappropriate touching, sexual assault (nonconsensual and violent behavior), or somewhere in between?
3. Context/environment: Is it in a professional/academic setting, such as a classroom or office meeting, or in a personal context such as party or in a bar? What is the culture of that environment? Is it sexist? Male dominated? Is alcohol involved?
4. Differences in status: Is the victim from a marginalized group (a person of color, lower socioeconomic status, an immigrant, or Lesbian,

Bisexual, Gay, Transgender, Questioning (LBGTQ) and the perpetra-tor from a privileged group (such as white men in faculty positions or CEOs)? What if a woman of color is a CEO and her supervisees are white men? How does race and ethnicity, sexual orientation, gender identity, and socioeconomic status play into the difficulty women may have in speaking up or being believed if they are victims of sexual misconduct?

5. Presence of others: Did the misconduct take place alone or were there others present? If others were present, how did they respond?

For example, in the case of Chanel Miller,[11] who was raped by Brock Turner, a Stanford student she had just met at a party on campus, two passersby helped apprehend the perpetrator and supported the victim's testimony. But what if she had been alone? Would it have been reduced to a "he said, she said" scenario? Even with eyewitness testimony, Brock Turner was given a light sen-tence despite the severity of the physical sexual assault. Why was this done? If he had been a man of color and she a white woman, would it have played out differently in terms of jail time?

6. Resources: Does the victim have or know of available resources that handle suspected cases of sexual misconduct, such as company human resources or campus crisis centers ? What if the sexual mis-conduct takes place in a social setting or a work setting without clear channels to report misconduct? To whom does the victim appeal?

7. Capacity of individuals involved handling the situation: Was the woman intoxicated to the point where she was not unable to give con-sent? Was she underage? Did she have a mental or developmental disability? Was she suffering from severe depression or acute anxi-ety? What about the offender? Was his condition such that he can't remember what he did? What responsibility does he have in terms of his behavior? What responsibility does the victim have in setting clear personal boundaries?

These are factors that clinicians and counselors may face when working with men and women where issues of sexual misconduct are present. It is often the gray areas encountered in the varieties and circumstances of reported sex-ual misconduct that make it challenging to deal with effectively in therapy.

Complex Issues Associated With the #MeToo Movement

To further complicate matters (or make them more interesting, depending on your perspective), the following issues make therapy additionally challenging. We know that many men (often in positions of power) have engaged in damaging behaviors toward many women. But, however important and necessary the #MeToo movement has been and continues to be, there are several issues surrounding the movement that leave many men and women confused. As these issues are addressed in constructive ways, the #MeToo movement will gain more power and will positively alter how women are treated in this culture.

1. Social Media Tends to Tell Only One Side of the Story

Women who tell their stories of sexual misconduct on social media are often women who have been victims of men who have abused them. While this is certainly true in most cases of #MeToo stories, it skews public perception in the direction of women as powerless victims and men as powerful aggressors. There is no counterpart to good men trying their best to work and socialize with women in appropriate and respectful ways. There is no "#WeToo" movement. Therefore men are too often seen as the enemy, and good men are lumped together with offenders or sidelined; not seen as active and crucial partners in stopping sexual harassment and misconduct.

2. Not All #MeToo Behaviors Are the Same

There are important differences among #MeToo behaviors; however, those differences and definitions are unclear. For example, when does sexual misbehavior cross the line into sexual misconduct? When does sexual misconduct cross the line into sexual assault? What definition of sexual assault is being used, since definitions of sexual assault vary from state to state? It is important to see the #MeToo movement as challenging a collection of bad behaviors—all disturbing but not all criminal or violent offenses—rather than combine them all into one concept (typically seen as men sexually assaulting women).

Like degrees of murder, degrees of sexual assault vary depending on the level of violence, the perpetrator's intent and the outcomes. For example, some of the names on the supposedly secret list of "shitty media men" (which everyone in the media world has seen) are of men who appear to be merely awkward, unskilled communicators who did not intend to harm the women involved, while others are alleged to have committed deliberate acts of violence and coercion.[12]

These distinctions—and the gray areas in which many #MeToo behaviors lie—must be understood by all of us working with offenders as well as those of us working with people on the receiving end of offenses. Furthermore, #MeToo behaviors are not always male to female harassment or misconduct: Women can harass men and women, and men can harass men. Women can be *disempowered* by being perceived as victims who need excessive protections. It is important to note that women who feel shame after experiencing sexual harm could also be viewed as survivors rather than just victims, an acknowledgment that may give them a more powerful view of themselves: They didn't cause it, but they survived it. Finally, the impact of sexual misconduct is not always the same, depending on the nature of the misconduct and the background of the victim.

3. The #MeToo Backlash Can Impede a Cooperative Work and Social Environment

Awareness of #MeToo behavior is welcome and essential. However, it can also lead to men withdrawing from contact with women both personally and professionally. Attractive women may be less likely to be hired by men for certain positions in today's climate because of how men think this might be perceived. Likewise, a male boss may be reluctant to ask a younger, attractive woman to join him on a business trip for the same reasons. The Center for Talent Innovation published a study in 2018 finding that 2 in 5 men and women agreed that "recent publicity about sexual harassment at work makes it even less likely that a male leader will sponsor a female protégée even if she deserves it."[13]

Some men resort to the "old boys' club" mentality to prevent contact with women if there's a chance that their behavior may be perceived as sexist. This kind of withdrawal into men-only "networks" is a reversion back to the days when men established business connections and ran institutions—excluding women. This strategy can lead to a reversal of the ability of men and women to work together in respectful ways, to confront potential problems between the genders, and to develop joint solutions.

Furthermore, normal and previously non-offensive playfulness or flirting can be restricted in ways that none of us intended. According to a November 2017 Economist/YouGov poll,[14] 17% of Americans ages 18 to 29 now believe that a man inviting a woman out for a drink "always" or "usually" constitutes sexual harassment.

4. People Often Assume That All Women Are the Same

One of the difficulties for men is that one woman may not have the same boundaries as another. What for one woman is attractive and desirable attention (mutual flirting) may seem to another like an invasion of her boundaries. What for one woman is comfort and support by a male hand laid on her shoulder might be seen by another as inappropriate touching.

One of the variables that we must keep in mind is the possibility that a woman previously has been the victim of sexual assault or misconduct, particularly as a child when she was powerless to confront the perpetrator. The figures vary, but many women have at some point in their lives been violated sexually in a number of ways and by different people. The scars of shame and helplessness that can underlie these situations may make women less able to assert good boundaries and more susceptible to internalizing sexual misconduct as their fault.

5. Accusations Against Men *Can* Be False or Exaggerated

The most prominent studies in the field conclude that the rate of false allegations of sexual assault is somewhere between 2%–8%.[15] So, 92%–98% of women claiming assault are being honest. And, given the nature of reporting sexual assault and the harm it can do the victims, it is probably far more common that offenses go unreported for a variety of reasons (not wanting to make waves, not wanting to hurt the offender, not being believed, a sense of shame about what happened, feeling they should have done more, making public the details, etc.).

However, there are ways in which the #MeToo movement, like any movement for social change, may have gone too far, leaving men without any voice if they are falsely accused of sexual misconduct. It is possible that a small number of claims may be exaggerated and embellished because of the accuser's motives or misunderstanding of the situation.

Sometimes, men are not believed when they speak up for their side of the issue. Some men are punished too harshly for #MeToo behavior that may be unintentional and minor. In one case, a professor gave a female student a big hug in an effort to be kind and supportive when she was having a hard time academically. This behavior was seen as sexually offensive by the student. The case was taken to the dean's office and then to the Title IX office. As a result of an internal investigation, the professor was put on probation. Is this what should happen? How could the incident have turned out differently? Where does the truth lie? This is one of the trickiest elements of the #MeToo movement and one that is still a work in progress. It is therefore important that clinicians objectively review the circumstances of their male clients who have been accused of sexual misconduct—and their female clients who report sexual misconduct.

6. Men Can Be Discouraged From Having a Voice in the #MeToo Movement

In an interview with Edward Helmore, Minnie Driver says "Let the women do the speaking up right now. The time right now is for men to just listen and not have an opinion about it for once."[16] This attitude exhibits a long-standing anger at a patriarchal culture that has encouraged men's opinions to take precedence over women's. However, this attitude gets in the way of men becoming valuable allies to women who have been the victims of sexual misconduct. The attitude that men are to be seen but not heard, that men belong in the movement as passive bystanders, does a disservice to both men and women.

The home page of the #MeToo movement[17] does not include mention men who can serve as role models, men who can help make institutional changes to empower women, or men who can confront other men on harassing behavior. But the #MeToo movement must include men on any number of levels. The movement should be seen as a societal problem that damages both men and women. Men need to step up and become involved, and women must encourage them to do so. Men must be seen as allies to the #MeToo movement and an important part of reducing the incidents of sexual harassment and abuse in our culture.

The Power of the Narrative

A predator is defined as "a person or organization that uses weaker people for their own advantage."[18] A perpetrator is defined as "someone who has committed a crime or a violent or harmful act."[19] An offender is defined as "a person who commits a crime, a person or thing that does something wrong."[20]

Do we refer to those who commit sexual misconduct as predators, perpetrators, or offenders? This depends on the context and intent of the person committing the sexual offense. However, for the purposes of this book, we will focus primarily on offenders or perpetrators (as defined by their behavior and not their intent) and not predators, whose intent is clearly ruthless exploitation. The intent behind sexual misconduct and the effect it has on its victims is often the gray area that we will explore in future chapters.

In thinking through how clinicians would handle cases, it is important to hear how the client describes her experience with sexual misconduct. The term "prey" is often used in conjunction with "predator," with prey defined as "one that is helpless or unable to resist attack."[21] What does the client think of the man whom she feels has violated her sexual boundaries? How does she see herself? Does she refer to her offender as a predator, and herself as prey, helpless and unable to defend herself? Do others describe her this way? Does she see herself as a victim or as a survivor? Could she eventually see herself as confident and resourceful, moving beyond just surviving, into a place of power and control?

Words have power, and how we and our clients use them in the therapy hour can shape a narrative that can be empowering or disempowering. Depending on the client and her case, it behooves us to consider how she refers to herself and to her offender, and how we either adopt that language or perhaps reframe it to help her move out of a place of shame, helplessness, and confusion.

The effects of a traumatic experience can be mitigated or enhanced by the narrative that accompanies the memory. Clinicians and counselors who work with trauma victims often encourage clients to think of themselves as *survivors*. The last thing we want for anyone who has suffered sexual assault, misconduct, or harassment is to develop an identity of a victim, because this can generate a self-fulfilling prophecy of disempowerment.

A survivor may look back at her #MeToo experiences and blame herself for being a willing participant, or as having brought it on herself because of her provocative behavior, or as someone who now feels permanently scarred and shamed. When she thinks of the person who hurt her, scared her, or took advantage of her, she may think of him as a predator, or being "just like all men," or sometimes as a good man who made a mistake, or even as a man she still loves and can forgive. It's our job to help survivors examine their stories, and to make sure that they have a range of possible narratives so they can find the one that may actually be the best fit.

Moving Forward

In this book, we chose to focus on several types of sexual misconduct (the gray area) and not on criminal actions such as rape or child molestation. How clinicians work with clients who are violent sexual offenders or victims of violent criminal sexual behavior is a book in and of itself, but not one that we are writing. We also chose to use the term "women" to refer to any person who is female-identified, and the term "men" to refer to any man who is male-identified. Although this does not delineate the different and perhaps more extreme ways in which transwomen experience sexual misconduct, we use the terms to simplify the narratives of men sexually abusing women. We will also be focusing only on behavior among adults, defined as anyone 18 years or older.

Instead, we will look at how to work effectively with adult clients who have experienced or conducted sexual misconduct that is nonviolent in nature—including unwanted or coercive sexual contact as well as sexual harassment. We will address the damaging behavior that men generate—from the calculated to the clueless—and how to help them become better men, with a view to taking positive and proactive steps in treating and stopping sexual misconduct and sexual harassment as it arises in all contexts. We will also look at how to empower women who have experienced #MeToo behavior. It is essential for therapists to understand the difference in attitude, behaviors, and contexts of #MeToo behaviors, and approach their male and female clients in ways that reflect those differences.

The #MeToo movement has taught us that there is a serious and often invisible problem in our culture surrounding conscious or unconscious violation of varying degrees of a woman's sexual and emotional boundaries. Knowledge of and respect for these boundaries is crucial in developing healthier relationships between men and women. Men need to know what these boundaries are. Women need to be clear about their own boundaries which vary from woman to woman. Organizations and colleges need to incorporate experiential and non-shaming mixed-gender trainings in order to identify and reduce #MeToo behavior.

As clinicians, we are on the frontline of cases where things have gone wrong in the area of sex, sexuality, and intimate communication between women and men. We see men who have committed varying degrees of sexual misconduct; we also see men who are simply confused about how to proceed with women in their lives. We see women who have been sexually violated or harassed by men; we also see women who don't know how to assert themselves or aren't clear about the rights they have to their bodies; and sometimes we see women who have chosen, at great cost to themselves, to be part of a social scene where disrespect for women is rampant.

The era of #MeToo has offered us an opportunity for change in relationships between men and women, where women can be more assertive with men, and men can be more respectful of women, where they can have a true and balanced dialogue about what they want in personal and professional interaction. It is our intention that this book serve as a guide for understanding what sexual misconduct is, with all of its gradations, and how to help clients who have experienced or initiated #MeToo behaviors. The time is right for clinicians to find ways in working with their clients to encourage women to speak up and assert good boundaries, and for men to listen respectfully and act sexually with a woman only with her clear and willing consent. Clinicians and counselors can and should be at the forefront of this paradigm shift as we help clients illuminate their own actions and motives and realize the impact they have on others. Ideally, we will work together to come to a place in our culture where the issue of sexual misconduct has dwindled, where men and women are neither victims nor oppressors, but are partners in a dance of mutual respect and understanding.

Chapter 2

Socialization Matters
How Gender Roles May Foster #MeToo Behaviors

In this chapter we will look at traditional gender norms and their impact on attitudes and behavior in the area of interpersonal relationships. We pay particular attention to how norms might contribute to the issues raised by the #MeToo movement. We will challenge the use of the term "opposite sex," commonly used by the general public, and use instead the more appropriate term, "other sex." There is nothing *opposite* about men and women, in fact they are the same in uteri until testosterone begins the process of making the fetus male instead of female. Seeing men and women as opposites only encourages separation of genders into two camps that have nothing in common.

In a famous study done 50 years ago,[1] mental health professionals viewed the norms for men (what they called "the competence cluster of confidence and independence") as healthier than the norms for women (what they called "the warmth and expressive cluster of kindness and concern for others"). The assumption that male norms didn't include the warmth cluster, that women couldn't show a competence cluster, and that male norms were superior to female norms segregated men and women into different and unequal camps. John Gray wrote a popular book[2] encouraging the idea that not only are men and women different, but they are *so* different that they might come from different planets. This is not helpful when trying to understand the shared ground between men and women, or their ability to take on roles associated with the other gender.

Why Is It Important to Know About Gender Role Norms?

Gender is one of the first things we notice about children. Socialization into prevailing gender roles begins early in a child's life. As our culture reinforces those roles in myriad ways, they can become invisible. As has been said in one form or another by many people (including Einstein): "Whoever discovered water wasn't a fish." When we are surrounded by our culture and rarely step out of it, we are often unaware of how we are socialized to act and think in ways that our culture says are appropriate for men or women. We then internalize these norms as part of our core identities without questioning these assumptions.

As all of us go through a socialization process within such contexts, our worldview is largely focused through the lens of gender. The role of gender and socialization as a boy or girl in shaping how the individual views and is viewed by others is vital to our understanding of the problems our clients present. As we proceed through this chapter, it is important to delineate between gender roles, gender norms, and gender stereotypes, although they are closely tied.

Gender roles are the parts we play as male or female according to the gender norms (what we are expected to do) we have internalized (usually as young children or adolescents). Gender stereotypes are often exaggerated views about men and women should act in our culture. Gender norms reinforce stereotypes, and stereotypes reinforce norms. Too often, counselors and therapists live in a world of the individual, paying more attention to the client's psyche and how the psyche was affected by their family of origin, and paying less attention to the world in which the client lives.

As social psychologists know, the individual always exists in the context of a larger picture. This includes the world they are born into, including factors such as race, ethnicity, religion, and socioeconomic status. Although courses on the psychology of gender do exist, their focus tends to be on gender roles for women, with less attention paid to male roles. Training programs in counseling do not always address the impact of gender role norms on client issues and behavior, or how to incorporate understanding of those norms in client treatment plans. Initial clinical assessments may not include client backgrounds in terms of how gender roles have played a part in the individual's socialization.

Treatment plans rarely include an in-depth exploration of gender role socialization. In the book *Bridging Separate Gender Worlds: Why Men and Women Clash and How Therapists Can Bring Them Together*,[3] the authors tackle this issue by conducting a "gender inquiry" to "clarify the variety of ways in which gender messages are transmitted across the generations."[4] We may be unaware of how we learned to act like boys/men or girls/women. Using a gender inquiry in therapy can help therapists look at how gender roles might play into problems of sexual misconduct with which your clients dealing. Sample questions include, "Do you remember talking to either of your parents about being a girl (boy)? Which parent? What are the some of the things you learned?" and "What did you learn about how you were expected to act with boys (if a girl) or girls (if a boy) and from whom?" If you think about your own clinical training, did the idea of conducting a gender inquiry ever come up?[5]

As you read this chapter, think about how you might incorporate a gender inquiry into your clinical practice. This could be particularly relevant with clients experiencing #MeToo issues where norms might play a significant part in what happened and why.

What Are Traditional Male Gender Role Norms?

There is an old saying that little boys are made of "snips and snails and puppy dog tails" and that little girls are made of "sugar and spice and everything nice." However we interpret this meaning, it essentially tells us that boys are different from girls—that girls are sweet and nice and that boys are outdoorsy and adventurous. According to Ron Levant,[6] a driving force for males to feel fully masculine is to not be like girls in any way. From that belief springs some of the key norms that shape behavior for men from an early age. Avoiding being like a girl in attitudes and behavior constrains men from incorporating the positive aspects of traditional feminine norms into their lives (such as emotional expression, nurturing others, and being able to ask for help), and encourages them to see women as less than men. This norm is damaging to everyone. When coupled with rigid adherence to male norms, it can cause men to disrespect women and to view themselves as superior to women. Misogyny may be the norm most responsible for what we see with male clients who have acted disrespectfully toward women during sexual interactions.

With this in mind, let's consider some of the main gender role norms that shape men's beliefs and behavior. Some, such as homophobia or misogyny, are never useful and cause much damage; others are problematic when they are too rigid or one-dimensional. For example, self-reliance is a positive trait—unless it becomes a rigid belief that allows no room for healthy dependence on others. Emotional control is useful when someone is feeling challenged or threatened unless it inhibits a man from healthy, appropriate emotional expression. As outlined in a recent report from the American Psychological Association on guidelines for working with boys and men,[7] traditional male norms which are rigid and inflexible are deleterious to the emotional and physical health of males.

There is considerable information about what constitutes male norms. Two well-established clinical measures have outlined the main norms. They are the Conformity to Male Norms Inventory[8] and the Male Role Norms Inventory.[9] These measures include the following norms:

- status seeking (including success, primacy of work, winning, and competition)
- self-reliance
- emotional control (or restriction)
- aggression (or violence)
- dominance (including dominance over women)
- nonrelational sexuality (playboyism)
- negative attitudes toward homosexuals

Other norms mentioned by just one of the measures include risk-taking and avoidance of femininity.

Let's look at these norms to see how they may shape a man's behavior in terms of relationships with self and others—particularly relationships with women—and how those associations may contribute to a man's decision to engage in some form of sexual misconduct.

Be aggressive (*I will take what I want regardless of the consequences*).
This can be done in healthy ways such as sports, risk-taking in business situations, or when standing up against bullies. The definition of aggression can be negative (hostile or violent behavior or attitudes toward another, or readiness to attack or confront). Or it can be defined in more positive terms (forceful and assertive pursuit of one's aims and interests, with synonyms including boldness, vigor, and zeal). Typically, however, aggression is seen as behavior that is intended to cause either physical or verbal harm. The most obvious way that this appears as a #MeToo offense is when a man forces unwanted sexual

attitudes and behavior on a woman. This can include anything from making continual lewd comments, to threatening a woman's career advancement or to actual rape. In this context, aggression is never a useful norm.

Nonrelational sex/playboyism (*I only like hooking up*).

Sexuality is a natural human trait and one which, when done consensually, can be very positive for men and women. Rewarding and respectful sex doesn't depend on long- or short-term commitment. It doesn't have to involve love; it can be seen as play with little or no emotional connection and is acceptable if both partners are operating by the same standard. This is not #MeToo behavior. If the *only* sex a man engages in is completely nonrelational, it can lead to problems for him and his partners. Strong sexual urges that can feel insistent to a young man, along with peer pressure to be a "stud" or "player," may lead to pushing sex on a woman in an uncaring, self-centered way. She becomes just an object to satiate his sexual needs but nothing else. This can be particularly damaging when the man initially presents himself as someone genuinely interested in his female partner, but is only using her as a conquest and for his own gratification.

Emotional control/restrictive emotionality (*I can suck it up*).

This is often referred to in the literature on the psychology of men as restriction in the range of emotions, in particular, sadness, need for help, and openness. Emotional restriction can be useful if one needs to retain a "stiff upper lip" in the face of adversity. However, if anger is the only emotion that men are conditioned to express, it does not allow a man to express a range of emotions without being seen as unmanly. Controlling one's emotions is context-dependent and, generally speaking, is more useful in a professional or adverse situation than it is in personal relationships that require the man to have accessibility to a range of emotions. This norm can be detrimental for men who need to work through behavior or emotions that are getting in the way of self-esteem and healthy relationships.

It is true intimacy when one can be vulnerable (as Brené Brown has pointed out in her highly popular *TED Talk,* "The Power of Vulnerability").[10] In order to be vulnerable, one has to be able to express a full range of emotions. If men are shut down by rigid norms, they can turn to more detached erotic satisfaction instead—which can lead to exploitation and boundary violations with their partners.

Self-reliance (*I can do it myself*).

This norm can be useful in situations that require the ability to be independent and self-reliant, and not lean on others for help. However, men are often afraid of seeming weak if they ask for help in any way. This can be a serious handicap if they need help such as seeking medical attention when injured or going to therapy when they are depressed or anxious. The consequences of a rigid concept of self-reliance can lead to a number of mental and physical health issues that undermine a man's ability for good self-care.

Status seeking (*I'm striving to be the best as viewed by others*).

Being competitive and striving for success in professional relationships can be productive for a man if it is done in moderation. However, the drive to achieve status can end up as a zero-sum game: if one person is better, it is at the expense of another. Collaborative thinking and teamwork (which are often the most effective way of getting things done) are at odds with the one-upmanship that status seeking can employ. This norm can be a major contributor to #MeToo behaviors. Instead of supporting each other in forming meaningful relationships with women, men may engage in locker-room talk, competing with each other about how many women they have had sex with as a status symbol of their virility.

Dominance (*I'm in charge*).

Striving to be dominant, especially toward women, can be a lonely and dangerous game. It assumes that a man must be in charge and his needs matter the most, regardless of the needs of others. This may be one of the most salient norms that can lead to sexual misconduct by men. It encourages a man to feel entitled to take what he wants from a woman, regardless of what she wants, since he believes he is in charge of what happens. This can turn into "gaslighting" (manipulative behavior) as a way of maintaining control of the situation ("I know you want sex, if you say you don't, you really do").

Risk-taking (*I'm game for anything*).

Taking risks can be positive if tempered with prudence. The man who climbed El Capitan solo without being roped in (depicted in the documentary *Free Solo*)[11]—where one misstep is certain death—had practiced his route almost 100 times and was prepared to take risks. Risks in business such as startup companies can pay off. But risks by definition carry the possibility of negative consequences such as failure, pain and even death. Men who strive to take risks unprepared—and perhaps do them to show off—can be damaged emotionally or physically. Some #MeToo male offenders are driven by the excitement generated by the risk of getting caught, such as a doctor conducting an inappropriate and sexually abusive medical procedure on a girl with her mother in the room. This is very risky (as Nassar found out) and can result in loss of career or significant jail time. In sexual relationships, it can lead a man to have unprotected sex with a woman—risking contracting (or transmitting) a sexually transmitted disease or causing pregnancy.

Negative attitudes toward homosexuals (*I don't think gays are true men*) and avoidance of femininity (*I don't want to be like a female*).

The underlying theme of these two norms is disrespect for women and a belief that women are inferior to men. Homosexuals may be seen as feminine, and the norm here is "don't be like a woman." It leads to disrespect of men who may act in nontraditional ways or who are seen as too "feminine." The worst insult on the playground is to tell a boy that "you're throwing like a girl," or to "quit crying like a girl," or the more blunt, "don't be such a pussy." Cutting off part of one's repertoire of attitudes and behaviors limits a man's ability to be a full person. Avoiding "feminine" behavior, such as asking for help and showing one's feelings, creates a gender role conflict[12] that can be confusing and can lead to demeaning women and gay men in order to keep one's sense of being a man intact. There is nothing positive about these norms; they interfere with positive relationships. Perhaps most importantly, they contribute to lack of respect for women, which is a key ingredient in sexual misconduct and harassment.

What Are Traditional Female Gender Role Norms?

Like traditional roles for men, lack of flexibility and nuance is a key issue. What is true, however, is that none of the norms for women appear to be directly harmful to men. This is food for thought as we examine how gender roles form a system that can reinforce roles for each gender in a negative and rigid way.

Recent textbooks on the psychology of women[13] suggest several key norms which center around not wanting to hurt or disappoint others. As we examine these, let's consider how they might limit or enhance relationships with self and others, particularly in the area of standing up to sexual misconduct or harassment.

Express one's emotions (*I can show my feelings—except anger*).

This can be healthy in appropriate situations, depending on the emotion. Showing feelings is one way of being vulnerable with others and can enhance intimacy and connection. However, the one emotion that women are often constrained in expressing is anger. An angry woman can be seen as threatening, bitchy, or even out of control due to her menstrual cycle. Showing other emotions openly—being able to cry, to be afraid, to show joy—all of these are healthy if done with awareness of context. But if a woman's sexual boundaries are violated by a man and she has difficulty in expressing anger, this can potentially lead to #MeToo behavior. She is inhibited by social norms in showing anger at being the recipient of sexual misconduct, and he doesn't respect her "no" because it lacks (to him) a sense of firm indignation.

Care for others (*I am there to help you, even at my own expense*).

Showing care of others, particularly those in vulnerable situations (such as children being sick) is a basic norm for women. Caring for others can be a positive norm without any negative aspects. However, this norm, if translated into "care for others even if it means I don't take care of myself," can prove harmful for women, especially in relationships with men. It dictates that women not speak their minds in order to allow the other person to save face. Many of our female clients have stated, "I didn't want to hurt his feelings, so I said nothing," and then suffered through continued harassment. Sexual misconduct can sometimes be stopped by speaking up and stating one's boundaries and needs. ("I would like to take our relationship further, but not yet. I don't know you well enough. I want to spend more time together before getting physical.")

Don't be too sexual (*If I show sexual desire, I am a slut*).

Sexuality and sex is a normal and healthy part of life. However it becomes confusing and limited if men are seen as sexually driven beings who dominate women, and women are seen as more passive sexually, trained to not be overtly sexual or allowed to take the initiative in sexual encounters. If women are sexually forward, they can be seen as being "too easy." The norm of "don't be too sexual" can cause shame in a woman who feels she provoked a man into sexual relations by acting sexual at all. Fortunately the norm of sexual reluctance is changing for a younger generation of women who feel more confidence in exploring their sexuality and sexual orientation (as well as gender identity) because the culture has loosened up its restrictions on female sexual expression. But traditional norms take a long time to change, and a number of women (especially older women) are confused about how to express their sexuality in positive and proactive ways, especially if they feel pressured to be sexual with a man they don't wish to be sexually intimate with.

Be attractive (*I have to look good for men to like me*).
Wanting to look and feel attractive is normal. This might involve putting on makeup, working out, wearing stylish clothes, or engaging in sports to stay strong and healthy. This is fine as long as it is primarily defined by oneself. However, if a woman feels she has to live up to a cultural standard of beauty (often unattainable) and judges herself or is judged by others solely on what she looks like, her sense of self-esteem can be eroded. Men may judge women solely on societal definitions of beauty, or mistake attractiveness for sexual availability. Being promoted as a commodity is demeaning and reinforces the view that women are there for men, that they are only sexual objects to be used by men.

Don't be too assertive (*If I speak up for what I need, I may hurt other people's feelings*).
If women are trained to be passive and submissive rather than assertive, they may find it difficult to speak up for themselves when men are acting inappropriately in personal and professional settings. Saying *no* is an important skill to learn at a young age, and girls are generally not taught to do this successfully. As adults they may be labeled frigid if they assert firm sexual boundaries. The acceptance of this labeling can prevent her from seeing that a man may be saying this in frustration at not getting what he wants rather than an objective assessment of her behavior.

Be nice (*I want to be liked and don't want to offend or annoy anyone*).
Being "nice" is useful if it means being kind or helpful. But if it simply means not making waves or not speaking up against men who are sexually abusive, then it limits women's ability to deal effectively with such men. This norm is reflected in other norms where women are told to not be aggressive, to tend to the needs of others at all costs, and to not show anger. In sexual situations, being nice can lead to either genuine misunderstandings on the part of men

who are clueless (rather than malevolent), or difficulty confronting predatory behavior, especially involving men in power.

Gender Norms as a Dysfunctional System

Traditional and rigid gender norms create a reinforcing feedback loop that limits both genders, but particularly women. As we've just described, these norms make women especially vulnerable in the areas of power, sexuality, and respect. If men strive to follow the norms of dominance, sexual conquest, and aggression, and women follow the norms of being nice, not being overtly sexual, and taking care of others' feelings, then following those norms can lead to situations of sexual misconduct. These situations are more likely be avoided if each gender had access to a range of attitudes and behavior. Let's see how these interlocking stereotypes might play out in reality, and what an alternative scenario might look like if each gender were able to rely on a full range of attitudes and behavior.

Scenario 1: Peer-to-peer interaction

Joe meets Jane at a fraternity party, is attracted to her, and wants to have sex with her. Jane is attracted to Joe but only wants to flirt and not take it any further. He comes on strong, responding to norms of aggression, dominance, and nonrelational sex. Jane tries to be nice and doesn't want to hurt his feelings, responding to norms of caretaking and lack of assertiveness. She also wants to take it slowly and see if they can get to know each other outside of a party setting before she is sexual with him. They both drink too much, impairing their judgments about what might happen. Joe suggests Jane come to his room and she follows, not sure she wants to but not wanting to be seen as mean. He closes the door and starts to take her clothes off. She resists but Joe continues, ignoring her pleas. At this point, sexual assault or rape might happen.

However, if each person were less bound by gender role stereotypes, Jane would not be so worried about being nice; she could have set better boundaries with Joe in the beginning. She might not have gone to his room, or would have been able to tell him that his persistence was bothering her. If Joe were better able to be more relational and less concerned with being dominant, he could acknowledge Jane's feelings and not push too hard or become defensive or ashamed if she said "*no.* " At this point, their relationship might get sexual, but it would be through mutual consent rather than force.

Scenario 2: Authority figure to subordinate interaction

Bill is a vice president in a large firm and is attracted to Susan, a woman who works for him. He has gone through a bitter divorce and wants to be sexual with someone who respects him and won't give him a hard time. He begins to pay special attention to Susan, taking time to converse with her about things outside of their professional relationship. He eventually starts touching her and commenting on how attractive she is. She goes along with his advances, not wanting to stir up trouble because she is worried about her job as well as about hurting his feelings. She wants to be seen as a team player, likeable and caring. While they are at a conference, they have dinner together and he suggests she join him in his suite for a drink. Not wanting to be rude and not quite knowing how to say *no* in a graceful way, she goes to his suite with him. Once the door is closed, he starts kissing her. She resists, but he continues. At this point, sexual assault or rape might happen.

If Susan and Bill could step out of their traditional gender roles, a different scenario would ensue. Continuing the story line, at a conference they have dinner together. Bill is still interested in Susan and, after a few drinks, suggests she come to his suite for a nightcap. Susan would tell Bill that while she appreciated his attention, it made her uncomfortable. Bill would back off, saying he was sorry, that he didn't know that she was feeling that way. At this point, Susan again says that she appreciates the offer but that she doesn't feel it is appropriate and might muddy the waters for their professional relationship, which she values. Bill agrees with her and says that perhaps they can get to know each other more on a personal level once they are not working together.

Both scenarios require each gender to act in a way that is counter to traditional gender role stereotypes. In the alternate scenarios, the women are assertive, clear about their boundaries, and do not walk into situations that could make it harder for them to keep those boundaries. The men are collaborative rather than dominant and take *no* for an answer. They understand that sexual contact might be possible in the future in different contexts, but respect the woman's needs and requests.

But unfortunately, these alternative scenarios are too scarce in the #MeToo era where following traditional gender roles in sexual situations can have devastating consequences. Men may believe they should control what happens in a relationship, believe they can act out sexually with no consequences, and that women's "no" can be overruled: Women may feel that they are unable or don't know how to assert themselves, can't confront gaslighting, and or go along with a man's wishes so as not to appear "bitchy" or hurt his feelings. If men are playboys and women can't be too sexual, then sexually active men reinforce sexually shy women.

In addition, if a workplace is composed largely of men, then women are often seen as the outsiders who threaten the status quo of the "boys club." This might create a backlash of sexual harassment as a way of putting women down by reducing them to sexual objects and not professionals of equal stature. In such an environment, women are likely to feel out of place and demeaned. Without resources or good training to confront harassment, women are likely to burn out or feel victimized and may choose to leave that setting.

Anger and sadness are normal human emotions when experienced and expressed in healthy ways, and can lead to more intimate relationships. When suppressed according to inflexible gender role norms, problems in relationships are more likely to arise. Women may have difficulty speaking up when their boundaries are violated, and men may have trouble expressing sadness or hurt and turn instead to anger or disrespect.

The Impact of Culture

In contemporary American culture, sexism still exists on numerous micro and macro levels. It can be seen in every area of life, from personal to professional relations, from the workplace to social interactions. Women are paid less than men and they hold significantly fewer positions of power in academia, business, and government. This is particularly true for women of color. Because of this inequity, men's voices are heard more than women's voices. In a society where men (typically white men) are in positions of power over women, where men are seen as primary and women as secondary, and when men in power feel entitled to see women as people they can control, sexual misconduct is more likely to occur.

Gender role norms are reinforced by parents, peers, schools, work environments, and media from an early age. It becomes difficult to change a system that encourages sexual acting out by men and objectification of women. One only has to look at the advertisements we see, depicting women as alluring sexual beings, often objectified, to be desired and used by men. Jean Kilbourne's lectures were made into a series of films called *Killing Me Softly,*[14] which spoke about the ways in which women are judged by their beauty (given variable cultural standards) and were used by Madison Avenue to promote products. She continued to be an inspiration for films along this theme, the latest being *Killing Us Softly 4: Advertising Images of Women.*[15] Unfortunately, 30 years has not radically changed that perception. All one has to do is turn on the TV or leaf through a magazine to see this in play. In popular culture sources, such as movies and TV shows, the pattern still emerges of women saying *no* but meaning *yes*. In a recent popular TV series,[16] the hero is depicted as having sex with his ex-girlfriend ostensibly against her will (she says *no* forcibly many times but gives in to his emotional and physical pressure and then clearly enjoys it). In another popular book, *Fifty Shades of Gray,*[17] the hero, Christian, is the master of Anastasia and controls their sexual interaction, which she learns to love.

What does this tell men? That women really want sex but have to resist at first against a man's advances? That women who say "*no*" will eventually say "*yes*" if they are pushed hard enough by men? That a man's desires come first, regardless of what the woman is comfortable with? These stereotypes, men as dominant and women as saying "*no*" but meaning "*yes,*" can contribute to #MeToo behavior. Popular culture (including movies, TV shows, books, and ads) and peer pressure (formed from gender role socialization at a very young age), and certainly pornography, all create scenarios where sexual misconduct is seen as permissible and therefore more likely to happen. When a man thinks he should be the sexual aggressor and take what he wants, and when women think they have to be nice and accept the man's behavior, the situation is ripe for sexual misconduct in a variety of forms, from disrespectful to destructive.

In a classic study,[18] female college students were presented with a vignette about a sexual situation and were asked to agree or disagree with the following:

> You were with a guy who wanted to engage in sexual intercourse and you wanted to also, but for some reason you indicated that you didn't want to, although you had every intention to and were willing to engage in sexual intercourse. In other words, you indicated *no* and you meant *yes*.

A whopping 39.3% of the respondents said they would say no but would really want to be sexual." This difficulty saying a clear *yes* to sexual intercourse may have a lot to do with a woman being socialized to not openly ask for sex because they are afraid they will be seen as being seen as too sexual. But this complicates how accurately a man can read a woman's signals of interest in being sexual.

Given this, how do we help our clients become aware of traditional gender norms that can be rigid, inflexible and assigned to just one sex, and can hurt the development of healthy relationships? How do we help them see that "real" men can listen and be respectful and not be afraid of showing traits typically seen as feminine, such as receptivity, vulnerability, and emotional openness? How often do we help women see that "real" women can speak up for what they want and what their boundaries are, especially in sexual situations?

In the second part of the book we will explore helping our clients understand how traditional gender norms may contribute to issues that the #MeToo movement has raised. In our clinical work, how often have you seen male clients resist delving into their emotional lives, or have said "I can do it myself," or "I just need to suck it up"? How often have your male clients been unaware of the consequences of their hurtful actions toward women? Where have you seen female clients hesitating to speak up if they think it makes a man feel uncomfortable? How often have you seen women put their self-esteem in the hands of men and forgo good self-care in the interest of wanting guys to like them?

Gender is just one facet of a person. We need to look at all aspects of our clients' lives, including the fluidity of gender, race, socioeconomic status, ethnicity, religion, and issues arising from one's family of origin. We need to take these factors into account when assessing and treating our clients. However, traditional gender norms represent a key variable that needs to be made more visible where matters of sexual misconduct are concerned. This is important so that our clients can examine their behavior and attitudes in the light of those norms. It is our hope that education around gender norms and their impact on our client's attitudes and behavior can help prevent sexual misconduct in the first place, or deal with it more effectively if it has already happened so that it does not happen again.

In the next two chapters, we will look at why some men engage in more predatory forms of sexual harassment and assault as well as which men are more likely to be perpetrators. We will also consider men who violate boundaries without realizing that they have done so and are often regretful and ashamed when they realize it. We will tell the stories of men who act out and the resulting consequences that impair or destroy healthy relationships with women. By examining this wide range of #MeToo behaviors through the lens of male gender role norms, we will be better able to work with our male clients (maybe not all of them but hopefully many) to help them overcome conditioning that inhibits men from respecting a woman's rights and needs in sexual interactions.

Chapter 3

Men Behaving Badly

Aggression, Threat, and Abuse of Power

Not every man who has committed harassing #MeToo-worthy behaviors has been driven by power or misogyny. In fact, most people who study these patterns have concluded that the majority of offenders are triggered by much more banal and benign motives than power, bullying, and aggression.[1] Plenty of #MeToo offenders are simply clueless—they misread cues and think that their victims enjoy their attentions. Presumably, education can change these men for the better. And certainly, most men are *not* harassers or rapists!

All these behaviors—the macroaggressions and the microaggressions—share the common progression of men crossing boundaries and women getting hurt. But the forces that drive these behaviors cut a wide swath. To understand and, ultimately, to change behavior, we have to make sense of these different forces.

The next two chapters lay the groundwork for understanding the range of #MeToo behavior: Who does it, why they do it, and what motivates them to do it. We will be reviewing behaviors that run the gamut—including cases that most counselors and therapists are unlikely to treat—so that we all know how the cases we actually do treat (as well as the victims affected by them) fit into the big picture.

We have organized these examples, and the variety of forces that motivate the perpetrators, into two broad categories. In this chapter we start with the most chilling and horrendous incidents and then move on to the more clueless and benign in the following chapter. Some of these stories are easy to classify. Others are not, because they lie somewhere in the gray area between monstrous and minor. Some of you might disagree with our placement of certain examples in one chapter rather than the other, and you might be right. In the long run, it doesn't matter—because most of us can agree that although all #MeToo behaviors are bad, some are considerably worse than others. We need to understand the differences so we can work most effectively with #MeToo violators.

In this chapter we examine power—but also entitlement, grooming, rationalization, delusional thinking, passive-aggressive avoidance of responsibility, and the perverse thrill of risk-taking behavior.

People who study #MeToo behaviors often debate the question: *Is it about power or is it about sex?* The consensus answer: *Yes.* It can be about either power or sex, and it is often both. Despite the term "sexual," usually the most lethal forms of sexual harassment are not *primarily* about sex. The worst of #MeToo behaviors are absolutely power based. Even suggestive comments or inappropriate touches are usually exercises in dominance.

We see the same distinctions in the field of domestic violence: The worst of the worst behaviors are driven by power and control motivations and employ a wide variety of abusive strategies to achieve their needs. But the majority of domestic violence offenders are often driven by conventional psychological forces, like fear of abandonment, jealousy, and insecurities.[2]

We now explore several examples of the most predatory and damaging #MeToo behaviors. We consider possible motivating factors and how they may be linked to gender roles in a culture of sexism.

Predators: Power and Sex in a Sexist Culture

In Chapter 1 we defined a predator as a person who ruthlessly exploits others: someone who injures, exploits, or plunders others for personal gain. We will look at some famous examples of predators, keeping in mind how their behavior is allowed, ignored, or even encouraged by a sexist culture in which women are seen as commodities, powerless, dependent on powerful men, and of lesser value than men. In these cases, power-based behavior has everything to do with quid pro quo. In every one of the situations we describe, the woman needs something from the man, and he dangles what he has to offer as a reward for her sexual compliance.

If she responds "successfully"—according to the needs of the predator— the rewards are significant. If she does not—if she does not comply, if she actively protests, or if she threatens to expose him—the loss to her can be devastating. Furthermore, predators adhere to the worst male norms: dominance, misogyny, nonrelational sex, and objectification of women. When you add all this up, it is a powerful combination of factors that generate the most damaging behaviors.

Weinstein and Hollywood

Harvey Weinstein perfected a system. He would call a meeting with an actress or other woman who was seeking career advancement. He would arrange for an assistant to bring her to a public setting, like an office, a restaurant, or a hotel bar. Then the script called for the assistant to leave—and the meeting would relocate to a hotel suite. Then he would make his moves. When a woman resisted or complained, she might be sent flowers in an attempt at mollification. If the flowers didn't work, there was always the threat of career damage—like bad-mouthing an actress to other producers and directors in ways that would sabotage the always fragile career possibilities of an aspiring artist.

Weinstein once trapped a woman in the hallway of a restaurant that was closed to the public and then masturbated in front of her until he ejaculated. Lauren Sivan[3] reports that he maneuvered her into a private room, then leaned in and tried to kiss her. She rejected that attempt and told him she had a long-term boyfriend. Weinstein then said to Sivan, "Well, can you just stand there and shut up?" Her exit route out of this room was trapped by Weinstein's body and she felt intimidated.

Weinstein then proceeded to expose himself to Sivan and began to masturbate. Sivan said she was deeply shocked by Weinstein's behavior—she was frozen and didn't know what to do or say. The incident in the vestibule didn't last long. Sivan says Weinstein ejaculated quickly into a potted plant and then zipped up his pants and they walked back into the kitchen.

The Harvey Weinstein method is the way El Chapo and Mafiosos often operate. You want something from somebody, you tempt them with bribes. And if they are reluctant to cooperate, you make them an offer they can't refuse by threatening them or their family. In the world of Mexican drug cartels, this is described as a choice between *plata o plomo*. You can go for the lucrative reward of the silver—and if that doesn't work, then the only choice is the bullets of lead. These are the "successful" operating principles of power.

For decades, Weinstein's behavior was either tolerated or sanctioned by Hollywood moguls who needed him to continue to grow their empire at the expense of more "expendable" people—like aspiring actresses.

Nassar and the USA Gymnastics Team

Larry Nassar was the USA Gymnastics national team doctor and an osteopathic physician at Michigan State University. He was accused of molesting at least 250 girls and young women (and one young man), including a number of famous Olympic gymnasts. He is now a convicted serial child molester who is serving decades of prison time.

In this case, a predator associated with a powerful institution was allowed to prey on young women and inflict abuse under the guise of training and treatment.

Nassar was the team doctor, and being under his treatment was compulsory for inclusion on the USA Gymnastics squad. Gymnast Jamie Dantzscher describes the environment at the training camps like this: "No one wants to step out of line because there's a group of people that make decisions that dictate whether you're successful or not. So you just comply with what you're told to do."[4]

Jessica Howard, the U.S. National Champion in rhythmic gymnastics from 1999 to 2001, described the price of staying in the good graces of the Olympic team decision makers: "You can't say anything. If you do, there's a chance you're going to get in trouble, and the last thing you want to do is bring more trouble onto yourself on purpose. You just don't cause trouble. That's one of the first rules of being an athlete. You need to be strong, silent, and let everything go on outside of you that's going on outside of you."[5]

The gymnasts (in most cases, years later) alleged that the "emotionally abusive environment" at the national team training camps gave Nassar an opportunity to take advantage of the gymnasts and made them afraid to speak up about the abuse. When several of them complained, doctors, coaches, and trainers brushed aside their concerns as if they were naive girls who didn't understand the special nature of Nassar's therapy.[6] This response exemplifies the power of another institution, like Hollywood, that chose to support an individual viewed as important and to dismiss the concerns of the more vulnerable and expendable victims.

Epstein and the Business World

Jeffrey Epstein became notorious for sex trafficking girls and young women in their teens and twenties. He mingled with the rich, famous, and powerful. He also had an instinct for what people wanted. One of his many ex-girlfriends said, "Jeffrey was brilliant in understanding how people felt. He could feel energy very clearly. But I think because he's a sociopath, he would manipulate that for his own needs. The average human population just doesn't operate that way, and thank God."[7]

Another ex-girlfriend was quoted similarly: "He always wanted to give the impression that he was an international man of mystery—'I control everyone and everything, I collect people, I own people, I can damage people.'"[8]

The men we are talking about here don't care what their victims want or feel. And many of them " . . . coerce others and actually relish the coercion . . . . For these men, it is precisely the power imbalance that's erotic."[9]

Narcissistic Entitlement

People who score high on scales of narcissism typically seem arrogant, grandiose, manipulative, entitled, and lacking in empathy. They are driven by a need to be perfect and constantly get others to enviously look up to them. In their desperate attempts to convince others of their superiority, many of these men are highly motivated to achieve much more than most people; this will give them something to really brag about. In respect to #MeToo behaviors, men who meet this description crave a response from women that, in some twisted way, reinforces their sense of being both powerful and desirable.

Narcissistically driven predators often pursue a career that provides unquestioned access to their preferred targets. These are men who found a way, or sometimes even stumbled their way, into rising to elite levels of power, success, and/or celebrity. And all this acclaim fueled their grandiosity and entitlement. Many of these men feel like they are entitled to getting what they want, whether it's the best table in a restaurant or the most desirable women. They don't really see their sexual transgressions as transgressions at all. Confronted with their exploitation of women, they often minimize and rationalize: *I have earned this. If someone else did this, I'd be concerned, but I know what I'm doing.*[10]

When a man finds himself in a position with increasingly more power and influence, he often starts to spin his relationships in a new and self-serving fashion in his own mind. With this personal version of reality, behaviors that at one time and in most ordinary life circumstances would seem ridiculous or outrageous can start to feel normal.

One U.S. president has famously espoused this philosophy of entitlement[11]: "And when you're a star, they let you do it. You can do anything. Grab them by the pussy. You can do anything." Likewise, when you are a famous director or a star doctor or an esteemed priest, you can do anything.

But . . . which comes first? Is the most typical situation one where the power-driven man strategically maneuvers himself into a position to exercise power via #MeToo behaviors? Or does this happen in reverse order: An "ordinary" (or maybe slightly narcissistic) man ends up in a position of power—and the perks, trappings, and norms of this position create the expectations and entitlement that lead to #MeToo behaviors?

With these competing narratives, the correct answer is that sometimes it is one scenario, sometimes the other, and sometimes a combination of the two. Obviously, men who have harassed and bullied women in the workplace have taken advantage of the perks and entitlement that their positions grant them. Yet the backstories of some of the most infamous abusers of the #MeToo era reveal that they engaged in abuses of women long before they were in a position to do this with reckless abandon.

Most sexual violators start with small steps, seeing what they can get away with. Before Larry Nassar ever found himself in abuser heaven (and adolescent girl hell) stationed as the USA Gymnastics team doctor, he already had engaged in plenty of sexual abuse. Before he even completed medical school and became a licensed doctor,[12] he allegedly molested a girl—under the guise of doing a study on flexibility. According to the woman's lawsuit, Nassar invited her to his apartment when she was between the age of 12 and 14. He asked her to participate in some medical research he was doing and offered her a free full body massage as compensation. She alleges that during the massage, Nassar penetrated her vaginally.

Several women accused Harvey Weinstein of sexual assault in the late 1970s and early 1980s, when he was a college dropout working as a music promoter in Buffalo, New York. These offenses occurred before he and his brother founded Miramax and long before he became a powerful and internationally influential figure. One woman, Hope Exiner d'Amore, told *The New York Times*[13] that when working for Weinstein in Buffalo at his former concert promoting business in the late 1970s, he invited her to come with him to New York City. When they checked in to a hotel, Weinstein claimed there was only one room available for them; she told *The Times* that he forced oral sex and intercourse on her in that room.

Bill Cosby got an early start too. A 71-year-old New Hampshire grandmother, Kristina Ruehli, told *Philadelphia Magazine*[14] that in 1965, when she was 22, she met Cosby while working as a talent agency secretary at Artists Agency Corp. She claimed that Cosby approached her and said: "I'm going to be on *Hollywood Palace* tonight, and I'm going to have a party at my home afterwards." He invited Ruehli, and she says she went. When she arrived, she said that she was surprised to find no one else there. Ruehli recalls that Cosby poured her two drinks and after that, states that she just doesn't remember much. She says she completely passed out and concludes he must have drugged her. When she came to, she alleges that she woke up in his bed and Cosby had his shirt off. "He was attempting to force me into oral sex."[15]

The potent combination of entitlement and then maneuvering oneself into a position of power and trust enables the worst of the worst of #MeToo behaviors. An ordinary guy in an ordinary job with ordinary levels of authority (who would want to exploit women this way) can only get away with so much. But when you are Harvey Weinstein or Larry Nassar or Bill Cosby, you have several key advantages going for you in your quest to exploit women. You have *power*—both victims and observers are afraid to deny you, challenge you, or report you. The potential consequences are just too intimidating. You also (certainly in the case of a doctor or a priest) have *trust*—often a blind and rather undeserved trust, but trust nevertheless. Many of the women who complied with Larry Nassar didn't simply do so out of fear. Many of them were convinced that he must have known what he was doing because he was a *doctor*. Because priests were viewed as actual agents of God, many used their stature and position as cover for egregious sexual exploitation for years. Bill Cosby managed to lure women to his apartment and "innocently" entice them to accept a drugged drink because he was . . . *Bill Cosby*. Dr. Huxtable. A warm and wise and respected man.

The sexually exploitative man who finds himself in combined positions of power and trust discovers he can successfully cross normal boundaries and, magically, nothing happens. The knowledge can be intoxicating and addictive. Unlike the sexually exploitative man in ordinary life circumstances, a man holding power and trust is allowed to take advantage of an astonishingly greater number of victims.

Dr. James Cantor of the University of Toronto claims that what distinguishes these powerful violators is not only that they fool themselves about what they're doing—that's an inherent quality in many who commit sexual misdeeds—it's that they can create an environment in which they go unchallenged. The more they get away with, the more they can push the envelope.[16] And we find that sexual situations trigger a specifically sexual narcissism; when these men are aroused, they engage in exploitation that they later justify to themselves. When men are socialized into being dominant, especially in sexual relationships (often glorified by peers and the media), it is particularly easy for predators to justify their behavior.

Rationalizations and Empathy Deficits

The capacity for extreme rationalization is essential for many sexual assaulters and harassers—because nobody, aside from an actual psychopath, can bear seeing themselves as a truly evil person. Harvey Weinstein famously told women whom he forced onto a bed, fondled, stripped (and then masturbated in front of): "It's just a little cuddling. It's not a problem. It's not like we're having sex."[17]

Even the men who did not begin a long career of exploitation early on, often found themselves seduced by the trappings and perks of being valued and powerful. Then as their position and power increased, they were able to act on it. This condition has been identified as "acquired situational narcissism" (ASN). It describes a person exhibiting narcissistic behavior *after* becoming successful or popular.[18]

Typically, a situational narcissist is someone who at one time behaved reasonably and respectfully, but developed an egocentric complex as the result of gaining a measure of accomplishment, fame, wealth, or other forms of external success. Situational narcissism can occur in just about any arena of life. Receiving elevated status (real or perceived) can instill a sense of superiority, entitlement, and privilege. The narcissist believes that he or she is now "above others," at least within their personal and/or professional circles. Male norms of being dominant and successful at all cost contribute to this sense of entitlement. And the entitlement is accompanied by—and often generates—a decreasing capacity for empathy. Exploitation becomes more possible and rationalizable by this depletion of empathy.

The bizarre pattern of comedian Louis C. K. can be framed as situational narcissism. Louis C. K. allegedly posed this startling question to female colleagues: "Can I masturbate in front of you?" Sometimes he got a stunned "yes," and he proceeded. His rationalization: "I said to myself that what I did was O.K. because I never showed a woman my dick without asking first."

Here is someone presenting himself as a "good guy" who has the decency and manners to ask for permission before engaging in a sexual act. But it requires superhuman levels of denial and superhuman deficits in empathy to convince oneself that this behavior is actually acceptable and welcomed by these women.

The true psychopaths are often brilliant at reading other people, but they simply don't care about anyone else's feelings. However, most of the men we are talking about in terms of #MeToo behaviors—and people who take advantage of others in many situations—actually do cling to a self-image of being a good person whose behavior is justified.

Another rationalization plaguing sexual predators is known as the "myth of uncontrollable arousal." Sexual predators often carry a toxic and inherently false belief that arousal is a kind of magical state that removes individual agency. Larry Nassar, in a court statement, used this kind of distancing language when he described his decades of penetrating young gymnasts as "a forest fire out of control."[19]

Jeffrey Epstein had an insatiable sexual appetite that included threesomes, and he reportedly required three orgasms a day. He told one of his girlfriends that "it was biological, like eating."[20] Once he felt comfortable with a woman, he often explained that he had a high sex drive and thereby could not be monogamous. One ex-girlfriend reported this: "He said everyone dates multiple people at the same time . . . that's how all wealthy and powerful people do it, he said kings and queens do it, and if I was less pedestrian and common we could have this beautiful, long-term relationship." She declined.

It's as if this type of predator, in a state of narcissistic delusion, feels that the intensity of his needs is a sign that he is entitled to such experiences. And of course, this preoccupation with satisfying one's own paramount needs—needs that cannot be controlled—sabotages any possible shred of capacity for empathy. The other person does not count and is solely an object for gratification. Our culture contributes to a predator's view of women because women are often presented as sexual objects for a man to use. In the groundbreaking film *Killing Us Softly 4: Advertising's Image of Women*,[21] Jean Kilbourne shows us how much women are objectified in the advertising industry.

What often accompanies this sense of uncontrollable arousal is a projection of blame onto the object (the woman). In Israeli director Michal Aviad's 2018 film, *Working Woman*,[22] the older male boss of a young woman steadily woos her and eventually tries to rape her. As he is blocking her passage from his hotel room, as he pins her against a wall, as he pulls her clothes off and ejaculates on her, he mumbles again and again, "You just drive me so crazy." Not, "I'm out of control." Not, "I know you didn't want this, but I insist on getting my needs met." The emphasis is on what *she* has created in *him*.

The mental gymnastics an individual must engage in to rationalize these behaviors (if you view yourself as a person with values and integrity) are best explained by the principles of "cognitive dissonance."

As most counselors and clinicians know, cognitive dissonance identifies the psychological distress experienced when an individual's belief clashes with new evidence. If you see yourself one way—and then you observe yourself acting in a way that contradicts this self-image—the dissonance is unbearable. You then either have to see yourself more clearly (painful as that may be) and make adjustments in your own behavior, or else you must twist your views into a pretzel to avoid uncomfortable contradictions.

In the context of #MeToo behaviors, if a man views himself as someone who treats women well, and then he makes a woman uncomfortable by coming on to her in the workplace, he is stuck with a disturbing dissonance. Psychologically, he is left with two choices:

He can tell himself that the way he is acting is acceptable and that:
- *everybody does it*
- *she is getting off on it*
- *she dresses provocatively and is asking for it*
- *if she doesn't like it it's because she is an uptight bitch*

This way he doesn't have to face the self-image of behaving badly in his treatment of women. Or...

He can recognize this darker side of his personality and the harm he has created, and he can then try to make amends and become more conscious of his own behaviors.

For so many people, and especially for the narcissistic men of #MeToo, the first choice is the more popular and the path of least resistance. It is so much easier to go the route that allows them to keep doing what they have been doing without feeling bad. The second choice requires more psychological maturity and humility. It requires the capacity to recognize and acknowledge dark aspects of oneself. With clients, it is much easier to work with the latter: In fact, true predators rarely show up for therapy because they believe that they are entitled to do what they do, so why would they need therapy? If they do show up (usually at the insistence of a girlfriend, wife, or employer), it's hard to work with them in any effective way other than to appeal to their self-interest in changing their behavior.

Gaslighting and Grooming: Alternate Realities

To give you an idea of how gaslighting works, we'll use some examples to show how this might play out. David Schwimmer, the actor most known as Ross on the TV show *Friends*, produced an outstanding series of six video vignettes entitled *That's Harassment*.[23] His team partnered with the Ad Council, the Rape, Abuse and Incest National Network (RAINN), and the National Women's Law Center (NWLC) as part of a PSA campaign to empower victims and bystanders to speak out against sexual harassment and provide tools for employers to create a safe work environment.

Written and directed by Sigal Avin (with executive producer Schwimmer), the film depicts various cases of sexual harassment in the workplace, each based on real events. The team created this project to highlight #MeToo behaviors and to end institutional silence and complicity.

Each video features a moment in an everyday scenario where acceptable interaction between a man and a woman subtly changes. Each vignette depicts a point when the man—the actor, the boss, the coworker, the doctor, the photographer, the politician—oversteps his boundaries in a way that confuses, demoralizes, and scares the woman he's talking to.

Most do not display any actual assault or macroaggressions—but they are all chilling. And they are all introduced with the tagline of "based on a real incident." One of the most disturbing is a scene between an actor and a wardrobe assistant. The actor, played by Noah Emmerich (*The Americans*, *The Truman Show*), is obviously adored by the younger woman who is helping him pick out his wardrobe for a scene. She talks excitedly about her niece, who desperately wants a video wishing her a happy birthday from this famous actor. The assistant is really apologetic, and so excited when he says he would be happy to do this for her niece: "You're so sweet, you're the best!!"

So far, so good.

The next thing she knows, she turns around and he has pulled his penis out of his pants. She laughs nervously. He tells her that "he just popped out to say hello!" With a smile and a laugh, she tells him, "Well, OK, he said hello, now put that thing back in."

We definitely see male entitlement and grandiosity here—he just assumes that (since she is being so friendly and admiring and since he's such a celebrity) *of course* she is going to be absolutely thrilled about having a sexual encounter with him.

But there's another theme here. He is grooming her. First, he is trying to establish a warm and friendly initial relationship, one where she will see him as a really good, safe guy. No predator has ever been successful by showing his true colors too early.

Now he starts to work on her a little more. He asks her for a hand helping his penis get back into his pants. Her says to her: "I can't believe you're so embarrassed." This is the next step of the grooming process. Here he is trying to establish a narrative about this encounter that goes something like this: "What I'm doing is totally normal and harmless. If you have a problem with it, that must indicate that you're really an uptight bitch who is sexually repressed. Haven't you ever seen a penis before? I CAN'T BELIEVE YOU ARE SO EMBARASSED. Your embarrassment is a statement about your personal hang-ups, not about my appalling behavior."

And it is extremely easy for the woman in this situation to doubt herself and cooperate, or at least to not strongly object to it or report it.

Then the grooming continues: "Don't you realize that I am attracted to you? . . . Look, I know you don't think a lot of yourself, but I think you are an incredibly sexy woman."

It is here that her face finally shifts from the original look of excitement, to nervous smiling, and now to hurt and betrayal. Fortunately, the grooming attempt hasn't been successful. But what he was trying to do is generate a narrative that actually might have worked with someone else: "I'm a stud movie star, and I get lots of attention. You're rather plain and just a wardrobe assistant. But I think you're so sexy! And my view of you as being sexy can lift you right out of feeling ordinary and propel you to a higher level and relieve your chronic doubts." That can be a very compelling offer, one that many women are easily susceptible to.

A gay actor on the *That's Harassment* project discussed that scene in an interview: "'I know you don't think much of yourself.' That line still sticks with me. I personally struggled with issues about being confident, my ego, self-esteem. A lot of times, I'm very hard on myself. I think we all are; we all have things that we don't like about ourselves. That line—'I know you don't think much of yourself'—really struck a chord with me. I've heard that before from people in my life. I remember hearing it from a guy I went out with. I didn't go out with him again."[24]

Grooming is a particularly insidious type of behavior because it pairs apparent concern for the victim with abuse, creating a confusing combination of kindness and exploitation that can be devastating. Larry Nassar was a deft practitioner of such priming. Former national team member Maggie Nichols documented the ways he "groomed" her by connecting with her on Facebook and complimenting her appearance on numerous occasions.[25] Her ally in moments of emotional distress was often the man assigned to relieve her physical pain, Dr. Nassar. "He was like my buddy."

Dantzscher says she began seeing Dr. Nassar after she earned a coveted spot on the U.S. Junior National Team. "He would put his fingers inside of me and move my leg around," she tells LaPook on the broadcast. "He would tell me I was going to feel a pop. And that that would put my hips back and help my back pain."[26]

Dantzscher says that, at the time, she didn't realize Dr. Nassar was doing something wrong. In fact, she says she appreciated his emotional support in an otherwise harsh atmosphere during training at the Karolyi Ranch.[27]

"I felt like we weren't allowed to even smile in the gym," she says. "So getting treatment [included] him just joking around and talking about how horrible they [the coaches] were. It was kind of like a bright light, I guess you could say."[28]

Because the athletes were instructed to keep a strict diet while at the ranch, Jeanette Antolin says Dr. Nassar would sneak them snacks and candy. She says the secret treats and friendly conversation helped build trust with the young gymnasts.[29]

"He was a buddy. He was someone that we would talk to when we were getting treatment, if we had a hard day. He was a listening ear. He would make us laugh. When it's such a serious environment that would be the world. It could fix your day."[30]

The doctor's grooming of the young women allowed him to create an alternative reality where black is white, up is down, and relentless sexual abuse is sound medical practice. Because these girls trusted him, they didn't think of his actions as anything outside of an acceptable medical procedure: "It was treatment. You don't complain about treatment."[31]

"We were manipulated into believing that Dr. Nassar was healing us as any normal doctor is supposed to do," Olympic gymnast Jade Capua testified.[32]

The conditions for "successful" sexual harassment are particularly ripe when the victim feels comfortable and safe with the harasser. Her ears and brain hear the words from a trusted authority and otherwise nice guy that this is safe and normal—but there's still this little signal emanating from her gut that is trying to call out that this is dangerous and wrong. It is so easy for a victim to lose her voice and doubt herself.

The victim knows that insertion of fingers into the vagina or anus in no way makes any sense as a treatment for the orthopedic concerns she had. But when she hears, again and again, that something is true, she starts to believe it—despite her intelligence and her better judgment and her inner compass for what is right and what is wrong. This can be especially true when the source of this bizarre narrative is a highly trusted figure like the doctor she depends on.

The examination by that doctor is the one single situation in her life—other than a sexual partner whom she has chosen to trust—where she has been taught that it is safe to take her clothes off and let somebody touch her in the most intimate places. Nobody else gets to do that.

One more example of altered reality: Olympic superstar gymnast Gabby Douglas sent a tweet criticizing some of the other gymnasts in a way that sounded like "victim shaming," stating that "dressing in a provocative/sexual way incites the wrong crowd."[33] She was later criticized by fellow Olympic teammates and later apologized for the tweet, declaring that she too was a victim of Nassar's abuse. But her original tweet would seem to have reflected the fake narrative that she had bought into: Nassar is good, and girls who were victimized and complain actually brought it on themselves.

Cognitive dissonance likely was at work here—it is very likely that Douglas could not accept the fact that she had been so exploited (and the shame that accompanies that) because she did could not see herself as a victim. So, like so many other victims in denial, her resolution (at least for a while) was to justify her doctor's behavior and blame the girls who complained.

Desperate Need for Narcissistic Mirroring

Another bizarre pattern (at least bizarre to most of the women who are on the receiving end of it) occurs when men actually masturbate to an audience.

Exhibitionist behavior in public or with strangers and more violent forms of assault by strangers are actually not the focus of this book or of the #MeToo movement. The genital exposure and masturbation behaviors we are focusing on here will always involve situations in a relationship context, and usually include a power imbalance.

Random creepy men who are exhibitionists are not a new phenomenon. Developmental risk factors for exhibitionistic disorder in males include anti-social personality disorder, alcohol abuse, and an interest in pedophilia. Many exhibitionists (almost exclusively male) engage in other paraphilias too, and this sometimes serves as a precursor to more serious sexual violence.

It is well known (although difficult for many of us to comprehend) that an exhibitionist perceives his victim's shocked response as a form of sexual inter-est. He deludes himself into believing that the woman is fascinated and excited by what she is seeing. He feels known and affirmed and recognized for what he sees as an essential component of his manhood, his sexuality. These feelings are connected to how men are culturally trained to view sex, and what they see as the epitome of sex, their penis. The status of having a large penis permeates many cultures, as is the ability to "perform" sexually. Small penises and lack of erections are a source of shame for many men.

"Someone who takes out his penis in a non-consenting way often says, 'Why did she stare? She must have liked it.'"[34] That is how narcissistic thinking alters reality for many of these men. They are desperate for narcissistic mir-roring (where they use women as a kind of mirror that, in their minds, reflects back admiration and excitement), and they manage to delude themselves into thinking that the staring of the repulsed woman somehow indicates approval.

One of Louis C. K.'s accusers reported (anonymously) to *The New York Times*: "It was something that I knew was wrong. I think the big piece of why I said yes was because of the culture. He abused his power."[35] So many women on the receiving end of his sexual misconduct invariably feel controlled, degraded, or ashamed—not to mention angry. The culture—a culture of men in power feeling entitled to these behaviors and women feeling like they had to go along—contributed to this abuse taking place.

We know that there are some men whose primary motivation is to express their hostility toward women and make them suffer. But the female experience of humiliation does not necessarily imply that the exhibitionist's main goal was to humiliate her. Many men just need to set up a situation, over and over, in which they can escape anxiety; they're not specifically out to make women suffer. Either way, the women just feel objectified and used.

In a similar way, when a woman is a "captive audience" and a man masturbates in front of her, he can believe she is enjoying the sight. This reality "works" for him because it offers reassurance that his penis, the symbol of his masculinity, is desirable, not noxious. With Louis C. K., as with other men who are compulsively drawn to this type of behavior, the underlying anxiety is likely so intense that his judgment becomes grossly impaired. Swept away are all other considerations, like the woman's feelings and the possibility of getting caught.

In a hilarious and biting commentary about Charlie Rose's propensity for wearing a bathrobe and exposing himself to his staff, comedian Seth Myers says this: "Here's a good rule of thumb: If your face isn't pulling in the babes, your penis isn't going to make the difference. Everybody's penis is 100 percent less attractive than their face."[36]

Risk and Thrill

There is no single explanation for motivations behind the most egregious acts of harassment and abuse. As discussed, power and entitlement honed by rationalization and alternate realities are the most common. But the pursuit of risk and thrill is another key pattern for many power-seeking abusers.

It would be foolish and inaccurate to classify all the most extreme macroaggressors as psychopaths, but some probably are. It is noteworthy that the excessive lust for risk-taking is a central trait of the psychopathic personality. Psychopaths simply do not get enough "charge" from the more normal activities of a person's life (such as passionate sex with someone you love and who has willingly consented).

Abuse of power is indeed intrinsic to #MeToo stories. But power alone does not explain why a man would choose to masturbate into a potted plant in front of a horrified woman rather than have sex with a willing one.[37] The possibility of getting into a little bit of trouble is definitely a turn on for many people—but fortunately, for most people, the possibility of getting in a lot of trouble is a turnoff.

Larry Nassar often had girls' parents sit in the room while he inserted his ungloved fingers in their daughters, blocking the view with his body or a towel. At his sentencing hearing, Michigan Assistant Attorney General Angela Povilaitis concluded the following: "To unnecessarily and without warning penetrate an unsuspecting minor for your own selfish sexual gains while her parent sat just feet away, unknowing, had to be part of the rush or the thrill for this defendant."[38]

Then there's Bill Cosby. The actor's modus operandi with his victims was to use his charm and benign persona to generate trust. Many of these women saw him as avuncular, turning to him for career advice. Once achieving that, he would lure a woman to a private place, usually his home or his hotel room. In a seemingly caring gesture to help her relax, he would offer her a beverage that was spiked with Quaaludes. And then, with his drugged and nonresistant victim, he could indulge himself without restrictions. He did not have to deal with a real person or a real person's feelings or needs.

For men who qualify as power-driven macroaggressors of sexual abuse, the lust for thrill is intense and generates risk-taking behavior that would terrify most of us. As if there weren't enough reasons for most people to not engage in this kind of behavior (like empathy, basic decency, potential shame, etc.), simply the risk of getting caught—by doing this again and again, with so many victims who had so many stories to tell—would certainly be enough to keep the average person on the straight and narrow. But, for these men, the thrill alone must be worth it. It is astonishing that it took so many victims and so many years for this incredibly risky behavior to finally catch up to Cosby.

Wrapping It Up

This chapter has covered some of the most powerful motivations for sexual predators—the psychopaths and profoundly narcissistic men who have typically inflicted the most damage over the longest period of time. While all of us in the counseling field need to understand these men and these motivations, fortunately, they represent the minority of #MeToo offenders. The next chapter illuminates the more common examples of men who violate sexual boundaries—the ones who many women have experienced in multiple every-day settings. Unlike the macroaggressors identified so far, the men we are about to discuss are motivated differently, and so we are more likely to get through to them in our clinical work.

But first we need to understand them.

Chapter 4

Men Behaving Poorly
Clueless, Inept, and Subtle Harassment

We have to make distinctions among the different types and motivations for #MeToo offenders. If we don't, we run the risk of demonizing men who are not predators and who are amenable to education and empathy. In the other direction, we run the risk of under-pathologizing more monstrous and power-driven behaviors (such as those described in the previous chapter) by being too accommodating or forgiving.

To understand and ultimately to fix what has gone so wrong for so many years, the last thing we need is to start—or perpetuate—a campaign against all men or all male norms or to imply that masculinity is inherently "toxic." As clinicians, we must expand our knowledge of the multiple motivations of the men who behave poorly, and better understand these clueless, inept, and subtle forms of harassment.

Attorney Debra Katz, who has represented Christine Blasey Ford and other sexual harassment victims, cautions us to recognize how #MeToo violations reside on a continuum: "All offensive behavior should be addressed, but not all offensive behavior warrants the most severe sanction . . . . To treat all allegations the same . . . feeds into a backlash narrative that men are vulnerable to even frivolous allegations by women."[1]

Many #MeToo complaints do not involve anything resembling criminal sexual assault or gross abuses of power. Men who cross the #MeToo line are not necessarily deviants, and the more moderate forms of sexual harassment and #MeToo behaviors don't necessarily stem from the darkest places of power and exploitation. They are sometimes passive-aggressive, sometimes generated by pure emotional and social ineptitude, and sometimes just plain clueless.

What makes this more challenging is what author Ijeoma Oluo describes like this: "Most abusers are more like Al Franken than Harvey Weinstein."[2] Likewise, writer Jennifer Wright[3] identifies the challenge and complexity in making sense of these events by saying that "(p)eople cannot wrap their head around the notion that likeable men can abuse women too."

Michal Aviad, director of the brilliant Israeli #MeToo movie, *Working Woman*, puts her own spin on the range of conduct that qualifies as #MeToo behavior: "Two of the most beloved actors in Israel were accused of sexual harassment recently. We all know these guys personally; they're not these movie villains. But you get an actor who flirts with an anonymous actress, she turns him down and then he tells the producer, 'I can't work with her.' That kind of stuff . . . . The subtleties are far more interesting than Harvey Weinstein, because how many of these insane criminals exist? It's more people who are doing things that used to be OK, but now are not OK."[4]

A central purpose of this book is to help both the clinician and client understand the deficits and internal voids that would lead a man to act inappropriately. But let's never lose sight of the core problem here. These behaviors are all sexual misconduct and are all harmful—whether they are the acts of the predator or the clueless. And of course, a man with integrity is responsible for never crossing that line in the first place.

Motivations for Boundary Violations

Why do they do it? What motivates someone (usually a man toward a woman) to cross a boundary and generate some degree of discomfort, disgust, annoyance, shame, or outright fear? The stories we will deconstruct here take place in a range of settings; we consider relationships at work, on campus, on the street, and with trusted figures.

Searching for Intimacy in All the Wrong Places

Many of the men who are #MeToo offenders are plagued with feelings of social and sexual ineptitude. They don't know how to go about relating to or courting women the respectful way, like being friendly, acting confident, showing genuine interest, taking some chances and risks.

In studies of attachment disorders, one form of insecure attachment is known as "avoidant" (or "dismissive"). The origin of this insecure attachment style often lies in childhood rejection or neglect, which led the child and then the adult to erect a "dismissive" wall around his heart. The adult who matches this profile wants to be in a relationship (he is not schizoid), but protects against this need and vulnerability by not consciously experiencing (and not demonstrating) much need for emotional closeness. He is more comfortable in emotional isolation, distancing himself from seeking meaningful relationships or from fully opening up when he is in one.

These are men who often have difficulty forming adult relationships. And even if they have somehow found themselves in a romantic relationship, they often cannot successfully integrate emotional intimacy and sexual intimacy into one package and one relationship. Conflicts about intimacy often lead them to seek sexual gratification elsewhere. Engaging in out-of-control sexual behavior (which could include porn addiction, soliciting prostitutes, anonymous sex, or exhibitionism) can serve to regulate the threat of emotional closeness.

The source of some of these #MeToo behaviors can best be understood as deficits in social and interpersonal skills—which have led to an impaired ability to establish relationships in a more conventional way.

Even reasonably healthy, secure, and confident men know that it is inherently risky to make a romantic or sexual move. There is the risk of rejection, and rejection can be difficult to tolerate. And if a relationship does develop, men fearful of attachment and intimacy may live in dread that they will not perform well enough—and that they will ultimately be rejected, hurt, or abandoned.

But everyone is still in need of connection, fearful or not. So getting even a rather primitive form of attention or sexual connection with a woman is much better than none—regardless if it's only the result of a power relationship where the woman feels obligated to respond positively (or at least tolerably) and the connection is inauthentic.

A client named Binh is a Vietnamese man working for a Silicon Valley company. He is in his 40s, and he has lived and worked in California since he was in college. He is shy, introverted, sexually repressed, and quite clueless about the mores of courting American women. He was put on probation at his workplace for making sexually suggestive comments to women with whom he worked. Part of his workplace probation involved counseling about sexual harassment issues.

For Binh, this inappropriate behavior had developed over a number of years. Although compatibly married since he was in his early 20s, his sexual relationship with his wife had evaporated years ago. Earlier in his career he was at a work conference at a hotel, where he and other team members were holding interviews for jobs at the company. He made what he describes as "a pass" at a woman he had been interviewing. Why? "Because I knew she was having sex with another guy at this conference, and I thought, 'She's available!'" When she ultimately did not get offered the job, she reported Binh's pass to his employer and he received a letter of reprimand.

A couple of years later, he made another pass, this time to the wife of another employee: "I knew she was sleeping with other men at the company, so I thought maybe it was possible she would sleep with me too." Some time after that, he perceived that a secretary working with one of the other executives seemed to be showing sexual interest in him and he responded with flirtation.

Most recently, he became interested in a 20-year-old female intern working at the company, because she "wore revealing clothing." He asked her out via email and followed up numerous times. She gave him a classic evasive response of "I want to think about it." When he persisted, she told him to stop. She later came into the personnel department with her father and quit her job. Binh said he felt terrible and ashamed to think that he had harmed her. He tortured himself thinking, "What am I doing chasing a 20-year-old woman living with her father?"

It became clear that Binh's was not a case of sexual predation. It was not a case of trading sex for career advancement. It was not a case of narcissistic grandiosity run amok. While the impact of his behavior was unmistakably destructive and profoundly inappropriate, everyone (his supervisees, his coworkers, his employers, and his therapist) understood that this was a case of social ineptitude. He reported that he actually thought his behavior was a normal way of showing sexual interest and that the women who worked with him would be charmed by this. He was horribly ashamed once he understood that he had offended and scared these women.

Likewise, a man who sends out photos of his genitals is often ineptly seeking connection and validation (while actually risking little). As Dr. Sarah Davies puts it: "Sending out dick pix can be a 'low risk' form of connection and intimacy (something we all have a deep, human, yearning for). But here it is protected behind a very masculine physical form, without the risks of being too emotionally vulnerable. Fear of rejection is natural, but if that rejection is in response to a lump of flesh, that is perhaps more bearable than the rejection being about a more meaningful part of his identity."[5]

One man interviewed for an *Esquire*[6] article describes his own behavior this way, looking back: "I realize now that it was more of a misguided replacement for trying to make actual meaningful connections with people who I felt I wasn't 'good enough' for." He goes on to say how he has changed over the years: "Overall, I have a much healthier take on relationships in general now that I'm older, which I'm thankful for."

Men who are cut off from feelings get confused about their natural human longing for intimacy. Many men have been socialized to believe that *If I feel close to her, that must mean sex.* In the movie *About Schmidt*,[7] Jack Nicholson plays a character who confuses friendliness and warmth from a woman with sexual interest.

In this movie, Warren Schmidt is an emotionally limited man who has recently lost Helen, his wife of many years. He is sad and aimless, and he tries to reach out to his daughter and other people in his life sincerely—but rather ineptly. He is befriended by a nice couple living in a trailer park. They spend a fun evening together over dinner and some beers. When the husband goes out for some more beer, the wife very sweetly tells Schmidt: "The feeling that I get from you is that—despite your good attitude, and your positive outlook, I think inside, you're a sad man." She goes on to say: "I see something more than grief and loss, something deeper . . . . fear . . . and loneliness."

Schmidt is deeply moved. He tells her, "I've only know you for . . . an hour or so, and yet, I feel like you understand me, better than my wife Helen ever did. Even after 42 years of marriage . . . . Maybe if I had met someone like you earlier."

And then he reaches over to her and starts kissing her. She responds with "Get off me, are you insane? God, what is wrong with you?" He is devastated and extremely remorseful. She kicks him out of their trailer.

The character Warren Schmidt technically committed an act of sexual assault on this woman. But this clearly falls into the category of emotionally and socially clueless men who confuse warm feelings with sexual ones. He may have caused harm, but intended none.

Madeleine Holden, a lawyer and writer, describes many of the men who offend in ways like this: "I think they are often clueless and desperate for female attention."[8] Although she acknowledges that many of the #MeToo men are certainly arrogant and entitled (and that making sexually suggestive comments, showing women porn, or showing or sending pictures of one's genitals is a peculiarly male arrogance), she also concludes that "I'm not sure that (many of these men are) exercising power in any deliberate sense."

Self-Centered Projections

People in general (and these men in particular) usually see what they want to see in others' behavior, and many #MeToo men project these assumptions onto the women that interest them. Men with high levels of narcissism (given their inflated positive self-image and perception of others through their own filter), or those with deficits in emotional intelligence, are likely to believe that most women find them sexually appealing. And, in what at first seems contradictory, a man with significant deficits in his sense of self desperately clings to the fantasy that women will find him appealing. So an individual with these deficits who thinks a woman is sexually attracted to him is likely to interpret her behavior as a sexual invitation, even if that was *not* her intention. When she dresses to be attractive, he perceives that her efforts must have been meant for him. When she is friendly or even mildly flirty, he perceives that this must be a clear signal that she is interested in what he is interested in.

Here's an example from a report about employee complaints in the San Diego County District Attorney's Office[9]: A senior IT engineer received a Letter of Warning in May 2017. He was cited for repeatedly tugging on the hair of a student worker at the office. He was also accused of making several inappropriate comments about women and their looks. He probably thought this was cute and that women would find his behavior to be somewhere between sexy and innocuous. He was warned not to make comments with sexual innuendo and not to touch other employees.

The problem of self-centered projections is especially relevant in making sense of men who send out unsolicited pictures of their genitals. For instance, Match.com generated a massive study on the dating experiences of singles who utilize their site and found that a whopping 49% of all women surveyed had been on the receiving end of a penis photo that they didn't request.[10] Why would a man possibly think that sending a picture of his penis could possibly be a turn-on to a woman?

There are probably some men who send pictures of their genitals to women as an aggressive, hostile, misogynistic act, hoping to shock and offend the recipient. Maybe somewhere there are a few men who get turned on by shocking the woman on the other end of the text: A 21st-century version of the old-fashioned trick of making obscene phone calls. This can be understood as an act of power and control—and the turn on is seeing (or imagining, in the case of genital photos), the shocked reactions from the women who get these pictures.

A man's motivations for this behavior are probably best understood by the discussions in the previous chapter.

But the prevailing profile of the man who sends dick pics of himself is one of self-centered delusion. Somehow the man we profile here has convinced himself that his package is spectacular and that the vision of this will impress and arouse the recipient. At best (and this is a stretch), he might just think that his gesture is cute and a cool way of saying "I like you."

As sex researcher Justin Lehmiller puts it, " . . . the most likely explanation is that men are simply misperceiving women's interest in receiving photos of their junk . . . . (M)en tend to overperceive how interested female strangers are in sex."[11] Research studies for decades now have told us that men consistently misperceive signals from women. Often, when a woman intends to signal friendliness, a man will perceive sexual interest. When this registers (often falsely, but registers nevertheless) as sexual interest, it follows (often falsely, often with disastrous effect) that her sexual interest means that she would really be interested in seeing his greatest sexual asset.

Deficits in Emotional Intelligence

In a podcast episode of *This American Life*,[12] the Australian journalist Eleanor Gordon-Smith confronted her catcallers in Sydney and found that most of the men were absolutely convinced that the women whom they singled out actually enjoyed the attention. She tried to explain to them that this was almost always *not* the case—in fact, just the opposite. Most of the men were not convinced, and their interpretation had everything to do with projecting their own experience onto the female experience. They know that if random women singled *them* out for sexual attention, *they* would be flattered—thrilled, even. So it follows that, because many men would be thrilled to get a photo of a woman flashing her breasts, they just automatically assume that she would be aroused by seeing his privates.

One said, "A guy just looks for a reaction, a smile, you're a dickhead, hi." When the interviewer asked him how many successful relationships have started from someone saying he's a dickhead, he laughed and sheepishly said, "Zero."

Another catcaller (who had made motions like air-grabbing a woman's breasts) said, "I like saying hello to women. I like being friendly to women . . . . It's a nice thing when a man says hello."

Another said, "Oh, you know, I want her to get enjoyment out of what I yell at her. I don't want her to be—in no way I want her to be offended, or feel in any way insecure about anything I say. It's always—like, I'm never going to say anything rude or abusive. It's always for the good of the night."

One other man described his habit of walking up to a random woman in a group and slapping her butt: "'Cause I try and put myself in their position, and I try and imagine what it would be like to just be walking and have some compliment thrown at me by whoever. I would get some type of compliment out of it. If they'd had enough balls, or had enough beers, or fucking whatever to be able to yell something out, I'd be like, yeah, fucking whatever . . . . I would feel a little bit special. If I was with a group of mates, I'd be like, ha, that's right. I've got a better ass than all you."

The interviewer concludes, "These guys didn't seem like sexist nut jobs. They didn't seem unreasonable. They weren't hard to talk to. And it occurred to me they've just like, made a mistake. They just got some kind of central fact about women wrong, and they think that we really enjoy this."

In another informal but interesting social psychology experiment, a blogger on Thrillist[13] was looking for a romantic partner on dating apps. Like many single women, she had been the unwilling recipient of an extraordinary number of dick pics. So, she decided to conduct a little experiment: She would show men what it was like to get an unsolicited photo of female genitals.

She found a picture of a "cute" vagina from the internet (somehow getting her friends and colleagues to rate the pictures and identify the "cutest"). After she matched with a series of men and exchanging some flirty texts, she sent the vagina photo. She was hoping to have these men experience the grossness of what she had been experiencing. She assumed that the typical response from the men would be getting grossed out and pissed off. And she assumed that most of them, like most women, would want nothing to do with her.

To her surprise, the men mostly responded with descriptions of how they planned to pleasure her and were eager to reply by sending very personal photos of their own (apparently thinking, *I would love it—so she would too!*). She even tried to get the desired response of disgust that she sought by sending the photo immediately after exchanging initial hellos. The results shocked her: There was no turnoff. Instead, the number of male genital photos sent in return grew considerably.

She considered her experiment to be a total failure. But of course it was not a failure—it just produced results that surprised her. She concluded that "given that men like to send dick pics, I suppose their enthusiasm for v-pics makes sense."

How do women on the receiving end of these photos typically react? Maybe, some women, somewhere, in some context, find them arousing or charming. But most are shocked. And disgusted. And scared. Some may just think it's stupid and do not feel particularly offended. Women often say that sending an unsolicited dick pic is one of the lamest and most pathetic moves possible—and they are mystified as to how a man could possibly think that it is anything but a doomed strategy.

Other women may just feel hurt and disappointed, because they'd thought they might be dealing with a guy who at least had decent manners and decent capacity for respecting women. A typical female comment: "I think men care way more about their penises than we do"[14] seems to sum up the differences fairly accurately.

The worst part of the experience is not the random creep who sends these, but rather the hurt feelings and sense of betrayal that so often accompany receiving these pictures. This is the same phenomenon seen in victims of childhood sexual abuse: The more you know the person, the closer you are to him or her, the worse it is. A blogger from a sex and relationships website articulates the experience this way: "[T]he problem for a lot of us isn't that we only wanted to be friends and the guy didn't pick up on that before sending us an unsolicited picture of his junk . . . . The problem is often that we are very interested . . . UNTIL we are sent an unsolicited picture of his dick. It feels . . . a little like assault. Not as traumatic as a physical assault, but certainly aggressive and nonconsensual. It's not that different."[15]

Former senator Al Franken is another case in point. A woman accused him of having forced an unwanted kiss on her during a 2006 USO tour. Particularly damning was the photo of him clownishly pretending to grab her breasts while she was asleep, which she described as humiliating. Seven more women followed with accusations against Franken; all of them centered on inappropriate groping or kisses.

But it *never* occurred to Franken (before the #MeToo movement and the identification of the behaviors described above) that he was doing anything that was remotely inappropriate or wrong. After Franken kissed a female acquaintance on the mouth in 2007, during his first campaign, an aide from South Dakota, David Benson, took him aside and said, "Don't do that."

"Really?" Franken said. Benson warned him that people might misinterpret it.[16]

Franken reports that he became somewhat more careful after that warning.
He realized that he might have been unaware of how his behavior came across.
"I'm a very physical person . . . . I guess maybe sometimes I'm oblivious."

When posing with kids, he jokingly put them in a headlock and the families
would often laugh about it because they knew he was just clowning around. But
once, when he did this in the Capitol, another senator, Chris Murphy, warned
him, "That looks like something that will bring joy and happiness to a thou-
sand families—until it ends your career."[17]

Obviously, he was not careful enough. But in the broad range of #MeToo
offenders, men who are inappropriately "touchy" are clearly at the less pathological end of the spectrum, and the pain and trauma of the victims of these
behaviors (while real and not to be dismissed) pales in comparison to many of
the other behaviors we have been reviewing. Some of these men (like Franken,
or like George H. W. Bush in the example that follows) are operating in some
fog of misguided norms regarding the acceptability of slightly rascally male
behavior, or some clueless belief that everyone wants to be touched by him and
will think it's just fun and friendly.

Boys Will Be Boys:
Conforming to Perceived Gender Role Norms

Anybody who has investigated cases of young men (as a group) who have
harassed or actually assaulted a woman knows that many of these guys would
never have done this on their own. A few predatory types might have followed
through, but the majority of young men who perpetrate these offenses get
swept up in the creepy and often violent groupthink that can possess packs
of men. Some #MeToo men are "overconforming" to common, if exaggerated,
notions of masculinity. They're doing a five-star rendition of what they think
manhood requires.

President George H. W. Bush, it has now come to light, had a long-standing
habit of groping women. He was particularly adept at surreptitiously getting
away with this during photo ops when he would put his arm around a woman—
and his hand would stray.

Multiple women came forward describing incidents that took place before
Bush was in a wheelchair and even while he was in office. One woman claimed

that President Bush put his hand on her rear end while having a photograph taken at a 1992 reelection fundraiser.

Another woman, Roslyn Corrigan, described an incident from 2003—when she was 16 years old.[18] She reports that her parents took her to an event in Texas and that she was looking forward to meeting the former president, until he groped her. Jenkins reports: "My initial reaction was absolute horror. I was really, really confused . . . . The first thing I did was look at my mom and, while he was still standing there, I didn't say anything. What does a teenager say to the ex-president of the United States? Like, 'Hey dude, you shouldn't have touched me like that?'"

When these reports first started coming out, Bush's spokesperson responded with a classic example of minimization and rationalization that we see all too often in these cases: "President Bush has been confined to a wheelchair for roughly five years, so his arm falls on the lower waist of people with whom he takes pictures."[19]

Later, as more reports over many years began surfacing, the same spokesperson offered up a new version of the behavior. Now we have an example of minimizing by reframing the intentions. The spokesman acknowledged that Bush had groped women repeatedly as accused but that it didn't mean what people thought it meant: He "has patted women's rears in what he intended to be a good-natured manner."[20]

These are hardly major sexual assaults, and these incidents do not represent the worst of the power-driven #MeToo violations that directly involve exchanging favors for rewards—but it is still sexual harassment, a #MeToo violation, and profoundly creepy. And these behaviors can still have a lasting impact on the victims.

For many men, the practice of making countless overtures of any form—relentless flirting, consistent sexual innuendoes, pursuing women relentlessly, even sending genital photos—and only being successful occasionally—is apparently good enough.

What motivates a mostly well-behaved man—a seemingly happily married family man under constant public scrutiny—to engage in this offensive behavior? There is nothing to suggest that former president Bush was a true sexual predator.

Maybe he just thought it was cute. He was confirming to an old-school notion of how "rascally" men behave, a kind of "boys will be boys" mentality.

They get a little frisky with the ladies, and (they think) the ladies enjoy it. Or at least the ladies will tolerate it as a naughty but not as an offensive nuisance. While many women have *never* found this type of attention cute, and many men now realize how offensive this is, it still does not mean George H. W. Bush is evil. It is just evidence that he was clueless and rather greedy, and it identifies him as destructively conforming to these perceived male norms. This is not a hopeless condition, and many men who get clued in are more than capable of challenging their allegiance to these perceived norms and reining in behavior that they never realized needed reining in before.

Here's another example from the report about employee complaints in the San Diego County District Attorney's Office.[21] The records show complaints of sexual harassment and inappropriate comments against a male paralegal between the years of 2011 and 2015. In the 2011 incident he received a letter of warning stating he'd violated the county's sexual harassment policy and was told to retake sexual harassment prevention training. A woman had complained that he had sexually harassed her over a period of time by making "inappropriate gestures and statements" among other things. When he was apparently upset about not getting a promotion in 2016 and told a female colleague who did get promoted, "Maybe I should grow a pair of boobs?" He apologized four days later, but still was interviewed by the Employee Relations Office for a hostile work environment allegation. He was counseled and later transferred to a different unit. His behavior represents his notion (mixed in with a dose of hostility toward women) that men should stick up for their rights against women encroaching on their territory.

Passive Aggressiveness and Abdicating Responsibility

Sexual harassment is often presented in a "playful" manner—so when the victim protests, gets upset, or reports it, she's identified as being "too sensitive" or "too feminist" or "no fun" or "too uptight."

Frequently, the offender is counting on the victim's self-doubt and confusion about what really happened to keep her quiet—and he knows that he can always claim that he was just doing his job or just engaging in playful banter. It's so easy for the offender; when accused of crossing a line or creating an unsafe work environment, he can just throw up his hands and say:

- Wow, I had no idea she would take it that way!
- I was just kidding.
- I'm the most feminist guy there is—Everybody knows I love women!
- I thought women *liked* to hear compliments!

In Michal Aviad's movie *Working Woman*,[22] one chilling scene portrays a boss insisting that his female assistant stay late to help him with a project. She can't say *no*. He has already tried to kiss her before, and he is turning this evening into a more sexualized and dangerous scene. He turns out the lights while they're working in his office.

> She says, calmly: "Can you turn on the light?"
> He says: "Sorry, accident."
> The light goes out again.
> She says, more forcefully: "Turn the light on, Benny! It's stressing me out!"
> After a few extremely long seconds, he turns the light back on. She is looking at him, terrified.
> He says: "Can't you take a joke? . . . I'm sorry . . . What? . . . So I can't joke around with you?"

This boss, in the power position, manages to engage in power-based exploitation of his assistant—and he does it in a way that can be labeled as just a "joke," intimating that she is just too uptight.

The scripts from the *That's Harassment*[23] videos (all based on true stories) capture the nuances of this confusion expertly. One scene disturbingly depicts a beautiful young model posing for a photo shoot. The photographer encourages her to adopt sexy poses and sexy looks—hardly out of line for a model photo shoot. But the instructions become increasingly graphic, to the point where he tells her to put her hand into her pants and pleasure herself for the camera. Particularly gut-wrenching is that the camera eventually pans wide and shows a group of about ten technicians and bystanders impassively watching this whole embarrassing moment. The model—whom we can assume is young and ambitious and desperately wanting to please this photographer as part of her career advancement—is again painfully silent. She is probably imagining that confronting the photographer would only lead to this response: *I do this all the time—it's my job to make you feel sexy and special. Don't be so uptight.*

One more scene from that video series depicts a female bartender in her 20s on the first day of her new job. She is getting trained by a male bartender in his 30s. We include a summary of the vignette here, along with commentary from a panel of *New York Times* experts.[24] Pay attention to the clever passive-aggressive ways in which the senior bartender gets away with sexualizing the encounter—that allows him plenty of room to defend his behavior as innocuous.

He starts out by establishing how he has worked at the bar for three years, even longer than the other staff.

Immediately, a power differential is established. All of us are taught to be polite and agreeable when we start a new job.

Robert Eckstein, lead trainer, Prevention Innovations
Research Center, University of New Hampshire

When she tells him that she knows one of the other bartenders, Liviya, because they went to surf camp together, he starts to turn the conversation in a flirty direction: "Surfing camp?! That's kind of hot. You and Liviya, little bikinis, catching waves . . ."

A common technique for harassers is to start with inappropriate but relatively benign comments. This allows them to claim they were just joking. They are also testing to see what else they can get away with.

Robert Eckstein, trainer

His next move is a little bolder. Under the pretense of "warning" her about life as a bartender, he imitates what they might do to her: "Guys are going to be coming up to you all the time . . . . Oh yeah. They're going to be like, "Hey, that's a sexy rear you got going on over there. Does that sexy rear have a number I can call?"

By imitating other men, he is framing his behavior as not his own. This tactic makes it easier to deny intent and get away with an action. She could say, "I understand you are trying to let me know how customers might treat me, but I don't need you to act it out."

Shannon Rawski, professor

Framing inappropriate comments as compliments is a powerful form of manipulation.

Gillian Thomas, senior staff lawyer,
ACLU, Women's Rights Project

During all this, she is lightheartedly protesting—never encouraging, but clearly reluctant to more assertively call him out. Then he actually gets physical. He says, "Yeah, cause you know guys. They'll be getting drunk, thinking they can have whatever they want. You know, the whole "grab 'em by the . . ." thing, and then out of nowhere they're just like . . ."

And he grabs her from behind. She's so surprised she's not even sure how to react. When she does protest saying, "Hey, you just fully grabbed me," he makes the classic passive-aggressive move. He acts like he was just joking. And he points out that he was just trying to look out for her. He even then insists that ("to make things even") she grab him from behind—as if that would be something she even remotely wanted to do.

Then he pulls out one final passive-aggressive maneuver: "O.K., good. 'Cause for a second there you turned around like you were going to give me some kind of feminist rant garbage. And I'm the biggest feminist I know . . . . Yeah, I love women."

It's all spelled out in that scene. The offensive male bartender has only engaged in behavior that he can credibly claim was no big deal or was misinterpreted. Many of the #MeToo offenders we study are masterful in this passive-aggressive behavior—exploiting the confusion and self-doubt of the recipient of the behavior. This mirrors domestic violence offenders who know how to inflict abuse that will not leave any bruises, which make their offenses much more difficult to actually prove.

The Continuum of #MeToo Behaviors: Sexual Assault or "Bad Date"?

And finally, there is simply the particular form of male ineptitude now popularized as the "bad date." The Aziz Ansari story discussed here is the most public example of this phenomenon. While "Grace," the woman who went public with the details of their date accused him of a kind of sexual assault, the prevailing consensus about this sequence of events has been mixed. Was this sexual assault? Sexual harassment? Sexual misconduct? A bad date?

Briefly, the story (according to Grace and never denied by Ansari) is that Grace and Ansari met at an after-party at the 2017 Emmy awards.[25] They flirted, she gave him her number. He called her and they got together for a date a week later.

After their date, they went back to his apartment. He started kissing her, then grabbing her breast, then started to undress her and himself. Within minutes, he said he was going to get a condom. She told him to chill. He went back to kissing her. He briefly performed oral sex on her and asked her to do the same for him, which she did. Ansari also physically pulled her hand towards his penis multiple times throughout the night. Grace reports that he wouldn't let her move away from him. She says she used verbal and nonverbal cues to indicate how uncomfortable and distressed she was.

Grace remembers him asking again and again, "Where do you want me to fuck you?" She excused herself to the bathroom soon after. Then she went back to Ansari. He asked her if she was okay. She told him that she didn't want to feel forced, because then she would hate him—and she didn't want to hate him.

Ansari responded sympathetically, and Grace thought the pressure was over. Then he pointed to his penis and motioned for her to perform oral sex—which she did. She said she felt pressured.

Then he asked her again, "Where do you want me to fuck you? Do you want me to fuck you right here?" He rammed his penis against her while he said it, mimicking intercourse.

She said that she wasn't ready to do this. He backed off, and they watched some TV together. While the TV played in the background, he kissed her again and moved to undo her pants. She turned away.

She remembers saying, "You guys are all the same, you guys are all the fucking same." Ansari asked her what she meant. When she turned to answer, she says he met her with "gross, forceful kisses."

Grace stood up from the couch, moved back to the kitchen island where she'd left her phone, and said she would call herself an Uber. He hugged her and kissed her goodbye, and gave her another "aggressive" kiss.

This incident stirred up controversy—especially among women. *The Washington Post* website, thelily.com, published two opinion pieces with different views about this story.[26] Then they collected over 150 comments and blogs from women reacting to these pieces. Many women viewed this as an assault because Grace never offered clear consent—and he certainly did not inquire about it. Many other women were deeply critical of Grace, believing that identifying this as sexual assault does a disservice to "real" victims of assault. They identified this as an account of a gross, regrettable situation that could have turned out terrible—but did not, and it is not actually assault.

While not in any way absolving Ansari for his pressuring and insensitive "bad date" behavior, they also saw Grace as woefully unassertive (e.g., "How can we find our voices as women, and become sexually positive and confident, and STOP sexual assault with accusations like these that minimize and trivialize the whole movement and bring us steps backward?")

The broadest range of women commenting recognized the complexity in this particular story. Here are some of the most valuable comments about the issues raised. They acknowledge that there is a spectrum of what is considered sexual misconduct—running from words and catcalls all the way to violence and rape—and that Grace's account likely falls somewhere between those:

I'm a victim of actual assault. This isn't assault, this is an awkward date. Not calling it out for what it is gives more fuel to the people trying to light a fire under #MeToo and calling it a witch hunt.

Her being much younger than him and not a celebrity played a big factor here. Maybe she wanted him to like her. Maybe she was confused as to what was happening, as his public persona is much different than the pushy, aggressive man he became. No, he clearly didn't rape her. It's complicated, but she let him know several times she wasn't digging the aggressive way he pursued her, physically.

This situation is an opportunity to look at our culture's sexual practices that are normalized while also being assaulting, coercive and rapey. This is why we talk about rape culture.' It's totally possible that he, like many men, was doing what he was taught to do. Despite that, it's incredibly wrong, and we should absolutely use this as a chance to educate about true consent. It's an opportunity, not a derailment. Let's make some positive change out of it!

Being a feminist does not mean that women are right all the time. This woman is not right on so many levels. She is a danger to legitimate victims.

I do think there's a place for this experience in a DIFFERENT conversation. How women feel like we owe men something sexually, how elusive consent can feel, how strange it is we sometimes lose our confident voices in sexual situations, how complex sex is emotionally even when we go in with different expectations . . . all of those issues deserve a platform in the feminist discussion. I can relate. And it's problematic and f—ked up. But this is an account of a gross, regrettable situation that could have turned out terrible. This particular account is not ASSAULT.

We don't know her history outside of this little snippet. Did you know, for instance, that people who've been sexually assaulted or abused in other ways in the past, especially childhood, often have trouble speaking up and removing themselves from situations like this? It's very common.

I have to disagree that assault is a lot about intent. Impact > intent. I think a lot of the conversation around this has to do with the fact that many men don't believe that they've crossed any boundaries and don't consider how the power dynamics play into the situation. That's not resulting in fewer traumatized women, though.

This case includes one's perception on subtle cues. How many times was I told I was flirting when I was just being courteous? How many times were my own actions perceived incorrectly? When she said she wanted to go home, he got her a ride. No sexual intercourse occurred. What more can one do?

If anyone thinks this type of scene is normal and just a bad date, they're making a really great argument for why #MeToo is so desperately necessary and how incredibly far we have to go.

While women do need to overcome socialization to be unabashedly vocal about what they do and do not want, men also need to give up their intentional obliviousness and magical thinking: Read nonverbal cues and check in often. Do not continue to act unless she is 100 percent enthusiastic in word and deed.

Wrapping It Up

These last two chapters have examined a range of #MeToo behaviors. We've considered the actions of the most despicable predators, men who are deeply wounded and seeking gratification, men who are clueless but definitely not predators, and men who misread the sometimes less-than-clear cues from their partners. While all these individuals have committed some form of sexual harassment, assault, or misconduct, they are clearly different in personality, style, and motivation—and they offer widely different possibilities for change and rehabilitation. For those of us who work with men, it is essential that we understand who we are dealing with.

In the next chapter, our colleague Leona Smith Di Faustino, from California State University, Long Beach, covers the ways that prototype #MeToo situations are made even more complex because of the intersectionality of sexual boundary violations with race, ethnicity, and sexual orientation.

Chapter 5

Two Truths

The Need for Intersectional Awareness

—Leona Smith Di Faustino, LCSW

In 2006, Tarana Burke established an organization focusing on sexual assault and harassment, particularly as experienced by girls and women of color. When she used "Me Too" as a bridge to connect the stories of survivors into a singular thread, she created space to examine the unique intersections of harm that exist for women of color. Members of marginalized communities navigate complex layers of systemic oppression and cultural variance that impact how they name and claim their histories of sexual harm.[1] This navigation is present in the Black community of the United States, where Black women and girls must negotiate the pressures of putting community first (at the expense of themselves) simultaneously with dominant culture norms that cause racial trauma.[2] Burke's "Me Too" put women of color's experiences at the center of these complex layers and provided a context for sexual harm that sits outside of the dominant narrative of white women's victimhood.[3]

In 2017, when celebrity social media users galvanized the public with #MeToo by linking women's experiences of sexual assault and sexual harassment in a collective virtual voice, Burke's intersectional framework of examining sexual harm of marginalized communities was erased. #MeToo became mainstream, evident in the expansion of awareness surrounding #MeToo being centered on white, Western women's experiences.[4]

In not powering itself from an intersectional framework, this momentum of #MeToo has in some ways hindered the influence and reach of Burke's original focus. When creating a template for interventions and programming, it is important that efforts are made to advance awareness of different cultural and racial experiences of sexual misconduct. When harnessing the momentum of the virtual community and channeling it into the tangible spaces of schools, offices, and institutions of daily living, we shift from the anonymity of the Twitter handle to the woman sitting across from us in our offices. Who is this person in relation to her history of sexual harm and how can therapists help her? Most importantly, how will her experience reflect what we are learning from the collective voice of #MeToo, and how will it hold a singular note that is unique to her experiences?

Please note that while the primary focus of this book is on sexual misconduct and harassment rather than sexual violence, this particular chapter covers research and theory about all forms of sexual violence toward women. What all these forms of #MeToo behaviors have in common is that they are committed by men who cause sexual harm of some kind toward women. And the vulnerability and impact of this sexual harm is often more complex and damaging for disenfranchised women—particularly women of color.

An Intersectional Framework

The act of helping victims is complicated by the fact that institutions of power are founded on principles that uphold systemic oppression based on race, class, gender, sexuality, and the variations of human experience that shift one away from the "dominant."[5] Policy and procedures that are constructed to help victims exist within frameworks that perpetuate disenfranchisement against marginalized individuals and communities.[6] The activists or academics who are well versed in critical theories are probably nodding their heads; clinicians may not be. If you are not familiar with critical theories, you may not be well acquainted with this crucial information, so this chapter is of particular importance.

However, this chapter is not intended to be a lecture about the structural inequities of our society that are perpetuated by a white patriarchal hierarchy of power; it is meant to provide an opportunity for everyone to lean away from their comfort zones and into their learning edge.[7] Our comfort zones are the things we know and how we practice what we know. They are static places because they are the areas of knowledge that we can control. When we lean into existing within a learning edge, we are creating space to be at the edge of our comfort zone.[8] This allows an opportunity for growth because it is in this place that we can begin to understand different perspectives. For people without a history of working in the sexual misconduct field, #MeToo is an example of existing within one's learning edge. The narrative of what has been acceptable is being reframed and reshaped to push people out of their comfort zones.

To help push that reframing to be inclusive, an intersectional framework is crucial. Patricia Hills Collins states, "Intersectionality as an analytic tool gives people better access to complexity of the world and themselves."[9] An intersectional framework is introduced in this chapter to help guide counselors toward a more inclusive practice of care. This is centered in a critical consciousness of practice that requires therapists to be more self-reflective when working with individuals who hold multiple social identities.[10]

The risk of not paying attention to the many ways that victims of #MeToo violations may differ because of intersecting identities and backgrounds is known as a "beta" error.[11] This occurs when race or minority status is extremely relevant to the presenting problem but is dismissed (or just ignored) by the counselor. That's why we teach about intersectionality, and why this chapter is included to help counselors and therapists in their work.

There is always a risk of what is known as an "alpha" error[12] as well: when the therapist assumes *incorrectly* that race or minority status is central to the presenting problem. This is a kind of microaggression ("Oh, you must be especially sensitive to this because you are Black"), even when this may not be attuned to the client's experience. While we focus on the nuances and differences, it is important that we never forget that the commonalities among survivors of #MeToo are more prominent than the differences.

The Value of Self-Reflection

Self-reflection is crucial when working to move out of one's comfort zones.[13] Comfort zones are the safe places where knowledge is known and the parameters of what is done fits a particular worldview.[14] Comfort zones do not spring fully formed from our consciousness but are instead created from how we interact with and are impacted by systems. Our environment creates what we know, and as mentioned previously, the framework of our environment is founded on principles of disenfranchisement for those that do not share identity with dominant society. Self-reflection is often difficult because it requires individuals to be honest when no one is watching and holding them accountable. Therefore, people often begin and end with the basics. "I'm not racist because I don't use racial epithets" or "I have Black friends" or "I voted for Barack Obama" (or, fill in the blank). That bar for self-reflection is low, but it can be comforting because it centers on something that can be controlled. If you don't do the bad thing, you are already winning.

Let's walk through how a therapist would practice self-reflection from an intersectional framework. We will use the social phenomena of sexual assault. Statistics are illustrative of how we make sense of social phenomena. About 1 in 4 women and 1 in 10 men experience contact sexual assault, physical assault, and/or stalking by an intimate partner during their lifetime."[15] These statistics provide facts on the social phenomenon of sexual assault based on gender but are devoid of the intricacies of who these "women" and "men" are.

Statistical averages do not always provide information on the multiple populations of individuals and communities that are harmed by sexual assault. Focusing only on what exists on the surface of rates of sexual misconduct in society leads to the creation of programs that fall short. These programs may address the problem but can lack the cultural relevance needed to improve the well-being of all members of a community.

Intersectional self-reflection requires one to go deeper and know and acknowledge that intersectional statistics speak to an issue that is far more complex than "male" or "female." These statistics include "American Indian and Alaskan women have the highest rates of rape and sexual assault victimization compared to all other race and ethnic groups,"[16] or "Approximately 1 in 8 lesbian women (13%), nearly half of bisexual women (46%), and 1 in 6 heterosexual women (17%) have been raped in their lifetime."[17]

When we work only from the starting point of "women," we aren't acknowledging how the systems of race, gender, and sexual orientation converge and impact how individuals process and cope with the trauma responses of sexual misconduct.[18] Social factors such as racism, sexism, and homophobia converge in unique ways. Intervention strategies based only on the generic concept of a woman will not meet the needs of individuals who have multiple intersecting identities, particularly identities that are systematically disenfranchised within larger society.[19]

It can be tempting to fall into the trap of "one size fits all" while riding the wave of #MeToo. In the digital age there are constant voices screaming into the void, but the voices that rise up are often those of the most privileged in our society. It is important that if counselors are using #MeToo as a catalyst for action, they are stepping back and listening for the voices they can't hear. Not hearing them doesn't mean they don't exist, but instead should raise questions as to why those voices have been silenced. It instead becomes an opportunity to explore why they may be silenced.

In working with #MeToo survivors, it is important to understand how holding multiple marginalized identities directly correlates to the silencing of marginalized voices. As referenced earlier, #MeToo has been dominated by the stories of women, particularly white women, that hold privilege in society.

Where does a clinician start when wanting to incorporate self-reflection in their practice? It begins with asking the following questions:

- Who is a survivor of sexual misconduct?
- How do I provide care based on my perception of a survivor of sexual misconduct?
- What are my strengths? What are my growth areas? What is my capacity to provide an intersectional framework of care?
- What continuing practices of critical reflection need to be implemented during and after therapy is provided to one's clients who are recipients of #MeToo behavior?
- If I do not have capacity to provide an intersectional framework of care, how do I ensure collaboration to offer this support?

If your perception is informed by generalized statistics, your concept of who experiences sexual misconduct is going to be broad. If your perception is based on your immediate community, it can create gaps based on who accesses and has access to resources. Members of marginalized communities typically navigate looking for the underrepresented in their community with more nuance than those who hold status as members of the dominant group of society. If you are clinician that holds membership in a dominant group, it is imperative to recognize this process.

What often occurs for people who aren't members of the dominant group is that their history of marginalization expands the parameters of who is known. Therefore, their ability to connect to different lived experiences is more developed than that of an individual who has only known a singular dominant identity and the subsequent privileges that are afforded because of that identity. Self-reflection builds awareness for those with a dominant group identity—knowing what to do begins with knowing what you *don't know*.

This reflection can be difficult. In fact it should induce some level of discomfort, because discomfort indicates growth. Muscles that are rarely used ache after exercise. Navigating where you feel comfortable and where you still need to learn should not be a solitary process either. It can easily devolve into feelings of inadequacy, or resistance. There is also the risk of reinforcing beliefs or practices that are inadvertently harmful. Consulting with someone who has a similar demographic to your client ensures there is accountability built into your self-reflection process. But it is also important to not tokenize your consultant. The Black woman you consult with may hold information you don't, but she does not represent all Black women— and she is not your magical guide, absolving you from doing your own, individual work.

The following are important questions to ask oneself when seeking consultation:

- What is it I don't know and how will this consultation improve my understanding?
- How will I ensure I don't tokenize my consultant(s)?
- How will I ensure that I incorporate the information my consultant(s) have provided?

When this process of critical reflection becomes a well-used muscle, clinicians can begin to analyze how they conduct therapy with #MeToo offenders and victims from an intersectional framework.

Good Therapy Practices

Positive therapy practices are informed by the critical reflection that therapists have engaged in by themselves or with consultants. Critical analysis should be used to determine if assessment tools and interventions do themselves perpetuate rather than reduce power inequities for survivors throughout the process of therapy. You should be sure to collaborate with other care providers when interventions are outside your scope of practice. Finally, it is important to ensure transparency of your therapy (how do you do this and to whom?), and to clearly define your own limitations and barriers (to whom?). Most significantly, it is more valuable and respectful to frankly acknowledge that, for example, you do not know much about the experience of Latinas who have entered the country illegally and live in constant fear of deportation. Clients will usually accept and even value your transparency about your limitations—but they will never accept you pretending to be someone you are not or to know something you do not.

Keep in mind that empowerment of #MeToo survivors is the focal outcome of assessment and interventions. It is the foundation of all interventions because it ensures that marginalized individuals are given access to power to make informed decisions about their care. Sexual assault and sexual misconduct are disempowering. This is where analysis begins; then intersecting identities are packed on top of this fact. Being a person of color in a society that is predicated on white patriarchal ideals is disempowering. Being queer in a society that is predicated on homophobic ideals is disempowering. Being poor in a society that absolves the mechanism of capitalist industry from accountability is disempowering. Each layer requires a constant analysis of power *with* versus power *over*, and there should be a clear delineation of where care can occur and where it cannot. Systems fail people who do not have access to privilege; therefore it is imperative within an intersectional framework of care that transparency is always present.

Practice may not always make perfect, but it can help in identifying where gaps of understanding occur. The following cases are presented as an opportunity to practice critical self-reflection. The purpose of this section is to start exercising the critical-reflection muscle. As you read the cases, take notes on where you sit in your comfort zone. Are you familiar with the information presented here? How, and in what way? If experiences of the individuals presented are new, what anxieties of providing therapy do you have? The purpose of these cases is to encourage you to lean into your learning edge. It is also an opportunity for you to begin the critical analysis of where you can be more intentional in an intersectional framework of care. All names and identifying information have been changed to protect confidentiality.

Case Analysis

Case Study 1

Tamara is a 23-year-old Black woman. She is cisgender, heterosexual, in a five-year relationship with a male partner, and mother of a two-year-old girl. She works as a cocktail waitress at a casino and lives in her grandmother's home with her partner and daughter. She is estranged from her parents and other family members.

While Tamara was serving drinks to a group of patrons at the casino, a male patron cupped her between her legs and stated, "I know how you can make a bigger tip." Shocked, Tamara dropped the tray of drinks she was holding and fled the area once the man released her. Tamara told her supervisor what occurred, but described not feeling supported, only told she could take a break before going back out on the floor. Tamara wants to quit her job, but her partner is currently finishing a training program and they need her income. She is anxious when serving drinks to patrons and describes feeling sick during her shifts. Recently, Tamara's grandmother said she needed to get over her "nonsense," because "you and your man aren't going to live for free in my house." Tamara has begun to look for another job, but she is finding it difficult to find employment that is flexible for her and her partner's childcare needs.

Case Study 2

Sarai is a 30-year-old Ecuadorian woman. She is cisgender, heterosexual, has a mobility disability, is a permanent resident of the United States, and is in the process of becoming a naturalized citizen. She is currently a student taking classes to be an LVN. She lives with extended family and has been in the United States for 10 years.

While seated in her wheelchair attending happy hour at a local bar with friends from school, a man rubbed his crotch on the back of her head and groped her breasts. One of her friends intervened and shoved the man away. An argument occurred between her friends, the man, and his friends. Sarai's wheelchair was almost tipped over, and the friend of the man that assaulted her threatened to call ICE. Concerned about more violence, Sarai and her friends left the bar. Sarai has found it difficult to go to school because the bar is near her campus, and fears she will see the man again. Her friends have encouraged her to file a police report, but Sarai doesn't trust law enforcement.

Case Study 3

Annette is a 20-year-old Chinese American woman. She is cisgender, lesbian, and is a first-generation college student. She lives at home while attending classes full-time at the local university.

While attending a party with a group of friends and graduate students, one of her teaching assistants (after a lot of alcohol), tried to pin her against a wall and kiss her. She pulled away from him, and he angrily snapped at her, "I guess they were right about you not liking men. Good luck when it comes time for grades at the end of the semester." His role as her TA meant that he had some influence over her grades. Annette was hesitant to report to the head of the department or any other college office, but her friends kept encouraging her to. She had begun to miss classes and her grades were beginning to suffer by her inability to concentrate and complete assignments.

Reflections on Case Studies

Let's begin at what your perceptions of each of these survivors are. How are you picturing them and their experiences? Are you in your comfort zone or are you starting to feel uneasy? There will probably be a combination of all those feelings, because even though all three women have experienced sexual harm, there are layers to each of their experiences that will elicit unique feelings of reflection. Starting with what you know is often the best way to begin the process of unpacking where you hold biases or have gaps of awareness.

Typically, in our first session with a victim of sexual misconduct we know or ask about the client's age, race/ethnicity, and gender identity. In subsequent sessions, depending on the client's presenting issue, we find out more about any information that seems relevant to the case, including sexual orientation, socioeconomic status, family connections, and (perhaps most importantly) any previous trauma history that might impact how the client understands and is reacting to the misconduct.

Without critical reflection, the broad generalization of what is known becomes the focal point of care. If the individual is a woman, therapy is based on cis-normative techniques for women. If the individual is queer identified, therapy is based on the needs of the LGBTQ+ community. With critical reflection, the known identities of individuals are linked in ways to provide better insight for therapy with a multifaceted approach. For Tamara, we know that her race and class status put her at risk for PTSD and somatic symptoms related to her sexual harm.[20] This is compounded with what we know regarding sexual harm toward the general population of women. As with Tamara, Sarai's gender is a risk factor for harm, but also as a woman with a disability, Sarai is at greater risk of experiencing a rape than a woman without a disability.[21] Annette's identify as a lesbian holds unique risk factors related to how the disclosure of her sexual orientation can impact the type of attention and response she receives in the aftermath of her sexual harassment.[22]

This intersectional approach to assessment also ensures that unintended consequences of care are minimized, and appropriate resources are provided to individuals in need. What could be an example of an unintended consequence of non-intersectional care? Tamara has described feeling sick and finding it difficult to work. Somatic symptoms are a common trauma response, and a clinician will use interventions that address this issue. Often, the first is having the client seek medical care. This is not a bad intervention, but when given to Tamara without critical reflection of her status as a Black woman, there are unintended consequences. Medical bias toward Black women creates health disparities that result in their medical issues being ignored or minimized.[23] Sending Tamara off to see her doctor works when clinicians view her as a woman, but when viewed as a Black woman, the intervention will need to be bolstered to ensure Tamara is not further harmed.

Now, let's work through the following critical reflection questions.

What are my strengths? What are my growth areas? What is my capacity to provide an intersectional framework in my therapy practice?

The answers to these questions are determined by the role you will have in Tamara, Sarai, and Annette's life. Are your clinical practice modalities inclusive of variation within cultural beliefs and practices? Tony N. Brown[24] uses critical race theory to explore the meaning of race in relationship to mental health and mental health problems. Clinicians must examine how racial stratification impacts mental health problems for individuals.

This analysis of practice is also useful for mental health professionals who work in an institution such as a business or university. Let's say you work in human resources at Tamara's casino. There has been a complaint filed against Tamara's supervisor by another employee, and in your investigation of this new case, you discover Tamara's story. What strengths do you have to help Tamara? What will an intersectional framework of care look like that keeps you within the scope of your job description? This can't be easily answered here because capacity to provide the appropriate intervention can only be determined by the individual and by the parameters allowed. You know (or you should know or be able to find out from legal counsel) what laws govern you and your organization, and you know what your organization is willing to expend time and energy on which pivots toward the next question.

What are the strengths of my organization? What are the growth areas of my organization? What is the capacity of my organization to provide an intersectional framework of care?

#MeToo has spotlighted organizational practices that minimize addressing sexual harm. Sexual harm perpetrators are either ignored or condoned in their behavior, while survivors are silenced or penalized for reporting. Tamara and Sarai's stories are illustrative of how organizations can have a direct impact on providing intersectional care. Tamara was sexually assaulted while working, and her supervisor's response was not appropriate. Sarai was harmed while at a bar, and although it is not the bar's responsibility to provide direct care, they have a responsibility to their community to provide a safe environment for their patrons.

When using Sarai's story to illustrate this point, there is the multifaceted aspect of her being at risk because of her disability, as well as her nationality. She was targeted while using her wheelchair, and her nationality was used as a threat to silence her complaints. As an organization, the bar she attended could very easily ensure they are providing an intersectional framework of care for their community with zero-tolerance policies. For example, signage could be posted that indicates what will and will not be tolerated in the establishment.

Annette's experience also serves as a point of analysis for organizational responsibility. She was harassed by a teaching assistant from the university she attends, and is now finding it difficult to concentrate because of his presence in her classes and on campus. She has yet to report to the university, but as an institution, it has a responsibility to meet the needs of Annette, even though the harassment did not occur on campus. In a later chapter, you will learn more details about how colleges and universities respond to #MeToo survivors.

If your organization does not have the capacity to provide an intersectional framework of care, the expectation isn't to dust your hands off and walk away. Instead, circle back to what strengths are present. Your organization may have a strong relationship with other community partners. Pull on that network. Your organization may have financial resources that can be used toward better professional development training, or hiring of consultants.

What critical reflection practices should the clinician implement during and after therapy?

As referenced earlier in the chapter, this means direct-action planning on the part of care providers. This is where the critical reflection of strengths and growth areas are analyzed for outcomes that meet the needs of individuals like Tamara, Sarai, and Annette.

If I do not have capacity to provide therapy from an intersectional framework, how do I ensure I am collaborating with a knowledgeable peer or supervisor to support an intersectional framework of care?

If my organization does not have capacity to provide an intersectional framework of care, how do I ensure my organization is collaborating with appropriate people to support an intersectional framework of care?

Consultation and collaboration with professionals who have expertise in the type of therapy needed for a population outside your purview is crucial. Inclusive collaboration is used intentionally because it requires individuals and organizations to continue to maintain an active role in collaborating. This is not achieved using a referral list that hasn't been updated in years; nor is it accomplished by contacting one clinician who is a member of a particular marginalized community and having them do the work—while you neglect to construct a formalized framework of care.

Sarai is trying to complete her education and to obtain her citizenship, while coping with the effects of her sexual assault. As her therapist, do you find legal services for her as part of your work with her? Is she bilingual—and is there cultural humility built into those bilingual services? What is your space like? Will Sarai be able to access offices while using her wheelchair? If any or all of those conditions cannot be met by you or your organization, what would collaboration look like? Will this be a warm hand off? If so, how do you ensure Sarai's needs are met?

Annette is struggling academically, and in triaging her care you may focus your interventions on ensuring she receives support at her university.

When referring her to the appropriate offices on campus for assistance with her sexual assault, it will also be important to determine if linking her to the campus LGBTQ+ center (if one is present), or to the local community LGBTQ+ center is needed. Annette's sexual orientation, and how her subsequent sexual harassment intersects with her sexual orientation, is as important as her failing grades.

Tamara is currently being triggered every time she goes to work, but she and her partner do not have a financial safety net that allows her to leave her job. Are you connected to resources outside of social services that can help? Are there affordable daycare facilities you are familiar with? Is there a program she and her partner can qualify for to receive additional financial services? Tamara's economic status has a direct impact on her ability to focus her attention on her healing process.

Once again, it is within this process of questioning and looking at all parameters of care for a client that gaps are identified. The intention is not to get you to work outside of your scope of practice but instead to be mindful in how and whom you ask for help.

Final Thoughts

#MeToo is a testament to the power of public feminism that forces society to center women's experiences of sexual misconduct at the forefront of our collective consciousness. As a tool harnessed to center the stories of sexual assault and sexual misconduct in a digital age, we are still unpacking how it will be used to hold institutions and individuals that wield power in them accountable. Therefore, it is imperative we don't replicate mechanisms of systemic oppression in our practices or institutions for which we work while we are mobilizing awareness for #MeToo. A shared narrative gives us context for our griefs, our joys, and our trials and tribulations. As we honor the sharing, critical reflection on whose stories are elevated into public discourse—and therefore what programs and interventions are created based on those stories—is paramount. #MeToo has the power of collective voices of victims of sexual assault, but it is the intersecting identities of those in the collective from which we should always be working.

Two Straight, Cisgender, White Clinicians' Take on
Working With Disenfranchised Clients:
A Commentary by Holly B. Sweet and David B. Wexler

As therapists who are white, straight, and privileged, the two of us often have clients whose demographics are different from our own. Much has been written and taught, in this chapter and in many other books,[25] about the profound value of both sensitivity and competence when counseling members of groups other than our own. This is true when treating clients who have different backgrounds or experiences from ours (combat zone vets, recovering alcoholics, fundamentalist Christians, etc.), but especially true when these different experiences are seeped with disenfranchisement.

Sensitivity, of course, is necessary but not sufficient. We need to read about or take classes on cross-cultural competence. We need to have learned (and continue to learn) about how our own beliefs, biases, and blind spots might impact our clients. Most of all, we need to be clinicians who genuinely know about and care about the experiences of disenfranchised groups.

But competence is more complicated. Competence means that not only is your heart and your mind in the right place but that also you have carefully thought through how your words and actions are likely to impact the client—not just what you were intending.

DAVID: *I once counseled a Black woman who was being physically and emotionally abused by her husband. She was in no denial about this. She wanted to get out of this relationship, and she was scared to leave him. But when it came to actions that involved authorities, like calling 911 when he assaulted her or the filing of a restraining order, she balked. I couldn't believe it, and I pushed harder because I cared about her. Until she explained to me something that was outside my experience, something that had never occurred to me: "I can't air my dirty laundry to white folks . . . . And I don't want to be responsible for putting one more brother into jail." It was only then that I realized how little I knew about the extra layers of pressure that this female victim experienced as she tried to navigate this complex situation. I had to be humble about what I didn't know and allow myself to be educated about her world.*

HOLLY: *I remember one client in particular, a bright young woman who was an immigrant from a Middle Eastern culture, currently employed in a well-paid technical job. She had been the recipient of sexual harassment at work and was feeling overwhelmed. As we started to work together, I encouraged her to speak up, thinking to myself that she's smart and well educated, and surely it would be relatively easy for her to work with her HR department. What I didn't consider until she pointed it out was that in her culture, women are not only expected to put up with male sexual misconduct but that it was considered normative and acceptable. To speak up about it would lead to being ostracized and shamed by both men and women.*

I asked her to tell me more about her culture in terms of gender relations. What was it like growing up as a girl in her country? Were there books I could read? Movies I could watch? I openly owned my lack of knowledge, expressed my willingness to learn, and let her lead me. As she became my teacher, she began to find her own voice at her own pace (not mine) and became better able to address harassment in her workplace.

The good news, we have found, is that most clients can bridge the gap of your differences if we pass the tests of "Do you really understand me?" "Do you respect me?" "Are you willing to learn about the real me and my culture?" and "Do you really have something to offer me?" Our experience has been that genuine human-to-human connection ultimately transcends the differences in class, race, religion, gender, and sexual orientation—but only when we are willing learners, able to own our biases, and open to the ongoing process of self-reflection and education.

Part II

FINDING SOLUTIONS: POSITIVE STRATEGIES FOR CLINICIANS AND EDUCATORS

Chapter 6

Working With Men
From Predators to the Misinformed

When it comes to treating men who have committed #MeToo offenses, we have to remember the range of possible stories here. Some men are probably untreatable; others are tough to treat but are still possible to get through to; and many others are amenable to education and confrontation regarding what they have done, why they have done it, and how their victims have been affected.

Those of us who are counselors, therapists, educators, employers, supervisors, and advisors have an absolutely essential job to do: We need to help #MeToo offenders recognize their own motivations and misconceptions, to become aware of how male norms may have shaped their behavior, and to be guided by empathy for the women they have affected. The ultimate goal is to change future behavior and to make amends for the past. And as their therapists, we have to know when intervention is possible and when it isn't possible.

In working with #MeToo men, keep in mind the following five guiding principles. Some may seem obvious, some more subtle; some may be hard for you to do, some might come more easily. Outside of cases involving psychopaths and pathological narcissists (see next section), these principles should apply across the board to *all* the men we treat:

1. Welcome them into therapy. You can't engage a man if you start with blame or shame.
2. Be empathic about their narrative. They need to be heard before they can change behavior.
3. Educate them about how gender role norms may have set them up for

#MeToo behavior. Many men don't even know about male norms that
can lead to #MeToo behavior.

4. Challenge their excuses. Once you have created the alliance, you can
    confront them when they know you come from a place of trust.

5. Help them take responsibility for their behavior, which often includes
    an effective apology and a commitment to change. This is the "action
    item" that may get overlooked in the therapy process and where a
    coaching style might work best.

How you implement these interventions depends on your clinical style, but all
five points should guide counselors in order for treatment to be effective with
#MeToo offenders.

Psychopaths, Pathological Narcissists, and Predators

While we adopt a fundamentally humanistic approach to human frailty and
male misbehaviors in particular, some men are essentially untreatable.

This is a short section because there's not a whole lot to say when it comes
to treatment for these pathologies. We know that predators like Harvey Weinstein, Larry Nassar, Jeffrey Epstein, and Bill Cosby are plagued with deficits
in central components of key human qualities, qualities that allow most of the
rest of the world to *not* engage in extremely disturbing behavior.

These men do not feel remorse or guilt. Their affective range (with the
exception, typically, of anger) is shallow and limited. They are callous and lack
the basic elements of empathy for others. They represent the worst of traditional male norms. But unfortunately, in the public eye, they appear to be very
successful professionally (a culturally valued male norm).

According to the internationally recognized findings of Dr. Robert Hare,[1]
these characteristics are the essential core qualities of the psychopathic personality. He calls this cluster of characteristics "aggressive narcissism," and
states that these traits are usually accompanied by glibness and superficial
charm, a grandiose sense of self-worth, pathological lying, acting in a conning
and manipulative fashion, and a failure to accept responsibility.

Of all the men in the world who have ever been accused of some sort of sexual harassment or #MeToo violation, this personality diagnosis represents a
narrow minority of perpetrators. Yet it gets a good deal of press since the men
(at least the ones who are caught and whose offenses have been made public)

are well-known and often admired publicly. But, as in many other criminal behaviors, this narrow minority usually commits the most shocking and flagrant criminal acts and—unfortunately—is the most unlikely group of people to benefit from any form of treatment or intervention.

The men in these personality categories are impaired. One trait, central to the likelihood of #MeToo behavior, is their impairment in capacity for empathy—defined as deficits in "the comprehension and recognition of other's experiences and motivations; tolerance of differing perspectives; and understanding of the effects of one's own behavior on others."[2]

The other central area relevant to this discussion is impairment in capacity for intimacy, defined as deficits in "the depth and duration of connection with others; desire and capacity for closeness; and mutuality of regard reflected in interpersonal behavior."[3]

Men like this do *not* benefit from treatment focusing on insight, empathy, self-disclosure, or improving self-esteem. They are unreached by humanistic treatment that tries to identify core positive qualities buried beneath the disturbing exterior. Because of these men's seemingly unlimited capacity for rationalization, entitlement, and projection of blame, typical therapeutic interventions are practically doomed.

Most disturbingly, studies have shown that the greater the level of psychopathic traits, the more *dangerous* it is to try to do what we do with practically all other clients struggling with their interpersonal behavior: teach empathy skills. Upon learning more about the experiences of others, anyone with psychopathic traits simply gains new tools to exploit the goodwill of others.

A therapeutic focus on "enlightened self-interest" is the only intervention with any track record for limiting the damage that these men can do. The few times that a psychopath (or pathological narcissist or predator) comes into therapy are seldom of his choosing. Generally he is referred because of criminal behavior, or workplace misconduct, or spousal abuse. Occasionally, a therapist can help him realize that continuing to engage in certain behaviors is likely to lead to negative consequences—incarceration, losing a job, losing a marriage, severe loss of status in a community important to him, financial loss, or some combination of these—and he is *sometimes* able to alter his patterns. The response cost of these consequences may have become too high for him and he may actually shift some of his behavior. However, beware that the patterns he may "choose" to alter for self-interest may not affect other patterns that the rest of society may want him to change.

Treating #MeToo Offenders:
Narcissistic Issues and Motivations

Now we move on to the actually treatable client. Not always *easily* treatable, but still possible to reach. This category of #MeToo violators is composed of men who have more redeeming social qualities than psychopaths do—and they are not as consistently dangerous—but they still are plagued with narcissistic entitlement. We in the counseling and clinical fields know something about treating and confronting contact-hungry, needy, powerful, moderately narcissistic men who cross boundaries—even if we lack success treating psychopaths.

Still, #MeToo offenders with strong narcissistic motivations are notoriously tough to treat. But since they are vulnerable to shame—and since they often desperately construct interpersonal worlds and internal narratives to avoid the experience of shame—the fear of shame can be used as leverage to help motivate them. Shame is a preoccupation in many men who come into treatment (given that it runs counter to male norms to ask for help) and is important to be aware of it in our counseling sessions. It is probably true that we need to be extra welcoming to men who may already be struggling with weak egos, which often underlies narcissism.

"Grandiose" Narcissism

We know the adult version of a narcissistic personality has two primary pathways. Although narcissists seem to be of radically different historical origins, they often lead to the same outcome. The first pathway originates from an overindulged childhood. They have typically grown up in an entitled environment, been treated as special, and have experienced excessive praise. Limits and boundaries growing up have often been woefully absent.

This pattern of narcissistic traits often borders on sociopathy. The anger can be cold. Avenging a perceived injustice can be a powerful motivator: "They get to do what they want: no limits, no boundaries, no rules, no consequences, so they grow up thinking that's the way the world works. These are the hardest to treat because you literally have to teach them to be uncomfortable, and it's hard for them to understand why." [4]

Plaguing this type of offender is a pattern known as "compensatory narcissism." Many of the narcissists that we see are the product of narcissistic parents—often parents who desperately sought to fulfill the holes in their own sense of self by living through their child. The child's perfection in achievement, looks, charm, and most significantly, impressing others, provided (or seemed to provide) something that the parents lacked themselves. When the child succeeded, the parent's self soared; when the child failed, the parent's self crashed—and the child was often shamed for this failure.

Under this parenting, the child learns that love is not at all unconditional, that their "golden child" status is actually only earned through performance. Often, as long as the child performs at high levels, he is allowed to engage in otherwise unacceptable behaviors like screaming, demanding, and entitlement. While not everyone with this personality pattern becomes sexually preoccupied and exploitative, many do. Sex—particularly emotionally detached sex, which is practically the hallmark of #MeToo offenders—can be self-soothing; a way to both stroke the ego and avoid emotional feelings and pain. Socialization into traditional male norms means that sex is particularly important to a man's sense of self and also may be one of the main ways he can experience intimacy.

"Vulnerable" Narcissism

The other primary pathway that creates a narcissistic adult emerges from the damaged and shamed self. This is best understood as the "vulnerable" subset of narcissism. Many of these men show patterns that overlap with borderline personality. Their anger is hot and reactive. Many of them have grown up in an abusive and shaming environment, and they are highly motivated by desperate efforts to overcompensate for this core of shame. They are extremely susceptible to narcissistic injuries.

According to psychologist Donald Dutton[5] and colleagues, male shame comes from public exposure of one's vulnerability. The whole self feels bad. If you were a boy whose father engaged in a pattern of shaming you, you can look back and probably figure that your father was desperately attempting to bolster or reassure his own shaky sense of self. Or maybe it was just force of habit, based on what was modeled for him. Regardless, for the boy who needs to feel loved by this main source of his male identity, the father's shaming forms a series of crushing blows.

Men who have been exposed to shame will do anything to avoid it in the future. We call this "shame-o-phobia": a hypersensitivity to the possibility of feeling shamed. If you were shamed as a boy, your radar is constantly on the lookout for the possibility of humiliation, and you may be almost phobic in your reactions. You project blame and perceive the worst in others. Tragically, you are especially desperate for affection and approval, but you cannot ask for it.

You can describe none of these feelings; you don't even know where they come from. Many men with this personality structure suffer from "normative male alexithymia"[6]: the inability to put feelings into words. It is common among so many men that researchers have labeled this as normative—not normative as in "healthy," but normative as in "widespread."

A number of researchers, clinicians, and writers have developed paradigms to understand this pattern in male psychology. Men who have been repeatedly shamed about their emotional states and genuine needs turn to various forms of addictive behavioral patterns to escape the intolerable negative emotions. Author Terry Real identifies the source of this condition as the "loss of the relational . . . that wound in boys' lives that sets up their vulnerability to depression as men."[7] This relational impoverishment creates a base for the feelings of shame, worthlessness, and emptiness that haunt many men. Many of these men are missing a capacity for tolerating frustration or connecting effectively with others—and these conditions can generate the objectifying and self-gratifying sexual misconduct of the narcissistic #MeToo offender.

Central Strategy 1: Empathy for the Self

The most valuable clinical pathway here is to find a way to reach, connect with, and develop respect for the damaged self lurking within almost all narcissists.

Keep in mind that, rather than being purely entitled and spoiled, most narcissists are overcompensating for deep wounds. They are shame-o-phobic. They are lonely. The grandiosity and entitlement almost always serves as a mask for the deeply buried natural longings for genuine intimacy.

Remember also that many of the narcissistic #MeToo men are unlikely to come in for any kind of counseling or therapy unless there has been a shock to their system. These men are often in foreign territory here, afraid of exposure and suddenly highly motivated to change. They are often raw. This provides an opportunity to connect with the more open and vulnerable self—at least for a while. Anyone who works with narcissists knows the joy of seeing a crack in the armor, or that window opening when the real person behind the mask is available. When that happens, we need to seize the opportunity to honor it, connect with it, and reinforce it—because it usually does not last long.

This is an important pitfall of treating (or being in a relationship with) someone who scores high on narcissistic traits. These clients sometimes seem to "get it" (demonstrate vulnerability, insight, impulse control, etc.) but they can't "hold it." It's like a rubber band that snaps back to its original shape. It is illusion to observe these changes or breakthroughs and count on them to last. Successful therapeutic intervention does not happen short-term here; when there is success, it is only after a number of "rubber band" experiences that steadily decrease in frequency and intensity over time.

The first move clinically is to engage the man empathically, so he feels safe in working through his behavior. Establishing a strong therapeutic alliance is particularly important for men who already have shame about their behavior. Many men (not just narcissistic men, but most men) are often inhibited about coming to therapy in the first place, since male norms value "going it alone" and see asking for help as a weakness. Knowing this about men tells us that the first clinical move should almost always be something like, "It's good you came in—this means you are at least willing to look at yourself and take responsibility. That's a sign of strength, not of weakness, and a lot of men can never go there."

It is important to take the position that this man has a core self that is valuable and lovable without relying on the trappings of power, or manipulation, or objectifying behavior. Difficult as it may seem, any counseling of the narcissistic #MeToo offender must communicate that this man is "good enough" without the steady stream of validation, confirmation, admiration, and feelings of power. The therapeutic relationship needs to send the message that he has never received growing up: That he is worthy of acceptance, imperfect as he is.

One strategy to bypass the inherent defensiveness of narcissistic #MeToo men is called "pacing and leading." This approach, originating from the work of Dr. Milton Erickson and further developed by neo-Ericksonian practitioners,[8] carefully mirrors the experience of the other person—followed by a leading suggestion for a new way to think or act. Based on Erickson's original work with indirect, naturalistic hypnotherapy, pacing means first developing empathy and rapport for the other person's experience by careful delineation—prior to making any correction or suggestion, prior to fostering a new perspective, prior to guiding new behavior.

Step 1: Offer pacing and "mirroring" responses that confirm the person's experience.

Step 2: Then—and only then—leading him into some new ways of thinking, feeling, or behaving.

When in doubt, return to pacing. It is hard to go wrong by doing this.

Here's an example. Dan was a successful attorney in his 40s, who consistently hired secretaries and paralegals that fit a certain type: They were female, they were young, they were attractive, and they (apparently) liked to party. He left his wife for one of these women, and he (and now his second wife) thought his partying days were finally behind him.

But they weren't; Dan continued to hire the same type, flirt outrageously, take selfies of himself and female employees with him in a Speedo and the women in bikinis at staff pool parties, and stay out late at "staff meetings" with a lot of alcohol involved. His new wife, of course, was hurt and offended. She pleaded with him to take a look at himself and how humiliating his behavior was to her (and to himself).

Inevitably, several of the female employees got together and compared notes about how creepy his behavior was and how obligated they felt to play along with him. Some of the women were motivated by just trying to be nice, because they actually liked him and respected his work. Others felt pressured to cooperate because they thought it would be career suicide not to. Others actually had no problem with it at all.

A group of the female employees came to him and his partners and reported their complaints. When the vise-grips of another marriage about to go down the tubes *and* the complaints from multiple employees came pressing down on him, Dan was ready for therapy.

Even when trying to ally with the healthier self buried in Dan's layers of narcissism, the therapist still had to set some parameters about the behavioral problem here: *OK, something that you're doing is really causing some problems, and it's our job to figure out what leads you to do this.* In the early treatment sessions, Dan talked about how much pressure he had always felt to prove that he was a successful man to his father. He painted a classic picture of a man reeling from narcissistic injuries, desperately attempting to fill something inside with nonstop validation—especially via the reassurance of female attention. The therapist worked with this picture to help Dan understand how society's expectations about what it means to be a "successful man" put a heavy pressure on both his father and then on Dan. Validating Dan's experience and putting it in a cultural context led to an initial wave of therapist "pacing":

- I can picture how much of a rush it was to have these women flirt with you.

- Getting that steady stream of positive response from them is such a high.
- And it probably made you consistently feel like you are cool, and lovable, and attractive, and interesting.
- And, of course, we all want to feel that way.
- And getting that from attractive women feels like it's pretty damn irresistible.
- And it has been really seductive, all along the way here, to keep telling yourself that this was no big deal, that your wife was just being insecure and jealous, that the women who work for you love how cool you are.
- Plus, it becomes really easy to not notice any signs that they might not all want to be treated like this by you, because that would probably make you feel ashamed.
- You put all these things together and it makes a lot of sense that this whole pattern developed without you realizing that there was anything out of line about it—even now, it's STILL hard to make sense of it.

And many more pacing statements about his needs, his feelings, his belief systems, and the like, for multiple sessions. The pacing is designed to show respect for the unmet needs that these behaviors are trying to fill, and to recognize that the needs (to be loved, to be valued, to be cared about) are absolutely valid. The pacing paves the way to conclude that it's just the desperation of these needs, and the execution in striving to assuage these unmet needs, that represent a problem.

With Dan, the therapist could have simply stepped in with the obvious lead: *You are in denial about your sexual harassment of your employees and it has to stop* or *Don't you realize the harm this is causing to these women?* And moved forward with that. These are totally valid statements, and ultimately ones we would want Dan to fully comprehend. But without proper pacing, this only activates shame and defensiveness.

To really impact Dan and the many men like him (and ultimately to reduce the likelihood of future victims of his harassment), he needs to feel respected and valued. Without pacing, the counselor or therapist lacks the leverage of emotional connection. With pacing, the narcissistic #MeToo offender is more likely to feel understood—and then more receptive to the value of the advice, guidance, or correction.

This echoes the fundamental principles of motivational interviewing: "Accusing clients of being in denial or resistant or addicted is more likely to increase their resistance than to instill motivation for change. We advocate starting with clients wherever they are, and altering their self-perceptions, not by arguing about labels, but through substantially more effective means."[9]

Central Strategy 2: Empathically Confronting Grandiosity and Entitlement

Most counselors and clinicians know this, but (just to clarify) "confronting" in our business does not usually mean getting in somebody's face and bludgeoning him so he knows how out of line he has been. Although once in a while that strategy may be called for, we usually have more nuanced and effective methods that we can finesse. Challenging a wounded man without first having established a good therapeutic alliance might mean he walks out of therapy.

Despite our primary orientation of respect, compassion, and empathy for the damaged self within, the purpose of the pacing is to set up the leading. We concur with author Terry Real who says: "I pay as much attention to issues of grandiosity in men as I do issues of shame."[10] Shame (and the failure to live up to the rigid and at times harmful expectations about true male behavior) may be the origin of many #MeToo behaviors, but it is the grandiosity and entitlement that emerges from this shame that is ultimately the social problem.

Why is this so crucial? Because grandiosity impairs judgment. The more self-preoccupied, the greater the impairment in empathy. A man who is desperately trying to bolster his undersupplied sense of self does not have room left over to consider the needs, feelings, or impact on others—and a breakdown in empathic accuracy is inevitable.

Virtually all grandiose men minimize and rationalize their behavior:

- It isn't that bad.
- You have to understand the circumstances.
- She gave me a lot of signals.
- I'm not the only guy who does stuff like this.

The narcissistically entitled man who manages to deftly generate these denials, minimizations, rationalizations, and projections of blame really doesn't understand why women are bothered by his behaviors, nor why these women are accusing him of assaultive or harassing behavior.

Sex researcher Michael Vigorito[11] makes the case that power feeds these rationalizations and justifications. This can make it more challenging for certain people to recognize that they have crossed the line. If people with power are able to avoid consequences, sometimes such insights may just not come.

When confronting offensive behavior, no matter how much we ally with the damaged self and show compassion, we eventually have to zero in on the central question: *Did you actually do this? Did you actually say this?* And stick with this question until the client really gets an undiluted picture of what he has done and how it has affected others.

And this is where the leading part comes in, after there has been sufficient pacing. In the example about Dan, the pacing sets the stage for the leading:

- Now that we understand where you were coming from and what you needed . . . we HAVE to help you figure out a way to manage these needs without taking advantage of these women and destroying another marriage.

In other cases, a confronting leading statement might sound like these:

- It sounds like you paid no attention to how she was affected when you kept telling her how hot she looked.
- Think about how you would have felt—and how would you have reacted—if you watched YOUR DAUGHTER'S boss get his dick out and ask her to touch it?
- You were his priest—that boy trusted you to know what is right and wrong, and it will be a long time before he can trust his own judgment again.

This confrontation stage is designed to teach narcissists about frustration tolerance, impulse control, empathy, other people's feelings, and about how to give as well as take. It often means saying, "Yes, you really did this, and you damaged someone, and it comes from a damaged place in yourself—and now that you know this, you can change it."

This only has a chance at making an impact if the therapist has passed previous tests and gained some trust. If the man has come to genuinely believe that his therapist values him, understands him, and appreciates that there is a better self within (this is where the pacing comes into play), then some bold in-your-face statements may actually get through.

The holy grail for this category of #MeToo men is to cultivate awareness of how they have victimized others and empathy for their victims—no small task when working with a narcissist. A primary aim we are working toward is to lead clients to recognize how these distortions prevent them from recognizing the damage their behavior causes.

Genuine change requires that the narcissist in therapy cultivate what Dr. Marsha Linehan[12] describes as "distress tolerance," or learning how to bear pain skillfully. Shame-o-phobia generates floods of intolerable shame. If we can make a connection with the healthier part of the self that is worthy of respect, the painful impact of facing what they have done becomes more tolerable. Even with a narcissist, this has at least a shot at prompting change.

Central Strategy 3: Educating About Perceived Male Norms

Another way to intervene with many men is to help identify and challenge perceived male norms. Too many counselors go into a therapy practice without ever having had a course in the psychology of men and how norms impact male behavior, especially in terms of difficulty with help seeking, restriction of emotional expression, and sexualization of intimacy. If the counselor is unaware of the impact of male norms on #MeToo behavior, they are missing the opportunity to help the man understand the cultural underpinning of his behavior, to assess how this has perhaps unconsciously increased his #MeToo behavior, and then to help him challenge those norms. The American Psychological Association provides worthwhile guidelines on counseling men and boys[13] and gives an excellent description of how to conduct therapy with males. In addition (as discussed in Chapter 2), conducting a "gender inquiry"[14] at the beginning of therapy can help educate the man about where his beliefs on manhood came from and how those experiences may have shaped his behavior in unconscious and harmful ways, affecting both himself and others.

Let's take a look at Benny, a man with a successful career as a waiter at a high-end restaurant, who came to the attention of the restaurant's human resources department for reasons that he simply could not make sense of. Two different female employees had made complaints about him.

He didn't get it. He had never touched them. He had never pushed for a date or cornered them in a supply room. He had never exposed himself. He didn't have any power over them in the restaurant hierarchy. *What did I do wrong?*

The HR counselor arranged a face-to-face meeting with one of the female complainants. She told him that she was uncomfortable with the way he leered at her. It felt like he was always checking her out. She wasn't worried he was going to assault her—it just made her feel like she always had to perform some sort of role for him.

Benny protested: "What's wrong with what I did?? Since when did a little friendly flirting become such a big deal? I can't tell a woman at work that she looks nice anymore? I hear other guys doing that all the time!"

His coworker tried to explain it: "When other guys tell me I look nice, it feels like a friendly compliment. You say it like, 'You look niiiiiiiiiice.' I feel like you're undressing me with your eyes. And your voice."

This froze Benny. He still didn't really get it, but this was the first time he had ever heard this kind of feedback: "I just thought I was being friendly too. That's just the way men talk to women to make them feel good."

When it comes to these misperceived male norms, this next point cannot be emphasized enough: A man who sexually misbehaves because he believes he is just conforming to expected male behavior is using a very lame excuse.

But the good news about this particular pathway to #MeToo boundary violations is that this is a relatively manageable and correctable condition. It requires education. And it relies on the assumption that a significant percentage of male #MeToo offenders actually intend no harm and are capable of self-correcting when they realize the harm. Benny was referred by HR to a therapist who worked with him to identify and then challenge some of these notions about how men are supposed to act. Our role as therapist or counselor in these cases is to make sure that the men talk to women about these unacceptable behaviors (especially, if possible, with the women whom they have hurt or offended) and that they get exposed to any educational materials we can provide that illuminate the issues. The series of *That's Harassment* videos, written and directed by Sigal Avin and executive produced by David Schwimmer is a good place to start.[15]

Of course, we have to be careful here about men who use the "boys will be boys" or "these are just evolutionary-programmed responses" as weak rationalizations for greedy and offensive behavior. Harvey Weinstein famously said in his attempt at an apology statement: "I came of age in the 60's and

70's, when all the rules about behavior and workplaces were different."[16] That era is well-depicted in the opening episode of the AMC show *Mad Men*, when the new secretary Peggy starts to initiate oral sex on her new boss, Don Draper. Fortunately, he refuses, but this scene tells us what Peggy had learned about the expectations of male bosses. While this may be a defensible explanation for men of a different generation who use outdated language like "I'll have my girl call your girl in the morning" or still refer to Asian people as "Orientals," this is a poor rationale for power-based sexual pressure and actual sexual assault. Reporter Claire Cain Miller observes about Weinstein: "As many people have pointed out, this is absolutely false. Never was his behavior acceptable. (Not to mention the fact that his behavior continued well past that time period.)"[17]

Harvey Weinstein can't say anything that would credibly explain any of his horrendous behavior, but there is actually something to this perspective of how some men blunder into more subtle offenses. In the past, many men in positions of authority were culturally reinforced in the belief that groping their female staff (or colleagues) and making salacious remarks were just part of being a frisky, fully masculine character. One woman we spoke to reported that, in a job interview, the male interviewer told her he didn't know whether he should hire her or date her—and it is quite likely that nothing about this statement seemed inappropriate to him.

Often, men like Benny have been shaped by what they have perceived is "normal" male behavior toward women—without ever actually checking this out with women. Much of this, of course, is shaped by the ever-present and ever-available access to porn. The standard porn "script" of a woman desperate for rough penetration from the man and offering him exactly what turns him on whenever he wants it easily slips into the consciousness of the boys and men who consume this. Also (as we discussed in the case of "Binh" in Chapter 4 and will discuss again), men are susceptible to the "she slept with somebody else at work (or in my dorm, or in my neighborhood), so therefore she'll want to sleep with me" rationalization. This is a disastrous form of male entitlement, as the man can easily justify his pursuit (and, worst-case scenario, assault) of a woman because he has come to believe it is unfair that he has been deprived of what other men have been able to have.

Examining the way a client is influenced by these male norms in a counseling setting can be an important component of education and treatment. If you're working with a #MeToo offender, it can be fruitful to ask "Who taught you that this is what women want? Who taught you that is what men are supposed to do?" This sometimes leads to an awareness that he learned this from watching porn, or from some alpha-male behavior in high school, or from his narcissistic father with many failed relationships. And the intervention's aim is to increase his exposure both to other men who can provide a different set of norms—and to women who can let him know what they actually find attractive and respectful.

Central Strategy 4: Applications for the Future

The behavioral application of these emotional connections, personal insights, and confrontations is ultimately the only thing that truly matters. Actions speak the loudest. The fundamental concern here is the impact of boundary violations on victims—and working with people who violate the boundaries is just our means to get there.

But how exactly do these discussions go? How do we help these clients change this behavior? It is a relatively simple task to give instructions to men who have not behaved well around women. This is just education and coaching:

- Don't touch unless clearly invited.
- Don't make comments about a woman's physical appearance in a work setting.
- Don't have any kind of sexual contact with someone over whom you have authority or influence.
- Pay attention to signals that the other person might be getting uncomfortable.

These suggestions might be given as questions first, asking the man to think for himself why he might do or have done these things (clarification of motivation) and the resulting impact on the woman he has offended (enhancement of empathy). For example, a therapist could pose these questions to Dan or Binh or Benny:

- What kind of response were you hoping to get?
- How do you think she felt?
- Why do you think she was uncomfortable with this?
- Where did you learn that this was a cool way to relate to women?

- Do you think there are any other ways you can be friendly with her?
- If your daughter (sister, mother, wife) said she felt uncomfortable with the way some guy at work talked to her, how would you feel?

Education about these behaviors are actually sufficient for some men, as we will discuss later in this chapter. But particularly with narcissistic men, it usually takes more.

One strategy that increases the likelihood of behavioral change (for men with narcissistic traits especially) can best be described as simply appealing to their self-interest: *If you keep acting this way, even if you don't understand why there is anything really wrong with it, you are likely to lose your job, lose your marriage, lose status in your community, and do harm to people you have no particular interest in doing harm to.*

This is known as having a "stake in conformity": The more you have to lose, the more likely it is that you will conform to social norms. We often ask men who are tempted to slip into old behavioral habits known to have caused harm to conjure up a "scare yourself" image: If a doctor is a #MeToo offender because of the way he touches his patients, we train him to picture what scary outcome will ensue if he touches a woman in this way again (public shame, loss of medical license, destroying marriage, etc.). Fear is a powerful motivator.

Another intervention to increase the likelihood of long-lasting behavioral change is to help the man with powerful unresolved needs recognize what he was dealing with:

- What was your assumption in this situation?
- What were you feeling?
- How did you read the situation, and was there a particular emotional need that you had at the time?
- Did you need a little extra dose of validation or confirmation that a pretty girl might smile at you if you said something flirtatious?

And then to frame this: *These are not pathological needs—except if it leads to damaging behavior. If that's the need, you've got to be aware of it so it doesn't get acted out, even in relatively benign ways. If you are unconscious of what's triggering you, you are not powerful. Self-knowledge is power.*

Another way to approach this involves finding ways to cultivate what is known as "empathic accuracy." This skill set, a cornerstone of emotional intelligence, represents how accurately one person can infer the thoughts and feelings of another person. This requires both the ability to understand another person's experience at some reasonable level and to have a cognitive label for that (*Wow, I guess that must have really hurt her feelings*). Empathic accuracy is an important aspect of what William Ickes has called "everyday mind reading"[18] and has been linked to positive peer relationship outcomes and stable romantic relationships.

The more self-preoccupied the person is, the more empathic accuracy is impaired. If you are feeling threatened or offended, it is hard to have any room left to consider the other person's experience. If you are plagued with your own anxiety or emotional needs, the same is true.

It should be obvious that these deficits make it more likely that a #MeToo offender will pressure a woman for sex, make vulgar comments about what she is wearing, touch her in ways that feel intimidating, and be clueless about how his position of influence or authority puts her in a bind.

So, the clinical strategy is to enhance the empathic accuracy. Have the client assume the role of the woman he has impacted. Even if he can't relate (*I would LOVE it if women would come up and touch me like that!*), compare these experiences to times in his life when he has felt intimidated or pressured. Ask him to imagine how his daughter (or mother or wife or sister) might feel in this situation. Better yet, have him actually ask these women how they would feel (or have felt, most likely). Have him read accounts of women's experiences. Watch videos together, like the *That's Harassment* series, and stop at key moments and zero in on what the woman in the scene is probably thinking or feeling at that moment.

One important issue in counseling men who are somewhere on the narcissistic spectrum is their desperate attempt to cling to a self-image of being "good." Many of the men we work with are actually capable of recognizing the harm they have done, generating capacity for the victim, and expressing remorse. But they often insist that it wasn't really all that bad because they didn't *mean* to do any harm. In their minds, since they didn't actually sit down and calculate in a methodical fashion how they were going to do harm to this woman, then they really are still decent and good.

While it is true that a sadistic psychopath is worse than a self-disordered narcissist (who is worse than some guy who is simply inept), this is scarcely a rationalization. We are all responsible for our unconscious motives (for superiority, for needing excessive admiration and recognition, for entitlement) as much as for our conscious ones. And the true litmus test of a "good and decent" man is his capacity to think a few chess moves ahead (utilizing his capacity for empathic accuracy) about how his behavior is likely to affect the woman, even if she doesn't specifically say something or protest. This is why therapy is so helpful: To make the unconscious conscious so that the client starts to have control over how he thinks and acts.

That said, all the empathic accuracy training or skill-set building in the world is to no avail when motivation is lacking. If there is a profound deficit in the man's capacity to care about how he affects others (as with psychopaths) or in his capacity to be aware of how anyone else is affected beyond himself (as with pathological narcissists), then none of this applies. Fortunately, many (if not most) #MeToo offenders do not fall into these two categories, and the cultivation of empathic accuracy really helps our cause.

Treating #MeToo Offenders:
The Clueless, Inept, and Subtle Harassers

Why would a man harass a woman whom he knows, whom he works with, whom he may actually care about? As we have reviewed, some men who do this are predatory and thrive on power and control. Even with more education in a counseling setting, they deny or simply don't care about the effects of their abuse; sometimes, they are actually aroused by it. Others are driven by complex narcissistic needs: They crave validation and feel entitled to it.

But beyond these types of men, it is likely true that a majority of #MeToo offenders are actually different. They are neither psychopathic nor narcissistic—but are simply clueless, inept, or uninformed. We are operating here on the assumption that many #MeToo offenders (maybe best described as "boundary violators") can use good judgment when they have more information about what harassment really is and how women are affected. Many men who learn more about the definitions and the impact of sexual misconduct had never realized what they may have done in the past—they thought they were acting within cultural norms and doing their best trying to "read her signals."

The more we can help these men talk to women or hear women's stories, the more enhanced their empathy for the female experience. And the more empathy (among these men), the more capable and motivated they are to actually recalibrate their behaviors toward women.

In a podcast episode of *This American Life*[19] in which a female Australian journalist decided to actually have conversations with the workers who were catcalling her (as described in Chapter 4), she concludes that these guys were not "sexist nut jobs." She could talk to them. They were respectful and open to the dialogue. She realized that they just got some kind of central fact about women wrong, and they actually were under the false impression that women really enjoy their attention.

Here's a quote of something she told one of these guys:

OK. So here's a thought that I think maybe hasn't occurred to you. There's quite a lot of violence against women, right? Like, we understand that. One of the things that happens when you feel afraid as a chick, and you're just walking around and a guy slaps your ass, is you don't know if he intends it as a compliment or if he's actually really violent.

And so something that we do, something that we've learned to do, is to not reject men. One of the strategies we adopt is laugh, smile, be collegiate, be appeasing, be nonconfrontational. Right? So I want to suggest to you that it's possible that a lot of the smiles and laughs that you see on the faces of the women who you slap or compliment are ways for them to get out of the situation rather than ways of thanking you.

And here was the catcalling, ass-slapper's response:

Well, I actually kind of feel a little bit bad now. Yeah, no, I do. Because I understand that. I understand that. That an ass slap cannot just be taken as a compliment.

For many people, men and women, therapists, and the general public, this revelation should fall into the "duh" category. But, if we are really committed to changing men (and ultimately protecting and honoring women), we need to take men where they are and work from there.

Let's return to our client Binh. Recall, he was a Silicon Valley electronics engineer, born and raised in Vietnam, who consistently crossed the #MeToo line by making inappropriate comments and overtures to women at his workplace. He was neither entitled nor a power-driven predator. He did not have any particular sexual pathology. He could not be accurately described as a narcissist, and certainly not as a psychopath.

The simplest, most essential treatment intervention for Binh involved education. The crucial factor that led to his offensive behavior was simply cluelessness about women and how to acceptably approach them. At the beginning of therapy, it simply had never occurred to him that coming on to attractive women who dressed in a way that aroused him was inappropriate. Fortunately, for his treatment plan, a lot of that work on his awareness had already taken place. He had received clear and unequivocal feedback that women did not welcome his advances. Human resources informed him. One of the women he pursued told him this. Seeing one of these women coming into the workplace with her father and quitting her job because of him left him no doubt. And he was, appropriately, humiliated and ashamed for having done harm.

The primary intervention with Binh involved individual therapy sessions. It became clear early on that he actually thought his behavior was a normal way of showing sexual interest and that his women coworkers would be charmed by this. He was mortified when it became clear that he had offended and scared these women.

So this recognition was progress. Because Binh was a man who would not consciously or deliberately choose to cause harm, receiving feedback about the harm he did instigate was already generating a new wave of self-monitoring. This was not just about staying out of trouble—he truly felt bad and did not want to repeat bad behavior.

The next phase of treatment for him focused on increasing his self-awareness. He developed his own "risk" inventory, identifying specific self-talk and feelings that historically made him more vulnerable to acting out (much like an alcoholic identifies their triggers):

I am at risk when . . .

- I know that a woman has had a sexual relationship with someone else at the workplace.
- She shows some friendly interest in me. (I am especially attracted to any woman who shows an interest in me.)
- I am feeling particularly lonely for conversation and companionship.
- She is attractive to me.
- I am bored or unhappy at work and need something more.
- I know that I would never have sex with her—but I'm just lonely!

I make mistakes because . . .

- I don't read signals accurately.
- I am unfulfilled in my sexual relationship with my wife.
- I am lonely and don't have much access to other people.

He learned to use these feelings and needs as signals where he was at increased risk to step beyond proper norms. He learned that, if he was not ultraconscious and ultracareful, he could easily slip into a mental fog and make bad decisions, decisions which would cause harm for himself and for others.

At last report, he said that he was still often tempted to use porn at work to "relax"—but now successfully distracts himself with other safer internet stimulation. And, as a result of his self-examination and therapy, he has never been accused of any other kind of sexual misconduct or inappropriate behavior for a number of years.

Let's go back to the Al Franken story. After the initial charges about his harassment emerged from Leann Tweeden, a number of other reports emerged about other incidents of groping or unwanted kisses. Franken told a reporter,[20] "My first instinct was 'This doesn't make any sense. This didn't happen.' But then, when they started adding up, I said, 'Well, maybe I'm doing something I'm not aware of.' But this was out of the blue for me."

This is an example of a man who acted poorly and crossed the line—but who does not seem to be motivated by some of the darker forces that drive other #MeToo men. The statement indicates that he does not get off on humiliating women, so he has a reasonable shot at eliminating these behaviors, now that the light bulb about the effect on women has turned fully on.

Apologies and Making Amends

One of the most valuable roles that any counselor or therapist can play for a #MeToo offender is that of an apology coach. Once you have gained the trust of your client and have empathetically explored his motivations and feelings about misbehaviors, it is time to instruct him on apologizing to the woman whose sexual boundaries he crossed. The #MeToo movement was started in part because men were not able or willing to understand their offensive behavior or believe in women's stories of sexual boundary violations—and women needed to be heard. It is critical for the victim to hear that the offender understands that what he did was wrong and the impact on her. She also needs to unequivocally hear his apology for hurting her and his commitment to changing his behavior.

Unfortunately, the landscape of #MeToo is littered with the poorly constructed, insincere, unemphatic, and highly defensive attempts at apologies. A clear, unequivocal, heartfelt, and empathic apology contains four major components. This is what we need to teach men—in public statements, in private conversations, with coworkers, or with intimate partners—about how to take full responsibility and at least begin the repair for the victim and for themselves. Victims of sexual misconduct need to hear that the offender is not only aware of what he did and understands that it was wrong but also that he demonstrates empathic accuracy for the harmful impact it had on her.

An Ineffective Apology

In the panorama of ineffective apologies, here are some classic "non-excuses" masquerading as apologies, which were made by men who have been accused of some kind of #MeToo misconduct or boundary violation.

- DENIAL: It never happened; she is just making this up.
- MINIMIZATION: She was too sensitive; I was just being affectionate. I don't see what the problem was.
- REGRET FOR GETTING CAUGHT: I realize I have hurt my career and my decisions have affected others around me.
- VAGUE STATEMENTS OF REMORSE: I am sorry this bothered her.
- PROJECTION OF BLAME: The #MeToo movement is being exploited by women making false claims, and I am the victim of a witch hunt.

Let's deconstruct some famous (or infamous) #MeToo apologies expressed by public figures—and see where they got it right or wrong. Many #MeToo perpetrators offer apologies filled with excuses for their behavior or explanations designed to cast doubt on their accusers. Harvey Weinstein has denied rape allegations but said he knows his behavior has caused pain. He blames his behavior on the culture in which he grew up, promises to enter therapy, then says he will channel his anger to fight the NRA, then says, "I so respect all women."[21] Kevin Spacey, accused of groping young men and boys, tried to deflect the focus of charges about his sexual molestation of a 14-year-old actor, Anthony Rapp, by publicly outing himself as being gay. It seems clear he was trying to change the subject.

Here are excerpted apologies from famous cases, followed by critiques and commentary. We start with Charlie Rose's apology statement on November 20, 2017.[22]

> *In my 45 years in journalism, I have prided myself on being an advocate for the careers of the women with whom I have worked.*

Just because you have the right politics does not insulate you from treating women poorly—as Harvey Weinstein and Bill Clinton can attest to!

> *Nevertheless, in the past few days, claims have been made about my behavior toward some former female colleagues.*

"Claims have been made" is the quintessential passive voice apology, like "mistakes were made." The most powerful apologies describe what the person has done, not what has been alleged.

> *It is essential that these women know I hear them and that I deeply apologize for my inappropriate behavior. I am greatly embarrassed. I have behaved insensitively at times, and I accept responsibility for that, though I do not believe that all of these allegations are accurate. I always felt that I was pursuing shared feelings, even though I now realize I was mistaken.*

Rose does clearly apologize, but it is full of hedging and defensiveness about how some of the accusations are not true and what a good man he is overall. He focuses exclusively on himself, about what he has learned, about how he has behaved, about his career, about his feelings. He mentions nothing—zero—that specifically identifies the experiences of the most important people in these events, who are, of course, the women he has damaged.

Apologies That Work

Now we present two public apologies that have likely had a positive impact on the victim or victims, or at least came as reasonably close as we imperfect human beings are likely to come. We have marked in bold the core messages that were expressed.

Al Franken

Senator Franken was accused of kissing radio broadcaster LeeAnn Tweeden without her consent, and he was photographed mimicking as if he were groping her breasts while she slept. Here are excerpts from his apology with commentary[23]:

> *The first thing I want to do is apologize: to Leeann, to everyone else who was part of that tour, to everyone who has worked for me, to everyone I represent, and to everyone who counts on me to be an ally and supporter and champion of women. There's more I want to say, but the first and most important thing—and if it's the only thing you care to hear, that's fine—is: **I'm sorry**.*

The actual words of "I'm sorry" with no equivocation is very welcome here.

> *But I want to say something else, too. Over the last few months, all of us—including and especially men who respect women—have been forced to take a good, hard look at our own actions and think (perhaps, shamefully, for the first time) about how those actions have affected women.*
>
> *For instance, that picture. I don't know what was in my head when I took that picture, and it doesn't matter. **There's no excuse**.*

Again, no equivocation whatsoever.

> *I look at it now and **I feel disgusted with myself**. It isn't funny. It's completely inappropriate. **It's obvious how Leeann would feel violated by that picture**. And, what's more, I can see how millions of other women would feel violated by it—women who have had similar experiences in their own lives, women who fear having those experiences, women who look up to me, women who have counted on me.*

Another welcome communication of empathy—accurate empathy—that is an essential component of a meaningful apology.

Coming from the world of comedy, I've told and written a lot of jokes that I once thought were funny but later came to realize were just plain offensive.

This is valuable personal insight, which gives the offended parties reason to hope that he has been genuinely moved and changed by this experience—and thus less likely to reoffend.

*But the intentions behind my actions aren't the point at all. **It's the impact these jokes had on others that matters**. And I'm sorry it's taken me so long to come to terms with that. While I don't remember the rehearsal for the skit as Leeann does, I understand why we need to listen to and believe women's experiences.*

"I remember it differently" starts to tread on the dangerous path toward rationalization and minimization—but the final conclusion is "listen to the women." Very respectful.

Dan Harmon

A public exchange between TV showrunner Dan Harmon and a former employee, writer Megan Ganz, led to an uncommon outcome of the #MeToo era: an effective apology.[24]

In an unusual move for many harassers, Harmon gave a full account of how and when he harassed Ganz. He was attracted to Ganz from the beginning, he said, and acted "flirty" and "creepy." While they worked together, Ganz expressed to him that his actions made her uncomfortable, but he didn't take it to heart. Instead, he broke up with his girlfriend and confessed his love to Ganz.

Ganz responded with a tweet, saying that being treated differently meant she was unable to evaluate her actual talent. Harmon didn't react well to this and recalls:

[I] treated her like garbage . . . I crushed on her and resented her for not reciprocating it and the entire time I was the one writing her paychecks

*and in control of whether she stayed or went and whether she felt good
about herself or not, and said horrible things . . . I just treated her cru-
elly . . . things I would never, ever would have done if she had been male
and if I never had those feelings for her.*

This apology lays out exactly what he did, and the insidiousness of it, with
no equivocation.

He goes on say:

*I lied to myself the entire time about it. And I lost my job. I ruined my
show. I betrayed the audience. I destroyed everything. And I damaged
her internal compass. And I moved on. I've never done it before and I
will never do it again, but I certainly wouldn't have been able to do it if
I had any respect for women.*

So valuable for him to identify how he damaged her "internal compass."

Harmon ended the apology by imploring listeners to think about their own
actions, "no matter who you are at work." He reported that he would have swept
it all under the rug had Ganz not called him out.

She accepted his apology and forgave him:

*What I didn't expect was the relief I'd feel just hearing him say these
things actually happened . . . I didn't dream it. I'm not crazy. Ironic that
the only person who could give me that comfort is the one person I'd
never ask.*

This reaction is so often unanticipated by abusers and harassers. His clear
and unequivocal validation of her experience—both the actual behaviors and
her reactions to it—is a major contribution to her healing.

A misguided, defensive, unattuned apology probably may do more harm
than no apology at all. Harriet Lerner says, "A genuine apology says: 'I get it, I
screwed up, I was wrong, your feelings make sense, and I want you to know I
won't do it again.'"[25] A true, sincere, and empathic apology does not undo the
damage that has been done—but it helps.

The Well-Constructed Apology

Now let's discuss the key components of a successful apology.[26] With each component, let's review how they played out in the apologies from the client Binh (described earlier).

Our primary assessment is based on the impact on the victim. Keep in mind the standard instruction from Step 9 of 12-step groups: "Making direct amends to such people wherever possible, *except when to do so would injure them or others. We don't want our actions to cause further damage, harm or stress.*"[27] So even though we usually encourage preparing and delivering a meaningful apology, sometimes that is actually more selfish than helpful and should not happen.

After consultation with his therapist, Binh came to the conclusion that his apology to the young intern he had pressured for sex would most likely be valuable for her to hear.

1. The Basic Statement: *I'm sorry.* No rationalizations, no excuses, no hedging. Just a simple statement that you are sorry and what you are sorry for having done.

For example, ask your client to start by describing exactly what he thought he did wrong. If he offers only vague descriptions (like "for anyone I may have hurt" or for "whatever actions I may have done that were inappropriate"), suggest that the impact is diluted and won't serve its purpose. The specific offense needs to be clearly identified—it will not work if the woman feels like he doesn't even know exactly what he's apologizing for.

Your client needs to accept responsibility, regardless of the provocation (no "but you have to understand you were giving me a lot of signals that you were into me"). Explain to him that if he adds qualifiers, it signals a rationalization, an excuse, and a focus on the other person's behaviors. While often the other person may have played some role in what has gone wrong, a true apology only focuses on your client's behaviors. Ask him what it would be like to take ownership of this behavior, to learn how his actions impacted the other person, and to begin to repair that relationship. What would be the benefit to her—to the woman they offended?

In the world of apology construction, your clients need to know that the motto is to get your *"but"* out of apologies in order for it to be a true apology. You can coach them by having them role-play the following statements:

- It was completely wrong for me to touch you the way I did, and I am really sorry for how I have hurt you by doing this. *(What would she say? How would she feel?)*
- Sending you that picture of myself was completely uncalled for, and I am so sorry for how that must have affected you. *(What would she say? How would she feel?)*
- HERE WAS BINH'S VERSION: I made a terrible mistake by coming on to you like I did. There's no excuse for me acting this way, and I am truly sorry.

2. Demonstration of Insight: It is necessary—but not sufficient—to issue the heartfelt apologies identified above (publicly or privately). In addition, the victim of your client's behavior (or the rest of the world, in some cases) needs to know that he is now a different person, or at least working on becoming one. Very few of us can change long-standing patterns of behavior simply by willpower or being told we have been bad. The forces within that generated these behaviors must be addressed, and any affected parties need evidence of this to contribute to healing and repair. Work with your clients on how to offer the victim evidence that he has learned something, or that there was some temporary circumstance that will not happen again, or at least that he will really be on guard against it the next time around:

- There's no excuse—but I realize now more than ever how needy I have been to get attention from women and how this need has really messed with my judgment. And I deeply regret that you had to suffer because I have not yet dealt with these issues.
- I have never actually taken the time to listen to women like I have now. I have only paid attention to what I needed, and not what you or other women needed. This is my problem, and I'm determined now to address this.
- HERE WAS BINH'S VERSION: I realize now how I got so off-track. I somehow thought that because you were young and attractive that this was an invitation to me. I am a married middle-aged guy—what am I doing chasing a 20-year-old woman living with her father? I know now

how crazy that is, and I know I will be a lot smarter about myself in the future.

3. Demonstration of Empathy: Your client needs to make it as clear as possible that he really understands the pain, anxiety, or mistrust that his actions have created in the victim. This is often missing from even well-intentioned apologies, when the apologizer focuses only on his own pain, shame, and ignorance. Identifying those are important, but the victimized party needs to know that the offender really understands what this experience has been like for *her*, not for the offender.

Help your clients be certain that they have listened to the other person's pain and that they clearly communicate the following message: "I want you to know that how I have made you feel is *not* going to slip out of my head or my heart." Suggest they rehearse this to see how it feels; does it feel genuine?—and if not, why not? Given that his shame can make him defensive, it might take some more time in therapy for a man to own up to what he has done.

Explore with them that when they express empathy (or try to as much as they can), it is vital to be specific about the feelings that the other person probably has. Explain that it is not sufficient to say, "I know this must be hard for you." Clients might think this is enough. But we need to let them know that to be an effective apology, this statement needs to be followed by a clearer articulation of the specific ways it has been hard, and the specific feelings that have been generated in the woman who has been a victim of the sexual misconduct. Discuss how it is important that the woman's feelings about the misconduct truly are recognized and honored by your client. Suggest he use the following types of statements:

- I realize now how hurt you feel and how hard it is for you trust me again. I get it now—or at least I'm trying to.
- I know I put pressure on you to take care of my needs, and I am probably not the first man in your life to do something like that. And I can see now how much harder I have made it for you to trust men in the future.
- HERE WAS BINH'S VERSION: I got so wrapped up in my needs that I just completely forgot about yours. When I heard that you quit your job, I realized how uncomfortable and probably scared you must have felt. And I can see how it might be hard for you to trust that other men who

you work for in the future are going to be safe. If I had paid attention to your feelings, it would have stopped me. But I didn't, and you paid the price for that.

4. Behavior Change: The proof is in the pudding. All the words and all the good intentions in the world don't mean a thing unless your client has genuinely learned something from his mistakes and is handling situations differently— maybe not 100% perfectly, but definitely doing better. His colleagues, friends, supervisors, and the public cannot feel secure until they have observed a consistent pattern of change in him over time. Obviously, the length of time this takes is directly related to how serious the offense was, but others need to know that his remorse genuinely translates into action.

> HERE WAS BINH'S VERSION: You're already gone from the company, so this won't affect you directly, but I promise to do everything I can so I don't ever repeat this with other women. I'm seeing a therapist who is helping me work on these issues, and I'm never going to forget the harm I have caused you and other women. Again, I am truly sorry and I wish the best for you.

Binh sent his apology to the young woman. He never heard back, so he has no idea how it affected her. But he thought it was worth a shot.

Working Toward Change

If men show up in our offices of their own accord, it likely means that they are aware they need to change their attitudes and behavior toward women, and are willing to take responsibility to change. We can work with these guys. These are the (relatively) easy ones. They need respect for making the effort to come into therapy, compassion for their shame, education around what they have done and why, and some strategies for moving forward in their relationships with women. And we (usually) like them.

However, we will get clients who are there because someone else (a partner, HR, a Title IX officer, college administrator, the legal system) has suggested or demanded it. Some of these men are going to say, "This is bullshit. If it was so bad, why didn't these women say something about it before? Look at all the ways in which men are being presumed guilty and have to be proven innocent.

Whatever happened to due process?" Of course, there's some validity to that. But there will always be some men whose way of dealing with any gender-politics issues that make them uncomfortable—or perhaps even culpable—is to say, "There go the feminists again!"

These are the men who are less likely to initially join with us. They may have shame that they are defending against, they may be angry that they feel they have been unfairly accused. They may see us as judgmental—and we may see them as arrogant, narcissistic, or entitled. We might not like them very much at first. But these are the men who most need our help.

In response to these men, and in the spirit of our ultimate goal of helping these men recognize the genuine #MeToo experiences of so many women at the hands of so many men, it is not productive to condemn them for being sexist or to insist that they must always believe the alleged victim. Rather, in classic pacing and leading style, it usually works better to acknowledge a portion of what the man is taking about, and to say something like this: "Yeah, there are some cases that we've all heard of where some alleged victim was probably making something up. That happens. But, you know, the most important thing is that for so long, so many women who've been harassed or abused or power-less haven't spoken up, and all those stories are emerging. Maybe some aren't valid, but it sure sounds like most of them are. Check this out with some of the women you know and love."

And then you can help them begin to shift toward an understanding of why they did what they did, the impact it had on others, and how change will be to everyone's benefit.

Ultimately men who have committed #MeToo behaviors need both our compassion and our challenge to help them become better men. Without com-passion, no one stays in therapy, but without challenge, no one changes.

A Female Clinician's Take on Working With Men: *A Commentary by Holly Sweet*

I'm guessing that many female clinicians reading this book have experi-enced some form of sexual misconduct or harassment. I know I'm in that category. Because of our history with experiencing sexual misconduct, we may have a strong negative reaction to the men we see in our offices who are responsible for causing sexual harm to women. I have worked hard to be objective with sexual offenders but sometimes I haven't been able to do it, especially if their misconduct mirrors something I experienced. I remember one client in particular. Instead of empathy, I felt anger. Instead of objectivity, I felt triggered. I felt like saying to him, "What a narcissistic arrogant prick you are to have done what you did. Shame on you!" Which of course is not a great way to work with someone.

If you have a gut reaction to a male client that causes you to feel like you don't or can't work effectively with him, or if you just plain don't like him, you may decide that the best thing to do is to refer him to another therapist. If you are in a clinical setting, this could be done through the intake and referral process. If you are in private practice, you may decide not to take on the case, or refer as quickly as possible to trusted colleagues who have knowledge and experience in working with this population. Or you may get supervision on the case, understanding your reaction and seeing if you can be more impartial.

However, if we hang in there with him, I believe that we, as female clinicians, have a special role to play in helping the offender learn from his conduct. Our own feelings can serve as a guide about how the victim of his offense might feel. Sharing this with him might help the narcissistic and clueless men understand how the victim might feel since we can talk from the perspective of a woman. We might ask "What do you think she felt?" or "What do you think your daughter would have felt if this had happened to her? Or even, "You know, if I were the person you harmed, I might feel X." This can help them gain empathy for their victims because it personalizes it to their own lives.

The transference the male client might experience toward us (which might show up as anger, dismissiveness, or defensiveness) could be a therapeutic asset if explored in a non-shaming way. We can serve as important role models about how women can be assertive yet compassionate. Maybe these men haven't had any female role models, or have seen women as either assertive bitches or wimpy do-gooders. Because of my own background, I tend to fall in the former category, but I think that might be a good thing, depending on the client. My client knows that I will be able to stay strong in the face of his anger, dismissiveness, or defensiveness, and my compassion helps him deal with his shame. Finally, a therapeutic alliance with our male clients, once established, can be a template for how to respect and connect with the other gender.

As for what helps me stay steady when working with male offenders, I have found that being in an all-female consulting group where we share our experiences has been invaluable. We can let off steam and process our feelings, share stories and think about solutions, and know "when to hold them and when to fold them." I also belong to a professional organization of clinicians and academics who are knowledgeable about doing therapy with men. I turn to them for research, readings, or informal consulting—which can help me better understand what male offenders might be going through.

I am lucky that I actually do like men (OK, *most* men). I have empathy for their struggles in trying to be "men" in a culture that punishes them if they don't act "manly" (i.e. be a stud, dominate, don't express vulnerability, don't ask for help, don't act like a girl, etc.). I know that some of the motivation behind their behavior might result from harmful socialization into what it means to be a man. The men I work with know this about me because I say it openly. I think they find my office a safe space to process what they did and where to go from there. Not always, but mostly.

Ultimately the question you must ask yourself is . . . do I really like men? Can I form an alliance with them despite their behavior and attitude? If you are not comfortable working with men in general, or men who have acted out sexually with women (or maybe you don't really like or trust men), you should definitely not take on this kind of case. We have to ask ourselves, no matter what he has done, can I work with this client in a compassionate, objective, and non-shaming way? This does not mean you can't confront him about his behavior and attitude. In fact, we must do this as part of the therapeutic process. We must be assertive and strong. But he needs to be able to trust that we are on his side despite his behavior and our calling him out on it. As hard as this might be, we know that therapy goes nowhere unless an alliance is formed and trust built. It can be a challenge for us and our clients, but I think it is critical to the healing process of men who have caused sexual harm to women.

Chapter 7

Working With Men

Did I Do Something Too??

Enlisting men as allies in the #MeToo movement involves the important task of having them conduct a careful personal inventory of anything they may have done that, at least by contemporary standards, could have hurt a woman, scared a woman, or made a woman feel uncomfortable. Gaining a level of personal awareness—the realization that there is at least a bit of this potential in many of us, it's not just a "them" problem—can be highly motivating and can help them show up in our clinical offices.

Many counselors and therapists now see men coming in after they have done a gut check on former behavior in light of the era of #MeToo consciousness and are worried about what they may have done. Often, this self-examination exercise causes some disquiet and they want to discuss any past interactions that could now be considered disrespectful, exploitative, or damaging to women in their lives. A lot of men say they're reviewing every sexual thing they've ever done in life to see if somehow they've done something inappropriate. Sometimes the introspection is motivated by having teenage daughters, so it seems important to review their own teen or young adult behavior and what that did to girls and women. Many of the men we see in a clinical setting have not been identified as #MeToo violators, but, as men of conscience, they are genuinely interested in reviewing their own histories to identify possible examples where they have even modestly crossed the line. For many of them, they're expressing anxiety, confusion, and not feeling like they can talk about it outside of therapy.

The men in this category are usually decent guys—or at least they are now, even if they haven't always behaved as such. And they care deeply about living up the standards of being a decent man. But when they hear all the stories of boundary violations and sexual pressure and outright assaults, they often have a sinking feeling in the pit of their stomach that cries out: *Uh oh, what did I ever do that has crossed that line?* or *Have I done things that at the time seemed like a funny joke or a prank or just normal guy behavior that by today's standards would be considered some sort of sexual harassment or abuse?*

So how do we hear these stories? Yes, plenty of men, of course, just like women, seek counseling or therapy voluntarily because they are unhappy with some aspect of their internal or external life. However, men often enter some form of counseling environment (groups, individual, couples, psychoeducational workshops, substance abuse treatment) because someone else told them to. Sometimes the outside pressure comes from social institutions, where men are ordered into treatment for domestic violence, parenting classes, sexual offender programs, or anger management programs. Other times men are pressured to seek services by their workplace, such as when they are required to attend sexual harassment counseling, a substance abuse program, or stress management. And, last but not least, many men are "ordered" into some form of treatment by the women in their lives. When we ask men who show up in a counseling setting the standard question of "What are you doing here?" the answer we often hear is "my wife told me I needed to be here."

Why are so many men reluctant to show up for our services? Shame. And the fear of being shamed further for being weak enough to need professional help: *I'm afraid I will be judged for what I have done wrong in my life, and I can't handle that.* Or, *If I am relying on someone else to fix me, I must be failing at some important life tasks.* Not to mention fear and anxiety about what will happen if he opens up: *I'm afraid I'm going to be changed against my will, and something fundamental to my well-being is going to be stripped away from me.* Or, *They're going to make me do something in that office that will make me feel stupid and incompetent. I'll be out of my element.*

Add shame about having skeletons in his closet for treating women badly, and the shame factor increases formidably. So, if a male client *is* in our office, and if he *does* reveal some behaviors from his past that he is now painfully revisiting, it is essential that we treat those stories and the feelings associated with them with tenderness and respect. It is almost always true that shame is not our friend—men who are shamed either withdraw or get defensive, neither of which gets us or them anywhere.

However, in the #MeToo situations we are reviewing here, sometimes shame may come in handy. When a man reflects and experiences disgust or shame about his own behavior, frame it as a good sign. It means he's realized that he had crossed the line as a boundary violator and has likely done damage. The disgust reaction stems from a healthy internal regulation system, and that sick feeling is the body's way of helping him know that this was wrong. The revulsion response is a helper and a sign of hope, and it should be reframed as such when men come into therapy. In almost every story we share here, the client reflects on earlier behaviors and experiences this wave of revulsion.

Many men have heard the story of Aziz Ansari—and how his pushy, clumsy, greedy, and unattuned behavior caused his date to feel like she was the victim of sexual assault. They ask themselves, *How many times in the past have I missed those same cues myself?*

And, inevitably, there is fear of getting into trouble because of the past. After hearing about the ghosts of past offenses that emerged about Brett Kavanaugh and Al Franken and others, they can't help but wonder: *What old story about me could be resurrected that could get me into trouble?* The more that they hear about—and feel—disgust at the dark behaviors of men and the dark effects on women, the more they struggle with feelings of shame about what they may have done in the past.

In an interview with performers and crew of the *That's Harassment* videos, one actor reflected on his past behaviors, which he had never really examined before. He realized that he had always treated female assistants on the set differently, sexualizing the encounters: "I will familiarize myself with the girls more, like, at the end of the day, give them a hug or something like that . . . . I don't know them that well. And I'm in a position of power. What are they gonna say? 'Listen, please don't touch me'?"[1]

With the influence of #MeToo consciousness raising—and particularly as a result of his work on these consciousness-raising videos—this actor realized the responsibility he had: "It's up to the men to educate men to be like, 'Be more conscious of your body with another woman.' Because 99 out of 100 girls are gonna be like, 'OK, well, whatever. That's the actor and I'm a PA (production assistant). I've gotta accept this.'"

That transition—from taking stock, becoming more conscious, generating more checks and balances on his own behavior, becoming more empathic with what so many women have experienced, and providing feedback and guidance for other men—is exactly what we hope to promote.

The men we consider here sometimes come to see us specifically out of their concern about their own pattern of #MeToo behavior; some are pushed into treatment by their partner, their workplace, their college counseling center, or their own failures in dating. More often, they are in counseling or therapy for something else—parenting issues, relationship conflicts, work issues, anxiety and depression—and the #MeToo stories just happen to come up. The counselor or therapist hearing these narratives needs to pay attention to where they land on the continuum of disturbing sexual behavior by asking questions like these:

- Was the behavior harmful only to the individual (a man with a porn addiction, excessive masturbation, etc.)?
- Was it exploitative of someone else (making sexist comments, staring at someone in a way that makes her uncomfortable)?
- Did this behavior actually turn into some kind of nonconsensual boundary violation of another person (touching somebody without consent, trapping someone in an enclosed space)?
- How much was the man's behavior influenced by perceived male attitudes (believing that he is supposed to be sexually aggressive, ignoring the sexually aggressive behavior of peers, making assumptions about women who dress attractively, etc.)?

Think of these questions as you read the following accounts of men reviewing their own histories of behaving badly toward women. These usually are not particularly complicated for the counselor and the client to figure out, but they can help both parties deconstruct what has happened.

At a time of cultural turmoil that the #MeToo consciousness has generated, having a good therapist can come in handy. In therapy, men can safely take stock of themselves (and examine their own missteps and boundary violations). These men often become powerful allies in the war on #MeToo behaviors—both as a positive influence on other men and as support figures to women.

When Men Wake Up in Counseling

The Power-Based Flirtation

One male client, who was turning a pre-#MeToo business encounter over in his head, recently met with his therapist about problems he was having with his teenage daughter. She was acting out sexually, and he was handling it poorly. This got him thinking about his own history of treating women.

He told a story from years back of visiting an office that had recently hired a beautiful young woman as an aide to a senior staff member. He was an important client of the business, and when the young aide took him into a back storage room to see some files, he said, "I can't believe they're letting me be alone with you!"

He told this therapist: "I swear I didn't make a move on her, I was just being flirty. She kind of laughed, she didn't seem scared or offended . . . . But I need you to straighten me out here. I mean, by today's standards, did I really do something wrong? Did I break some #MeToo rule?"

Clinical Themes

The therapist's response: "The answer is *yes*, it was wrong. You were an important client of this business, so she probably felt like she had to be nice to you, and you were taking advantage of that power. It wasn't a criminal act, and many have done so much worse—but that was an abuse of power."

How to run a gut check here: "Picture your daughter. Picture her in the position this young woman was in, and imagine some middle-aged, important guy saying this to her while she's basically trapped with him back in a storage room with nobody else around. How would she feel? Picture that, and you have your answer."

And then it almost always helps to follow up with words of encouragement for the very act of self-examination. The therapist said, "It is really a good sign that you are actually asking this question. Not every guy can do that, and not every guy is able to use this to avoid making mistakes like that again."

The therapist had treated this client off and on for years, through different relationship crises, acts of infidelity, and family of origin issues. This story had never come up before, and it was significant that he had never brought such an interaction up in therapy prior to #MeToo. One of the byproducts of #MeToo movement consciousness raising is that everyday guys (who might have bumbled into some situation in which they slightly abused their power) are now paying more attention to their behavior and to what effect such actions might have on the woman, past and present.

Fortunately, we clinicians can help men examine and confront many of these fears, as the first step. Next, we educate them, in a non-shaming and respectful way, that their behavior was inappropriate; most men are actually appreciative of this: It's helpful for them to get a straight answer from someone they trust during these confusing times.

The Secret Stalker

Another client, Jack, came into therapy because of his history of sexual obsessions—and the compulsive behaviors that he generated as a result. One disturbing behavior was the habit of "discreetly" following attractive women around in supermarkets. He wanted to make sure that he got as much time as possible experiencing the rush of watching this target of his interest. If the woman he was stalking got out of his field of vision and left the store before he had a chance to observe her for very long, he was depressed. It was a painful missed opportunity. He also had a relentless porn habit, which would sometime keep him from going into work because he needed to stay home and masturbate.

Jack was sure that his sleuthing was so skilled and subtle that the women he pursued were never aware of his secret observations.

It *might* be possible that, in some of Jack's stalking, the women he focused on were not aware of what he was doing. However, most women who have been in this situation (and there are many) would say just the opposite. Women can often *feel* the presence of a man watching them, lowering his gaze to her breasts, positioning himself in a particular way to get close or get a good look. This is even true when being watched from a distance. Many report having been relentlessly observed from a "safe" distance in a *public place*, and yet they still feel so uncomfortable that they are compelled to leave the area.

Jack made the decision to enter therapy, more ashamed than ever. He had been observing and obsessing about a female employee of his who was wearing a low-cut top. He managed to maneuver himself so that he was looking over her shoulder while she was on her computer, with the excuse that he was helping her review what was on her screen. While in this position, he pulled out his phone. He made some reference to checking a text that was coming in—but he was actually sneaking in a photo with a view down her top.

This was a breaking point moment for Jack. He was disgusted with himself—and, as mentioned before, here is when shame and disgust actually serve a valuable purpose. And, importantly, the shame was directly triggered by his increased awareness and consciousness stemming from the flood of #MeToo stories. Discreetly stalking anonymous women in the supermarket was one thing, and creepy in its own right. But actually taking invasive photos of a woman with whom he had a professional relationship—someone who looked up to him and trusted him—pushed even Jack over the edge.

Yes, Jack was a perpetrator—but he wasn't looking for power over his employee or any of the other women. He would be horrified if any of them were in any way aware of what he was doing. His guilt levels peaked, and so did his remorse. For some people, this just leads to self-punishing behavior, like emotional and social withdrawal or substance abuse. But Jack sought professional help at this point because he was now in a relationship that he desperately wanted to keep, and he knew how much was at stake.

Clinical Themes

Jack's clinical intervention involved group treatment for out-of-control sexual behavior. He also engaged in individual therapy to explore what was so desperately missing in his life and why it drove him to get his needs met in such a dysfunctional fashion. Here were the key treatment components for Jack:

> Normalizing the healthy component of the needs: *You think about women a lot. You get aroused a lot. That's not the problem—plenty of men think about sex a lot!*
>
> Putting the "shame" into perspective: *I know you feel ashamed. The only value of shame is that is has gotten you off your ass to do something about this way of relating to women. After that, remember that "shame is not our friend." Guilt, remorse, OK. It's good that you feel bad. But if you get stuck in shame, you're likely to retreat into despair and just give up, or you might get defensive and deny the problem because the shame is too great.*
>
> Discovering the core need: *You're trying to do something for yourself, and because of the oversexualization in your family when growing up, your brain has been programmed to turn to sexual arousal for self-soothing and self-stimulation. It quiets something inside of*

you. We need to figure to what you are really looking for: Valida-
tion? Stimulation? Real connection? When we figure this out, it will
help you get more creative about how to find what you're really
looking for.

Jack has emerged as a watchdog for #MeToo violations. He preaches to the men in his group to help activate their empathic accuracy about what so many women have been through. And he has become an outspoken advocate at his workplace for more attention to these issues.

Accessing Shame About the Past

Another client—happily married, socially progressive, devoted father to daughters—showed up at an individual therapy session very troubled. He was uncharacteristically subdued. He had just read an account of women in low-paying jobs (housekeepers, waitresses) who often had to tolerate random groping by men in the course of their daily work. The article had triggered his wife to tell him about times when she was a teenager, tolerating random groping from men pressed against her on subways and buses.

For the first time in decades, the following shameful memory flooded him: "I don't think I have ever told anybody this. Not my wife, none of my pals, nobody. But for some reason I don't want to take these secret stories to my grave.

"When I was about 12 or 13, my friend and I would ride around the streets of the St. Louis neighborhood where we grew up. We would spot a reasonably attractive young woman, then target her by riding by her and each grabbing one of her breasts while we sped by. Then we would zoom off down an alley so she could never get a good look at us. I think I must have done that five times over a few months.

"Then I also remembered doing exactly what my wife described: men rubbing up against girls and women in crowded buses. Always in a way where they knew it, but it was never quite obvious enough that I could actually be accused of anything."

He paused and looked down: "I just started to picture someone doing this to my wife when she was young. Or anytime. Or my own daughters. I would never want them to feel that fear, and to learn to mistrust boys and men so much. And I'd want to kill a guy who would do this to them."

Clinical Themes

If you were counseling this client, the good news is that a lot of the work has already been done—by him. He is recalling the past events clearly. He is taking responsibility. He is feeling appropriate levels of shame about what he has done in the distant past. And he is feeling a surge of empathy for his wife, his daughters, and all the other women of the world who have been put in these positions. The therapist, here, just needs to follow along and support his growing awareness of himself and others.

The remaining clinical step is to make sure he does not stay locked down in shame mode. That emotion has served its purpose, but dwelling on it will either cause him to withdraw from what he is facing (because it is painful) or start to deny, minimize, rationalize, or project blame (because the shame becomes unbearable).

The best clinical message here sounds like this: "It is brave of you to face this. Many men could never go there, but you are doing it. We have to remember that you were young and hormonal and immature, and you are not that boy any more. The best amends you can make is to put your disgust with your own behavior to good use, by being a positive influence on boys and men and being more empathic and allied with girls and women. And that's exactly what you're doing."

When Understanding #MeToo Encourages Men to Tell Their Story

In 2018, just after Christine Blasey Ford went public with her accusations of sexual assault against Brett Kavanaugh, *The New York Times* invited male readers to tell them whether they had ever behaved toward girls or women in ways they now regret.[2]

The response was enormous. Some of the stories summarized here are further examples of men's recognition of their own misbehaviors and the steps they take in effective therapy—exactly what we are aiming for in this chapter. The submissions were striking in their candor; the narratives were by men who appeared to genuinely question why they had once conducted themselves in ways of which they now felt ashamed.

We can use these stories, like the clinical accounts above, to help men reflect on past boundary violations and offensive behavior—toward the ultimate goal of becoming better men, influencing other men, and becoming better allies to women. Here are some of the memories from men looking back.

When the Tables Are Turned

"Clark" recalled how, when he was 16, "a high-school party devolved into a kind of group wrestling match," and he took advantage of the scramble to "grope" the body of an attractive girl who he always felt was out of his league and, therefore, would never actually be able to touch.

Clark didn't think he was doing anything wrong, and he does not know whether this girl knew that he was the culprit, but when she promptly climbed out of the pile and left the party, visibly "hurt, disappointed, indignant, and bewildered," he realized how wrong it had been. He has regretted it ever since.

Years later, a coworker made an unexpected aggressive sexual advance to Clark. That unwelcome experience made him realize that the girl long ago had probably felt not just upset, but "violated, unclean, and disappointed that someone with whom I had previously been friendly turned out to value me only as an object of his desire."

Clinical Themes

Clark has already done much of his own self-examination, and he is past the stage of resistance, denial, minimization, and rationalization. So the clinical task would be to help him integrate what he now understands and can tolerate seeing about himself. You would then use this for two main tasks—making sure he would never respond like this again, and developing an even greater depth of empathy for anyone who has experienced what he did and what was done to him.

The Power of Rationalization

In another story, "Carlos" looked back at a date he went on in 1949 when he was 17.

Carlos asked a shy girl from his school to go with him to a movie. But he picked her up with one of his guy friends in the driver's seat, and rather than going to the movie, he drove to a dark street, where, with his friend still sitting in the front seat, he huddled up next to her in the back seat, spouting raunchy suggestions about what he might do with her. He never intended to assault her, and he didn't. But at some point, her fear of what he was suggesting he would do became palpable, to the point where his friend in the front seat told Carlos to stop. Carlos drove her home and she couldn't get out of the car fast enough. Carlos now realizes that, sitting in a car with two guys she didn't know, on an empty street in an unfamiliar neighborhood, with one of them talking forcefully about having sex with her, his date was probably terrified that she was going to be raped.

At the time, Carlos rationalized his pressuring and threatening behavior by telling himself that he was never going to follow through on his sexual suggestions—but decades later, he realizes that the perception of threat was damage enough, and he is full of regret. But he also knows that he has never done anything like that since, which leads him to believe that it is definitely possible for people who behaved badly as kids to mature and eschew even serious youthful misconduct, if they admit to wrongdoing. "If I were to see her today," he says, "I would apologize sincerely with no excuses."

Clinical Themes

Carlos responded to the newspaper's request for stories of men regretting their behavior toward women, and he is not necessarily sitting in a counseling office processing this. But, if he were, the same principles outlined in these clinical tips would apply. An additional suggestion would be to encourage him to share his story with other men—just like he has done for *The New York Times*. He is in a position to be a role model to men of all ages who have acted like this and have repressed it out of shame. It helps us all when people are brave enough to come clean.

The Frozen Bystander

This final story is from "Ian", who recalls a story not about his own behavior directly, but rather about his complicity in the behavior of others.

Ian and three of his male buddies went over to the apartment of a young woman he knew. She had a friend there with her who had a reputation for being "fast." The second woman's demeanor that night made clear that she was not interested in playing around. Nevertheless, his buddies pressured her to go with them into the dark pantry and eventually led her in there despite her evident reluctance. Ian remained outside with the woman whom he knew. They were both "frozen."

Ian never knew what actually went on in the pantry, but he was ashamed then and he remains ashamed of his failure to go in and intercede. Years later, Ian can't explain why he just stood by, other than a feeling that the situation was out of his control and it was not his place to reprimand them. But he is sure that "if it happened today, I would intervene."

Clinical Themes

So, if Ian came into your office with this story, shameful about what he didn't do, there are several key themes for you to work on with him.

> First: The message of respect: *It is brave of you to do this. Many men could never face the feelings that you are choosing to face.*
>
> Second: The message of self-forgiveness: *You were young and scared and inexperienced. At least you knew something was wrong—even if you did not act on that instinct at the time.*
>
> Third: Deepening the self-knowledge: *We need to figure out what froze you, to make especially sure you would not freeze like that again. Fear of social ostracism? Maybe it was some sort of confirmation of warped male norms? Maybe you didn't want to stand out?*
>
> Finally: Putting this all to good use: *How can you take what you have felt and learned and create value from it? Talk to other men about this. Recognize the instinct to freeze in challenging situations and be prepared for it—so you can push through it as much as possible. Take women seriously when you hear their stories. Elicit conversations from the women you love and care about the most to hear and understand what they have been through.*

Wrapping It Up

These are the men—the men who have self-examined in counseling sessions, the men who have written their personal accounts to a newspaper, and all other men everywhere who are reviewing their past—who are uniquely positioned to confront other men and serve as positive role models. In the stories we've presented, you hear a consistent theme of "now I realize how this must have affected her"; "I would apologize now if I had a chance"; and "I was so ashamed that I've never done anything of the kind since then." Fortunately, most of these histories of misconduct were short-lived, and most of these men have gone on to treat women well. They are also the ones most likely motivated to be respectful colleagues and partners. And they are the ones most likely to come through as effective bystanders for the women—in their personal lives and throughout their communities and workplaces—who have been on the receiving end of sexual misconduct. They are the compassionate allies much needed in a #MeToo culture.

Chapter 8

Empowering Women
Strategies and Challenges

The online Cambridge Dictionary defines "empowerment" as "the process of gaining freedom and power to do what you want or to control what happens to you."[1] Finding ways to increase one's sense of empowerment is highly applicable to the work we do with women who have not felt strong and confident in the face of #MeToo behaviors. This particularly applies to those whose demographic profile (i.e., transwomen or women of color) may marginalize them and may increase how often they are the victims of sexual misconduct. Chapter 5 looks at the importance of specific factors that make these populations vulnerable, and the need for clinicians to understand those factors.

Anything that helps a woman take charge of her situation, act in a strong and confident manner (even though she might not feel that way), and claim her rights—especially to her body—is empowerment. Empowering women means helping them learn to practice good self-care, honor themselves, and ask for help when needed. It means teaching assertive skills so they can handle sexual misconduct that has occurred, or might occur, in a strong and confident way. It is worth remembering that empowerment does not necessarily mean that a woman rejects sexual touching or sexual comments. The key word is "consent"—consensual sex and sexual touching between adults who are capable of giving consent is not a criminal act. It may be inappropriate, a bad use of judgment, or people might regret it later, but it is not sexual misconduct.

Helping women take charge of their lives as much as possible is sometimes seen as blaming the victim. This is a false assumption. Blaming the victim implies that somehow she was responsible for #MeToo behavior directed toward her. No woman *ever* deserves to be the victim of sexual misconduct.

It doesn't matter how drunk she is, what she is wearing, how much she is making out with someone, what room she goes into, whether her *yes* turns into a *no* at the last minute, what parties she goes to, or how many men she has dated or slept with. Sexual misconduct is *never* justified, ever, no matter the circumstances.

Shouldn't Men Be the Ones to Change?

While #MeToo offenders are 100% responsible for their own behavior—women have a role in speaking up, establishing boundaries, and holding offenders responsible. Arguments are often raised (and with good reason) about why women should be expected to do any work in changing their own behavior. Shouldn't men be doing their own work in changing their #MeToo behavior? Yes. Should they have to change? Yes. Shouldn't institutions be held responsible for educating men about why they assume they can do what they want? Yes. Shouldn't boys be socialized to respect girls? Yes. But the reality is that helping an individual female client gain more power in her life takes place faster than changing a sexist system—and in fact is one way in which that system will change. The more that women gain power in their lives, the faster the system is likely to change. The #MeToo movement has already shown that. In a flawed system, women may have to take action to protect themselves since the consequences of not doing so can harm them. This is empowerment in a damaged and sexist system. Changing that system is crucial, but it takes time.

In the meantime, women must do what they can to protect themselves and other women and to do what they can to fix the broken systems. One hypothetical way to do this in a campus setting would be for women to take charge of setting the stage for sexual interactions at fraternity parties. It is interesting to think about what would happen if no women showed up at those parties until men acted in a more respectful fashion toward them. Probably not much of a party, right? Think about the Greek play, *Lysistrata*,[2] where women withheld sex from their men until the Spartan and Athenian men ceased to fight and negotiated peace. Although it is a comedy, not necessarily a social commentary, it does contain an interesting lesson about the collective power of women to shape the actions of men. So empowerment is not just for one woman, it is empowerment for all women. Women have the power to take control of sexist situations, even if they aren't yet aware of the power they can individually and collectively wield.

They can and should be aided by good men who can act as allies and effective bystanders: This isn't a "women-only" club. In fact, men *need* to be an integral part of the #MeToo movement, to understand the varieties of sexual misconduct, the damage it causes women, and how they can help as allies and proactive bystanders.

The Impact of Trauma History in Our Clients

Before we discuss treatment and counseling issues for #MeToo survivors, we should address the issue of taking a trauma history (thanks to Sandra Brown, MA, for supplying much of this background information). A trauma history is important since approximately 8% of girls have actually been the victim of completed forced penetration, attempted forced penetration, or alcohol/drug facilitated completed penetration prior to age 18[3]—and this figure does not account for the much more frequent incidents of sexual harassment and misconduct that also leaves a mark. If we do not investigate the possible ways in which previous experiences with sexual misconduct at a young age might be triggers for our clients' current reaction, we miss how we would conceptualize appropriate treatment. An untreated trauma history can often impact clients' abilities to deal with new experiences of sexual misconduct.

Some clinicians reading this and treating survivors have extensive experience with trauma, while many of you may not. Some survivors of #MeToo experiences may not have any significant clinical trauma reactions, but many of them do. People who are triggered by previous trauma experiences may be highly reluctant to report it—in many cases, they are not even conscious of it themselves—unless we introduce the subject.

When treating a client who has experienced or viewed sexual misconduct, you might inquire at the appropriate time in treatment about any history of sexual trauma she might have. If the term "trauma" might feel too extreme, you can ask her about "severe life events"[4] or simply "events in the past where you have felt this way before." It is often helpful to utilize a simple PTSD questionnaire, like the PCL-C,[5] which is readily available on the internet. This intervention would of course depend on the client and the sexual misconduct she experienced since one size does not fit all.

For women who have some lingering trauma symptoms, therapists can treat the reactions by making the client aware about how her previous sexual trauma might impact how she views and handles current sexual misconduct. However, a true trauma disorder with a diagnosis of PTSD probably needs to be referred out to a trauma specialist. These issues should be addressed early in treatment to help identify her reactions to the event, so that if they are indicative of ongoing distress, ancillary treatment and referrals can be generated early. For resources on trauma assessment and treatment, one of the best sources is the International Society for Traumatic Stress Studies.[6] Other resources are listed in the Resources section.

Suggestions About What Clinicians Might Do

Here's the good news: Counseling victims of relationship violence, abuse, and harassment usually helps. Therapy can reduce PTSD symptoms and depression.[7] It can provide lasting improvements in social support and quality of life.[8] And it can improve emotional and social functioning.[9]

When women come into our offices after an experience with sexual misconduct to self or others (or concerned about future sexual misconduct), our role is to get a clear picture of the situation that brought them to us. We help them understand what they feel and why; listen carefully and compassionately to their situations; and work with them to reduce any sense of shame, confusion, or of feeling overwhelmed or helpless. In addition, it is important to assist them in increasing their self-efficacy by helping them formulate a plan as to how they want to handle what has happened, or how they might handle a similar situation in the future.

Listed next are suggestions about how you might work best with your clients. This is not a comprehensive list. You may not agree with all recommendations. You might have ones of your own we've left out. Not all suggestions are appropriate for all clients. You may have a different counseling style. But these recommendations are worth considering. For a more comprehensive list, consider reading materials that cover ways to handle sexual misconduct: Recommended readings are listed in the Resources section.

- Listen and believe her story: The therapist must first and foremost believe the client's account—even if we discover later that the report was exaggerated or even untrue. Damage is done to a victim whose account is not listened to or believed. The power of the #MeToo movement lies in victims speaking up, being heard and validated for their reactions to their experiences, and being part of a group of people who share similar experiences. Telling the story and being listened to by a nonjudgmental and supportive person is key to recovery.

- Explore any past trauma that might be relevant to the current situation: According to trauma theory,[10] current assaults can trigger memories of previous assaults and lead to a "freeze" strategy, or make her feel that she somehow deserved the assault because she didn't say *no* as it was happening. It is important to gently explore any previous experiences of sexual assault if that seems appropriate to your client's experience, and to know the limits of your expertise so that a proper referral can take place for ongoing work around trauma.

- Offer education about gender role norms: Many women are not aware of how norms for women play into how they perceive and handle a potential #MeToo situation. Providing psychoeducation about how women learn to be a woman can create a greater awareness of how traditional female norms might inhibit assertive actions. It can be helpful to conduct a full or abbreviated gender inquiry about this process if you feel this is warranted for your client.[11]

- Explore ways she can stay safe: Depending on the issues that the client brings in, the therapist might help her learn how to keep herself safe in the first place. For social settings in college, this often involves not drinking too much, having people around her watch out for her if she does drink too much, or avoiding situations where a lot of drinking is going on. For workplace settings, this might include not being alone with a supervisor in a nonwork private setting. Learning how to stay safe is good self-care and will help her make informed and wise choices. If she has already been assaulted, it is useful for her to know how she can best protect herself (and her friends) in the future.

- Review guidelines about consent: Women and men both are often unsure of what "consent" really means or how to communicate it. Exploring what consent means to a female client, why she is entitled to give it, and how she can give consent in a clear way are fundamental to avoiding miscommunication in a sexual situation. Men need to learn what consent means, since too often they don't know how to read the cues, they misinterpret them, or assume that a lack of a response equals a *yes* to further sexual contact. Helping men and women understand the parameters of consent is particularly important in a campus culture where sexual interactions often occur in a social setting where consent can be muddied by alcohol and conformity to group standards.

- Help her locate allies: Allies can range from friends who protect her from drinking too much, from going alone to a man's room or car, or going outside with him unaccompanied. Supporters can include men at parties who are "good men" who help police their drunken buddies from doing sexual damage to women. They can also include male and female bystanders (better named "active bystanders" since they are doing more than just standing by), who can witness what is going on, intervene where possible, and work with authorities to help the victim.

- Explore appropriate resources: If the harassment occurs in a campus setting, resources could include student groups, college crisis centers, or university compliance (Title IX) offices. If the harassment occurs in the workplace, resources might include lodging a complaint with her Human Resources Department, or the professional organization to which her harasser belongs.

- Consider ongoing support: This can include individual therapy, joining a group for survivors of sexual misconduct, or being part of the #MeToo movement in whatever capacity works for them. The shared stories on the #MeToo website[12] or reading a book about similar stories (*We Believe You*[13]) can help them know they are not alone and show how others have dealt with similar situations.

- Teach assertive skills: This can be done by utilizing workbooks,[14] role-playing in the office, or referring her to assertiveness training groups. These suggestions can be helpful for a client to have tools to stand up for herself if she has to confront sexual misconduct again.

- Explore ways to increase self-esteem: In a patriarchal culture, women are often seen as less than men. In that social construct, women may doubt their own value, because they've learned that a man's assessment is more important than their own sense of self. It may also lead them to believe that they need to have approval from men to feel good about themselves. Helping your clients understand why they feel this way and how it might play into handling sexual misconduct effectively can be an important part of moving a client from seeing herself as a victim to viewing herself as a woman with power.

- Operate from a team approach: In feminist therapy, having egalitarian relationships is important—this means that the therapist and client share a level playing field. Therapists may choose to judiciously self-disclose about the issues at hand if they feel this can make the client feel less alone or better understood. It also empowers the client to be an active member of the therapy process.

Overcoming Obstacles to Empowerment for Women

Following are some assumptions that women might hold about dealing with sexual misconduct, followed by possible clinician responses. These suggestions and prompts are designed to help clients reassess their beliefs and behavior, and to identify times where they might think and act in a stronger and more confident manner.

I have to be nice: The desire to not hurt someone's feelings is a big part of gender role norms for women: Nurture others, be nice. Women too often, because of this norm, do not say *no* quickly enough or express their real feelings because they don't want to seem mean. *Educate your client about cultural gender role norms for women. Help her see that being nice is often done at her own expense in terms of speaking up for what she wants and needs. Ask her why she is worried about hurting others when they don't seem to care about hurting her. What makes her think she is hurting others? What does that mean to her? Is there a way for her to approach the harasser that would feel more comfortable for her but still get the point across? Challenge the idea that being liked is more important than being respected. Examine what it means to her to be liked and the cost to her for acting as a "nice" person.*

I'm afraid of retaliation: This is particularly difficult for women who are in institutional settings (college, corporate, government) and are victimized by powerful advisors or supervisors who are deemed indispensable. Women may be concerned about saying *no* to a potential offender for fear the man will make fun of her, shun her, or get back at her through gossip. If he is an authority figure, this is a more difficult situation to handle. Women know that their job security, career advancement, grades, or letters of recommendation may very well be on the line if they don't go along with sexual activity. *Explore the reality behind her fear in the particular situation in which she finds herself. Is she unnecessarily afraid or unable to find allies to confront any reprisal? Work with her to locate appropriate resources to deal with possible retaliation.*

I don't want to "out" the offender: This is linked to the norm of being nice—worries about what will happen to the offender if she speaks up. *Reassure her that it is not her job to worry about him and that, in fact, speaking up may help him understand the consequences of behavior so he doesn't repeat the behavior.*

It's my fault: A woman may feel a sense of shame about what happened; particularly, shame that she should have done more to stop it. *Explore that shame and help her see that she is not alone and that other victims frequently feel the same way. Work with her to recognize that she couldn't stop the man's actions for a variety of reasons. The shame should belong to the offender not the victim. Explore why she would feel guilty for an action taken by someone who has power over her and should know better—have her think about a friend who was in a similar situation—would she advise her friend to continue to feel guilty?*

I shouldn't make a scene: Being polite and careful not to upset others is part of gender role norms for women. Too often women see standing up for themselves as confrontation. *Discuss with her how "making a scene" can simply mean saying no and refusing to go along with what the man wants. Use language that may make it less uncomfortable for her to say no. In this case, you might suggest she reframe "making a scene" as "being assertive."*

I will just ignore the unwanted behavior: This is a mistaken belief that unwanted behavior will just go away on its own: that the man will intuitively know that his behavior is unwanted. *Suggest that she would do better to speak up and say no—if she doesn't, how does he know unless it is egregious behavior? This is where informed consent comes in. She has to say no. No means no. And no response is* **not** *a yes.*

I'm afraid he won't stop if I ask him to: Depending on the circumstances, this can be a real fear, for example if she is in a precarious situation (i.e., alone in a man's dorm room or a supervisor's hotel room or in the office after hours). *Explore how she might stay out of an unsafe situation, how to be assertive and do whatever she needs to do to get out if she is already in one. Offer her a list of possible behaviors. Have her role-play saying no.*

I don't have a right to speak up: Many women feel they don't have the right to say *no*, that men determine who has that right and who doesn't., *Explore with her that these are false beliefs that should be debunked. Remind her that good self-care in fact involves speaking up, that women who stand up for themselves are standing up for all women, and that men do not have the right to judge her. Explore with your client what it would be like to speak her mind. What are the benefits? Disadvantages? How could she speak up in a way most likely to be acknowledged? Who have been or are her role models for assertive behavior? Suggest she do some exercises from assertiveness training books to identify what her strengths and deficits might be in the area of feeling empowered to speak up and know how to do it.*

I feel responsible for what happened because I led him on: Your client may feel that she led her offender on if she dressed in a sexy outfit at work, or engaged in some flirty banter with a coworker. Clarify with her that this does *not* make her responsible for the harassing, pushy, or retaliatory response from the other person. *Ask her why she feels that she is responsible for* **his** *sexual behavior that is out of line. Ask her to imagine if the tables were turned—if she were supervisor, would she feel that the "victim" was responsible for what happened? What if she were the guy who pushed himself on her sexually and pinned her down? Would she think the girl being molested was responsible?*

Maybe it wasn't sexual misconduct: When sexual misconduct happens, too often a woman is confused about what happened and doesn't trust her gut that something was wrong. *Help her look at what her gut said, why she didn't trust it, and how she can learn to respect what* **she** *thinks and feels in a difficult situation. Go through the list of what constitutes sexual misconduct and see how her situation might correspond.*

If I show anger, I am not feminine: in our culture, women are usually taught that anger is not an acceptable emotion to show (although it is for men). Angry women can be seen as bitchy and unlikeable. *Talk with her about gender role stereotypes for women and how they can get in the way of being assertive. Help her see that anger can be powerful and courageous, that it is not unfeminine but rather a healthy response to sexual misconduct.*

I will be ostracized from my team/social group: Most people want to be part of a team or social group, and if that team or group doesn't want you, for whatever reasons, it is difficult to know your truth and speak it. *Work with your client to explore the reality behind this assumption. If it's true, suggest she talk to someone on that team or in her Human Resources Department. If there is only rejection, help her find allies, a new team or social group, or move to a different environment that does not explicitly or implicitly condone sexual misconduct.*

I won't be believed: The power of the #MeToo movement is that it publicized the many voices of women who have been sexually assaulted. The overwhelming number of testimonies has helped sideline the once-standard disbelief about women's accusations. If one woman complains, it can be dismissed. If 10 women complain, it is much harder to dismiss. If 100 women complain, it can become impossible to dismiss. *Help her look at who will believe her and what her institutional resources are. Help her find allies on her campus or at her workplace who are likely to believe her and might be able and willing to take steps to confront the situation. Have her read stories from other survivors. Discuss how to find others who have experienced something similar and work with them to confront the perpetrator.*

Challenging Disempowering Comments by Men

Therapists also need to help women handle comments and attitudes from men that diminish her or show disrespect, factors that might make it more difficult for her to say *no* if she buys their assessment of her. Listed below are some common things a woman might hear from a man who has or is about to transgress her sexual boundaries. They are followed by suggestions a clinician might make to improve her response to these microaggressions.

- **You're too sensitive:** This is a classic statement that men make to invalidate a woman's feelings that something is wrong. If women take what men say as the truth (at the expense of their own), it diminishes a woman's worth. Why should a man's opinion be considered any more correct than a women's? Why isn't "you're too sensitive" seen as a way of deflecting a man's role in an uncomfortable situation? *Suggest that* *the best way to handle this might be by saying "that might be, but I need _____" or, "I'm sorry you feel this way but _____" or even, "It sounds like you are uncomfortable with what I am saying." This allows the woman to be assertive without directly contradicting the man's statement. If he continues to say "You're too sensitive," she can keep repeating her statement (known as the broken record technique). You can do some role-playing with her so she can see how this might look in real life. Any of these statements puts power back in the hands of the woman.*

- **Our sexual contact was consensual:** This excuse is used too often in cases of sexual misconduct where the man tries to deny the charge by assuming the contact was consensual. It is not consensual unless the woman gives informed consent (i.e., she must be in a state where she is mentally and physically able to do this). *Teaching your client the value of knowing the guidelines of how to most effectively give or not give consent will help her gain more control over a potentially dangerous situation.*

- **You owe me:** Does a woman owe a man anything in terms of sexual contact? Why would she owe him for sex? This is a man's way of making the woman feel guilty and ties into the gender norm for woman of "being nice." And saying *no* seems like not a nice thing to say. *Teaching a woman how to say no and know they are entitled to say no in whatever sexual situation they find themselves is a vital part of empowering them.*

- **This isn't a big deal:** Yes, it *is* a big deal if a woman is being coerced into a sexual situation she doesn't want to be in. He may not see it as a big deal, but he is speaking for her, which he cannot do. *Remind your client that she can say, "Yes, it's a big deal to me," and stick with that statement, regardless of whether he continues to go back to saying, "it isn't a big deal."*

- **No one will believe you:** This is complicated because if it's a "he said, she said" situation without witnesses (as is common), and he has some power that she doesn't (such as advisor to student) she may not be believed. *Suggest to her that the best way to handle this might be to document what she can, find allies and witnesses where feasible, and make a complaint through the appropriate channels as soon as possible.*

- **You asked for this by the way you drank/flirted/were dressed:** These are common excuses used by men to blame the women for leading them on. No matter what a woman wore, drank, or how she flirted, no one is asking for it if they don't want it. *Explore with her the injustice of having to police what she wears, how she flirts, or the quantity she drinks. Ask her why men aren't accused of "asking for it." Why isn't the burden on the man to ask permission? Helping her get angry about this can be useful in realizing she has a right to be angry rather than ashamed.*
- **You wanted this:** This is a common excuse which is "gaslighting"— telling the victim that she isn't feeling what she feels. *Explore with the client about why she didn't want or ask for the sexual contact. Surmise with her what the motivation is behind the man saying this to her. Suggest a response such as "I did not want this; I never said I did, and you must respect the fact that you were not acknowledging my lack of interest." If he persists, she can say "You don't know what I want or don't want, so don't make an assumption about what you think I want."*

Respecting the Stages of Change

This message is for everyone in the helping professions, but especially for men: We all need to be very respectful and patient with a victim who is trying to make sense of what has happened to them, and what the best course of action is—if any. Friends, family members therapists must learn to view the victim's decision-making as a *process* and realize that she has to proceed at her own pace. We have to respect the insights derived from the "stages of change" model,[15] which outlines the stages of precontemplation/contemplation/preparation/action/maintenance. We can't push someone into the action stage when they are at precontemplation or contemplation. It is tempting, because the stakes feel so high, but it usually alienates and backfires.

The sound alternative stance is one of respect for the process. Women in physically abusive relationships usually convey that the decision to stay or leave the violent relationship was a *highly rational* choice that carefully and accurately considered the pros and cons of the situation, particularly the potentially lethal consequences of leaving. The same applies to victims of sexual harassment and misconduct. None of us really knows the potential cost to her of shame, of shunning, of practical consequences like loss of job or career advancement, of reactivating past trauma, of fear of something shameful about her past being exposed. She is the only person who can explore on her own terms all the complexities, including benefits and costs to her, of taking or not taking action. We are there to help with that process, not assume we know what's best for her.

A Male Clinician's Take on Working with Women:
A Commentary by David Wexler

As a man, I am afflicted with an action-oriented mentality. Men (speaking in generalities, of course) particularly like to lean in to solving problems. And there is nothing more compelling for most men than helping a woman. This mindset often makes it particularly challenging for me and other male counselors and therapists to work with a woman struggling with some sort of sexual boundary violation or any kind of abuse. It's easy to get protective—and, if we're not careful, we can end up unconsciously focused on relieving our own anxiety and meeting our own needs than on being genuinely attuned to hers.

More important for the female client who has been badly treated by men is this: The most potent ingredient in healing often is this new positive interaction with a male who is caring, understanding, protective, respectful, and safe. When I work with a woman who is reeling from being damaged by men, I realize that I have a responsibility to build a relationship with her that can help repair this damage.

This is a different contribution, of course, than a female therapist can offer her. A female therapist is well-positioned to offer safety, empathy, and kinship, all of which are priceless. But we men (while unable to say that we know what it is like to be a woman harassed or traumatized by men) have something else to offer.

I can't say that very many of my female clients who are dealing with histories of sexual trauma actually say to me, "Wow, now that I feel safe with you, it helps me recognize that it is possible to have a positive relationship with a man." But I know that this is a key element in what is taking place, unsaid or not.

But I will add one caveat. I have supervised male therapists who have become intoxicated with being the "one good man" in the woman's life, and this has led to them excessively critiquing other men in her life. This dynamic has fostered an unhealthy dependence, in which the female client starts to see the male therapist as the only man who can and will ever really understand her. I have some profound advice for male counselors and therapists out there: *Don't go there.*

Chapter 9

Sexual Misconduct on Campus
Stopping the Spread of Sexist Behavior

In this chapter we will examine how counselors can help undergraduate women who have experienced sexual and sexual harassment on college campuses. Although peer sexual misconduct probably makes up the majority of campus cases that clinicians see in their offices, we will also include several examples of sexual misconduct based on an imbalance of power in the relationship. We will look at constructive ways for women to address the crisis, specifically what women can do to take charge of their lives in campus cultures where sexism and demeaning attitudes toward women exist. As therapists, we know that we can work primarily with our clients, but empowering them to take a stand against sexual misconduct will help change campus culture in small and large ways.

Peer Sexual Assault: The Case of Chanel Miller

It is important to reiterate that the focus on our book is on the gray areas of sexual misconduct, rather than on cases of forcible physical assault or criminal behavior such as rape. However, we felt it useful to start this chapter with the public face of peer sexual assault because many of the factors involved in this case are common on college campuses across the United States.

Chanel Miller (who was known only as Emily Doe until 2019) was sexually assaulted by Brock Turner in 2015, after they both drank extensively at a Stanford fraternity party. While she lay unconscious and her assailant was in the process of sexually assaulting her, two male bystanders came by, accosted the perpetrator, held him down until the police arrived, and were able to give third-party testimony about the assault. Despite the clear evidence that she had been sexually assaulted, she was a woman of color without any status on campus because she was not a student there, whereas her offender was Brock Turner, who was white and well-known as a champion swimmer on the Stanford campus. Turner was given a very light sentence which drew widespread outrage.

Miller bravely wrote a book[1] to give a personal voice to the incident in the hopes that other women will find the courage to report sexual misconduct whenever and wherever it happens. Her victim impact statement went viral shortly after BuzzFeed picked it up. In it she said that she hoped that sharing her experience would give other young women a sense of solidarity and hope, and help them know that they were not alone and would be listened to. She also said that she was grateful that two bystanders found her and helped restrain the perpetrator until the police arrived. She said that she (and other women) needed to learn the words her rescuers used, "What the fuck are you doing?" as a prototype for calling out sexual assault in no uncertain terms.

Although Miller was not a student on the campus when she was raped, the issues raised in this case are common to the incidents we face on campus that are on the spectrum of sexual misconduct. These factors include the following:

- There was nonconsensual sexual behavior by a male student.
- Both parties were young.
- Alcohol was involved.
- The victim was a person of color and the male was white.
- The assault took place within a male-dominated social setting.
- The victim experienced humiliation and shame after the assault.
- The assault and how it was handled caused ongoing psychological harm to her.
- The legal system was difficult for her to negotiate.
- The perpetrator received minimal punishment.

The prevalence of sexual misconduct on campus includes its multiple variations, such as the demographics of the offender and victim, the context in which the misconduct occurred, and the emotional consequences to the victim of the offender's behavior. As we look more closely at the factors contributing to sexual misconduct on campuses and the ways we can empower women, we must keep in mind how intersectionality can play a part.

Sexual Misconduct on College Campuses: The Impact of Demographics and Culture

There is an epidemic of sexual assault and sexual misconduct on American college campuses. According to the National Criminal Justice Reference Service[2] and the AAU Campus Climate Survey on Sexual Assault and Misconduct,[3] approximately 1 in 5 women (and 1 in 16 men) are sexually assaulted while in college due to physical force, threats of physical force, or incapacitation. Many more—as many as 59%—experience sexual harassment and sexual pressure (the wide range of #MeToo offenses), which don't always meet the criteria for sexual assault and thus don't make it into typical statistics about sexual assault.[4] Although this book does not cover the full range of sexual assault, we believe that there is a continuum of sexual harms that have common themes: acceptance of violation of women's sexual boundaries, disrespect of women, entitlement on the part of men, and a culture of sexism that encourages sexual misconduct without consequences for the perpetrators.

Let's start with the demographics found on many campuses that may contribute to the high incidence of sexual assault by men on women.

- The undergraduates are typically between the ages of 17 and 22. This means they are emerging adults, so are in transition from adolescence to adulthood. A report from the America Academy of Child and Adolescent states that research shows that adolescent brains lack the same degree of executive functioning as do adult brains.[5] Therefore, qualities that are essential in managing the complexities of relationship issues, peer pressure, hormones, and alcohol and drugs are not always well-developed when students are trying to make decisions about sexual behavior.
- For freshmen in particular, college is probably the first time they have been away from home, so are likely to be operating under less structure than what was provided by their parents. Students are freer to experiment with their sexuality and may not be ready for the challenge of setting healthy limits for themselves.
- Students tend to live in residence halls with levels of peer pressure far beyond what they probably experienced if they lived at home. That said, residential private high school culture can have the same impact and perhaps be even more damaging to women due to the younger age of the students.

- A peer culture on many campuses encourages the use of alcohol at parties (particularly at fraternities). First-year students may not be used to the effects of drinking a lot of alcohol. It impairs their capacity to govern, inhibits their behavior, and certainly impairs judgment about the consequences of any of their choices. Binge drinking on many campuses is so common[6] that it has become not only accepted but expected behavior.

- On many campuses, young men live in all-male fraternities which can encourage the adoption of unhealthy sexual behavior. Traditional male gender role norms often encourage conquest of women—and sharing bragging rights about this—as a sign of manhood. This seems to be particularly true for male athletes. While not dominant for all men in the college world, rigid and proscribed masculinity norms can play into the oversexualization of contact with women.

Depending on the institutions, orientations and trainings about sexual misconduct may not be very effective, especially if they are one-time offerings or only focused on the negative aspects of male behavior. The impact of gender role norms are not usually identified in trainings. Definitions of sexual assault and sexual misconduct are inconsistent. Standards for consent are not always clear or offered frequently enough. As we can see, all of these factors may contribute to the high rate of reported sexual misconduct (and this doesn't include #MeToo behavior that goes unreported[7]), so we can guess that the actual incidence is higher.

Campus #MeToo Behavior and Individual Clinical Work: Five Vignettes

An important part of working with victims of sexual misconduct involves helping the victim move beyond feeling powerless, contaminated, and ashamed into a stronger stance about what happened to her, to reframe the narrative of what happened to put her in a more powerful position. This is moving from victim to survivor, and moving from survivor to empowerment. This can include thinking about how to handle a situation of potential misconduct in the future should it arise for her or one of her friends. However, we always need to keep in mind that there is a fine line between acknowledging that she is truly a victim of sexual misconduct (and has not caused or encouraged it), and educating her about how she might handle any similar cases with greater self-care and personal power.

These vignettes are based on actual cases of sexual misconduct and harassment that took place at different college campuses. Three vignettes are about peer misconduct, two are about misconduct by authority figures. The vignettes are designed to show not only how clinicians might work with student victims of sexual misconduct but also some of the internal and external barriers that might limit a victim from handling sexual misconduct from a position of strength.

If our goal is to help the victim handle the aftermath of the assault in ways which strengthen her sense of self and her ability to move forward with her life with confidence, how do we help make this happen? As you read these stories, consider how you might work with these five clients. What might you have done the same, differently? How might your approach be different depending on their sexual orientation, race, ethnicity, and so on? What if the student is a commuter student and does not live on campus? What might you need in terms of consultation or supervision? What resources do you need to be an effective counselor? And what can you do to help change the culture of sexual assault of your campus, both inside and outside your office? We have offered some questions at the end of each vignette to stimulate thinking about the variety of clients we may serve and their particular needs.

Peer Sexual Misconduct: *Why Does This Keep Happening to Me?*

Ashley was a 25-year-old college junior who came into her counseling center because she was having trouble dating. She said she was the victim of a campus sexual assault two years ago, but didn't want to talk about it, saying "I have already dealt with it and don't want to go over this again." Although the therapist could see the link between the assault and Ashley's issue with dating, she respected that decision and worked out a treatment plan with Ashley for dealing with her presenting problem, dating. They began to explore Ashley's thoughts about why she was cautious around men. She said she didn't trust men—and wasn't sure that they would be "good men." She said that she always ended up in situations with men who "put the moves on me," were overtly sexual, and made her feel uncomfortable. But she admitted that she had a hard time speaking up because she didn't want to hurt their feelings. She didn't understand why she repeatedly dated "bad men," saying "why does this keep happening to me?"

Gently and gradually the therapist suggested they explore the past assault when Ashley was ready, since the therapist thought that sequelae from the previous assault may be interfering with her current inability to move forward. The therapist let Ashley talk about it at her own pace, reassuring her that her feelings of shame and her difficulty addressing the impact of the assault on her were normal. In several instances the therapist would say, "we women . . ." as a way of bonding with her client and to let Ashley know she wasn't alone in her experience or her feelings. She also educated Ashley about the different types of emotions survivors may feel following sexual assault, and provided techniques to calm herself when she felt overwhelmed.

Eventually Ashley came to realize that she was interpreting all her dates' behaviors in a malevolent light, that most weren't like her perpetrator, and that she could see them for who they are—"good men" who were unsure about how to tell her that they were attracted to her or how to move forward with physical contact. Ashley began to speak up when on a date when she felt uncomfortable, asked her dates to take it slow, and started to trust that she had enough confidence to take control in an uncomfortable situation and not get overwhelmed.

In this case, the therapist intervened in several ways that helped Ashley move past her assault: She went at Ashley's pace, she allowed Ashley to tell her story and she listened in a nonjudgmental way. She framed some of her comments as applicable not just to Ashley but to many women. And the therapist helped Ashley explore how staying silent for fear of hurting a man's feelings was embedded in traditional and restrictive gender roles that served no one. She employed one of the fundamental tenets of feminist therapy[8]: That the therapist and client are a team, and the client has agency and expertise in her own recovery.

Imagine Ashley is from a highly religious family where sex is only permissible in the context of marriage, and any girl who is assaulted is "asking for it" and is shamed. How would this affect your interactions with her and how she understands her struggles?

Peer Sexual Misconduct: *It Was My Fault*

Michelle is a freshman who belonged to a popular sorority where members often went to fraternity parties on campus. She and her friends had fun, drinking and flirting and enjoying letting loose after working hard all week on their studies. She knew the guys in the fraternity and felt comfortable being with them in a social setting. One Saturday night she and some of her friends arrived late to a party. Everyone had been drinking fairly heavily and she and her friends felt they were behind in the fun. Michelle had several drinks in quick succession and began to feel relaxed and happy. She was attracted to Steve, a star member of the football team who was confident and fun, and considered a "catch" by anyone's standards as far as she could see. She made out with him for a while, enjoying the buzz of the alcohol and having a good time in general. When he suggested going to his room for a little "fun" she was hesitant but knew him to be a good guy and believed he wouldn't do anything that she didn't want to do. When they got to his room, he shut the door and proceeded to undress her, feeling her breasts and starting to put his hand on her genitals. She felt uncomfortable and said "*No*, this isn't what I want."

To which he replied, "You know you want this."

She said *no* again and he proceeded to take off her dress and unzip his pants. She panicked at this point and said "What are you doing? Stop!" Although he didn't penetrate her (the legal definition of rape), he touched her in places where she felt violated.

At some point, he said "I hope you enjoyed that as much as I did," and left her to go downstairs. She stayed in the room, unable to believe what had happened, telling herself that she didn't say no soon enough, that she shouldn't have gone to his room, that she led him on by kissing him in the fraternity lounge. As she went downstairs, she felt sick and asked her roommates to take her home.

For a long time she told no one, filled with shame and wanting to forget that it ever happened. Her homework began to suffer. She finally told her friends what had happened and they all agreed she should contact the university counseling center as soon as possible. She wanted to see a female therapist because she felt the male therapist might not understand or would judge her. However, only male therapists had appointments available and she decided to take one.

The therapist at the center listened carefully to her story, allowing her to disclose what had happened at her own pace. He explored options with Michelle about what she wanted to do at this point, giving her a range of possible actions and resources on campus, and working with her to see what the benefit or disadvantage was in each case. He helped Michelle see that what had happened was not her fault, that *no* meant *no*, that she had done the best she could, and that the shame should belong to Steve, not to her. He said that healing might take time and that she was welcome to continue to see him or get referred to another clinician outside of the campus clinic. His suggestions and empathic listening helped Michelle work through the assault, But he also provided a positive male role model for Michelle, showing her that there are men who could listen to and support her. This is something that male clinicians can bring to the table in dealing with female assault victims and may be an important part of the client's recovery.

Although Michelle ultimately decided not to file a complaint, she discussed the incident with her sorority sisters and they agreed to have a "buddy" system in the future to protect each other from incidents like this. In the meantime, the therapist discussed the case with his colleagues at the counseling center and with campus administrators who ran sexual harassment trainings to see how they might improve the programs so that these kinds of assaults that involve heavy drinking might be less likely to happen.

What if Michelle is a first-generation Latina college student with little experience of what it's like to be on a college campus? How might you see this case differently? What are the issues you would address?

Authority Figure Sexual Misconduct:
I Couldn't Say No Because He Might Retaliate Against Me

Paige was a senior doing her thesis in biology. She went to consult her advisor about a problem she was having with her data collection. He was friendly to her and chatted about what her future plans were once she graduated. He suggested that they go out for dinner later that week, saying it was a way to get to know his students better. Paige was uncomfortable with this plan because she felt that it was inappropriate and crossed professional boundaries. However, she agreed because she didn't want to get on his bad side. After all, she told herself, a good recommendation from a highly respected professor in her field would be really helpful in furthering her career. "I can be really helpful to you in getting a job," he said at dinner, and suggested that they have drinks at his place afterward to discuss on which companies she should focus, given her interests.

Again she felt this inappropriate but didn't want to seem unfriendly. Once she was in his apartment, he suggested that they sit on the sofa so they could talk more easily. She went along with his suggestion since she didn't want to offend him or cause a scene but felt increasingly uncomfortable. At this point, he began to touch her and say how attractive she was and how it would be fun for them to explore being sexual with each other. She didn't know what to do at this point. She was worried about making a scene and not wanting to offend him for fear he would turn against her. She went along with the sexual contact up to the point where he suggested they have intercourse. She said she had to get home. He said "Ok, but don't tell anyone about the incident—no one will believe you anyhow, and I just want to make sure nothing gets in the way of the help you need finishing your thesis."

Paige talked to her friends who told her to contact the campus counseling center for help. Her clinician listened carefully to her account, asked a few questions, empathized with her situation, and said that Paige could contact the campus Title IX office if she wanted to. She didn't know what Title IX was, so the counselor discussed with her what the office did and how it was set up to handle these kinds of cases. Paige said she was afraid her advisor would punish her if she did report him, but the clinician reassured her that the Title IX office was there to protect her.

Paige ended up going to the Title IX office and received the support she needed to file a complaint. She also switched advisors. She continued to see the campus clinician, who worked with her to understand the emotional impact this experience had on her, how to deal with that impact in a positive way, and to appreciate her courage in being assertive and taking active steps despite her advisor's threats. They explored future resources for her, including joining a local #MeToo group for support. The clinician suggested that Paige might consider continuing therapy to help her work through some of the painful issues that the experience brought up for her, since Paige had been sexually abused in high school by a teacher. She thought this was a good idea and they worked together during the rest of her senior year to help her process her assaults and gain more confidence in being assertive.

What if Paige were an immigrant from a war-torn country? How might this impact how she views an authority figure? Her ability to be heard? Her safety if she speaks out against the harasser? How would you help?

Peer Harassment: *Maybe I Don't Belong Here*

Emily was a college sophomore, referred to her campus counseling center by a friend who had heard her complain about sexist comments made during study sessions and in social settings. Emily was reluctant to go, wondering if, in fact, she didn't even belong at the university—that maybe her admission had been an administrative mistake—or that she needed to "toughen up" and learn to roll with the punches. As she discussed this with friends, she realized that they, too, had similar issues. In one dormitory, the men had put up pictures of women in the dorm with sexual comments next to their names. In another, women were rated as to how good looking they were. In study sessions, women's comments were dismissed or ignored. Guys would follow her around, making inappropriate comments or not taking the "hint" that she was not interested in them. Men would show pornographic films in mixed-gender dorms, citing "freedom of speech" when women complained to their faculty advisors.

These situations made Emily (and many of her friends) feel unwelcome at the university. Finally she'd had enough of what felt like a hostile environment. When she went to the campus counseling center and explained her situation, her counselor labeled the actions of the students as harassment and showed her the campus guidelines. They explored what she might want to do, including going to the campus ombudsperson to lodge her complaints. Emily followed the advice of the counselor and saw the ombudsperson. She felt listened to and she felt validated; she learned about sexual harassment and the laws that govern it, and she saw what action would be taken to address her concerns both on an individual and collective level. Emily felt more in control of her environment and more confident that she had institutional support in dealing with the harassing behavior. Campus personnel increased the effectiveness and frequency of sexual harassment training in dormitories on campus. In addition, Emily met with a group of female students who worked together to stop the sexist behavior in all areas of the campus.

Imagine that Emily is a Black student who is enrolled in a mostly white college campus. How would that change how you might see this situation and handle it?

Authority Figure Harassment: *Am I Being Too Sensitive?*
Danielle was an undergraduate at a prestigious university, staffed with professors whose research was nationally known. In one of the lectures given by a chemistry professor, slides were shown that used women's naked bodies to illustrate key points. Danielle felt very uncomfortable with this and considered stopping attending class. The atmosphere felt toxic to her, but she wondered if she was just being too sensitive. She brought up the issue with her friends who urged her not to do anything about it. "You'll get in trouble if you report this to the dean," they said. "Just let it go, it's not a big deal." Danielle felt at a loss about what to do: On the one hand, the slides made her feel like she, as a woman, was a sexual object. On the other hand, she worried she was overly

sensitive and that maybe this really *was* ok. She talked to her resident hall advisor about the incident who suggested she see a therapist at the counseling center to explore what had happened and what to do next.

The counselor she saw listened carefully and respectfully to her issues with the slides, how they had made her feel, and what she had done with her feelings. They discussed what the campus policy was concerning this kind of behavior; he labeled it "sexual harassment" and showed Danielle the information that the university had put out about what constituted harassment. He then asked Danielle what she wanted to do, listing several options for her. She felt she had an ally with him, trusted his judgment, and went to the Title IX office to lodge a complaint. Apparently, the professor had done this before, but because he was internationally known, no one had done anything about it. At this point, the dean of his department stepped in, realized that the professor's behavior was ongoing harassment that he could no longer turn a blind eye to, even if the professor was highly respected by other faculty. The professor was placed on administrative leave and no longer lectured in that subject.

Danielle went back to see her clinician one more time to discuss what had happened and how she felt. He was supportive of her actions, and told her that she was welcome to come back at any time to continue to discuss any further ramifications she had from the incident.

Imagine that Danielle is from a small working-class town, the first in her family to go to college. She doesn't know anyone in her community who has gone beyond a local two-year community college. How might this alter how you work with her and understand her reactions and feelings?

Stepping Outside of Our Offices

Unfortunately, some of the programs, although well-meaning, can divide the genders rather than unite them in effectively addressing issues concerning sexual misconduct if all men are seen as potential offenders.

As clinicians, we probably do most of our work on an individual basis in our own offices. However, we may be an underutilized resource. Because of our professional training and expertise, we can collaborate with college personnel to explore different and effective ways to reduce #MeToo behavior and empower women. We might consider how to become more involved, given our skill sets and interests, time constraints, and potential support from our centers and from campus leaders. We know our time is limited, but participating in a few of these programs and classes might be worthy additions to our schedules. Suggestions for involvement are italicized. Finally, consider how your clients who have dealt with issues of sexual misconduct could make use of these resources in ways that empower them without making men the enemy.

Training Programs: Reducing Cases of Sexual Misconduct

Each campus should have at least one program dedicated to finding effective ways to reduce the incidence of sexual assaults. These on-campus prevention programs are probably the primary way institutions educate students about this topic, and the types of programs (and their success rates) are varied. Although we provide a listing of specific programs in the Resources section, we felt it was worth mentioning one in particular. The Enhanced Assess, Acknowledge and Act Program[9] was developed by Professor Charlene Senn at the University of Windsor to reduce the incidence of sexual harm to young women. The program ran facilitated discussions and role-playing sessions led by faculty and staff; in these, women students learned to "understand their own sexual and relationship desires and recognize factors—like isolation, or sexual entitlement in men's behavior—that can raise the risk of sexual assault. It helped the young women overcome emotional barriers that might keep them from resisting coercion from men they know, and to learn effective verbal and physical self-defense strategies."[10] The reduction in assaults was significant: Students who took part in this intervention were 30% to 64% less likely to experience rape, attempted rape, or nonconsensual sexual contact over the next two years than were women in the control group.[11] A list of several different types of campus training programs is included in the Resources section. *Consider how you might work with the trainers, bringing in a psychological perspective developed from your own experience as a clinician.*

Classes: Education as a Tool for Change

A variety of classes on the psychology of women, the psychology of men, and the psychology of gender are taught on American college campuses. Learning about #MeToo behaviors in an educational setting can be a non-blaming approach to creating greater understanding of other genders and exploring how rigid gender norms increase situations of sexual misconduct. Classes which offer an experiential component are particularly useful since students can interact the material in a more substantial way. *You might think about whether you want to offer or help create and lead an experiential seminar on those topics.*

Groups: The Importance of Commonality
Several models include groups for sexual assault survivors, assertiveness training groups, and women's groups. Groups are often an excellent way for victims of #MeToo behaviors to support each other. *You can offer support groups in your counseling centers on either an ongoing or drop-in basis for women who have experienced sexual misconduct.*

Hotlines: The Value of Anonymity
Most campuses have some kind of 24/7 confidential hotline, often run by students. Campus hotlines are places where people can share incidents of sexual misconduct when the victim feels too embarrassed, shamed, or confused to bring her experiences to the counseling center. Hotlines are also a resource if an individual wishes to discuss how to help a friend who is a #MeToo survivor. *Staff supervision of the hotline phonebank is essential; many of you are already helping students run these services. If you are not, consider how you might become involved.*

Freshman Orientation: The Importance of a Non-Blaming, Experiential, and Ongoing Approach
Most colleges have some kind of orientation for freshmen that focuses on how to prevent sexual misconduct on campus. Typically, these are one-time offerings and do not include follow-up sessions. These sometimes have a negative aspect to them (men as perpetrators committing sexual assault, women as victims) and may not present the wide variety and complexity of #MeToo behaviors. *Think about ways you could work with orientation leaders to evaluate and revise current orientation programs to be ongoing, more experiential, and tailored to your student body and college.*

Women's Centers: The Support Provided by a Single-Sex Environment
Campus centers for women have been around since the early 1970s, typically serving as a space where women can come to relax, feel safe, and connect with other women. Feeling safe and connected can help women be better able to handle sexual misconduct because they can share their experiences and strategies. *Consider being a staff advisor for one of these centers.*

Bystander Trainings: The Value of Allies

Learning how men (and women) can step in and stop #MeToo behavior is a crucial part of reducing sexual misconduct. These trainings have been shown to effectively reduce #MeToo incidents, in part because they make use of peer pressure to highlight and bolster respect for women. More detailed information about bystander training will be covered in Chapter 12. *Consider how you might help students learn ways to stop #MeToo behavior by speaking up and stepping in as needed, as well as some of the barriers they might encounter when doing so.*

Education and Prevention:
The Importance of Consent in Sexual Situations

Women are empowered when they understand what consent to sexual behavior looks like, how to best communicate consent, and what actions to take if their consent is not heard or respected. All definitions of sexual misconduct (and there are many, as we have described in Chapter 1) include the use of the word "consent." Consent is critical to understanding whether sexual misconduct has happened.

But what is consent exactly? Definitions vary among academic institutions and between states, so it is hard to pin down exactly what will or might constitute consent in a particular situation. The Rape, Abuse and Incest National Network (RAINN) gives a working definition of consent as "an agreement between participants to engage in sexual activity." Some of the core elements of consent they describe are (1) the ability to consent (in particular not being incapacitated) (2) frequent verbal and non-verbal communication, and (3) the ability to change one's mind at any time. It is helpful to look at the RAINN website to see a more detailed description of the components of consent.

Here is a brief example of what consent might look like for two young adults on a college campus[13]:

- Both Eric and Samantha are engaged in sexual activity enthusiastically, after both agreeing to have sex.
- They have continuous communication every step of the way while sexting, hooking up, or while in a committed relationship.

- Both Samantha and Eric are capable of making informed decisions, are not intoxicated, incapacitated, or coerced.
- If Samantha does not say *no*, says *I'm not sure*, or remains silent, Eric does not continue with sexual activity of any kind until they communicate about what she needs.

However, there are gray areas that can lead to misunderstandings, even with the best of intentions. For example, what kind of physical cues would the recipient give to the initiator? Are there cultural differences about those cues? Could men and women have different ideas of what a certain cue might mean? What if the communication is made in vague terms or misinterpreted? These are issues that can lead to sexual misconduct. It would be helpful to have a copy of your institution's guidelines for consent in your office, as well a copy of the consent section from the RAINN website. These could be used as adjunct material to help students think through what consent means to them personally.

Resources for Clinicians: Helping the Helpers

Referrals: Making Use of Campus Programs

In most colleges, there are a range of offices and programs that deal with sexual misconduct through disciplinary and legal channels, including Title IX offices and campus assault programs. Getting to know personnel associated with handling cases of sexual misconduct and how they operate would be important, since part of your counseling might include referrals to appropriate resources on campus.

Consultation and Supervision: The Value of Collaboration

You don't have to handle your cases alone. Share specific cases for which you need feedback with your colleagues and supervisors. If a case feels too much for you to handle, for whatever reason, consider referring the client to another clinician. Countertransference can be prominent in these situations, so having good supervision is important. There is nothing wrong with being triggered by a client's case, but we need to handle it with objectivity.

Consult with other professionals about the issues raised in your cases; these resources might include Title IX administrators, as well as personnel who work with issues regarding respectful conduct between the genders in classroom, housing, and social settings. Attend sexual-assault trainings and read literature written by assault experts to broaden your knowledge.

We must be alert to the demographics of our clients in terms of the intersectionality of race, sexual orientation, socioeconomic status, sexual identity, and ethnicity. This shapes not only how we feel about the situation—such as the blind spots we might have toward clients who are different from us—but also how we tailor our treatment to best meet their needs. It is important to get good consultation from a peer, or request supervision from an experienced therapist who is part of a particular intersectionality, and to use the "self-reflection" mentioned in Chapter 5 as a tool to see our blind spots so we can work more knowledgeably with our clients.

Finally, we can listen nonjudgmentally, and our efforts to empower clients through education and other resources are skills and methods most of us have. We don't need to be experts to help victims of sexual misconduct, but we do have to know our limits and limitations, and seek guidance in our cases where needed.

Where Do We Go From Here?

Sexual misconduct is a problem that needs to be addressed on many fronts, including more effective trainings about assault and harassment, better channels for reporting and handling sexual misconduct that does occur, and changing a culture of sexual misconduct that encourages men to act toward women in sexual and disrespectful ways. However, the majority of men and women in college settings are not offenders or victims. If 20% of women on college campuses report having suffered sexual assault,[14] that leaves 80% who have not. Even when accounting for underreporting, it is likely that the majority of women have not been victims, and the majority of men have not been offenders.

There is a great confusion about what a #MeToo behavior actually is. This has left us unclear about what is or is not appropriate behavior with the other gender. Women can too often group men into the general category of "perpetrators," rather than their more likely role of potential allies. Men can be confused about the rules of social behavior. When is a compliment seen as a nice gesture and when as harassment? Since women's opinions vary in terms of what might offend versus flatter them, how does a man assess what is appropriate? What behavior creates a hostile environment for women on campus? Is it the same for all campuses? Are good men ever falsely accused?

Men are fearful of being seen as offenders; women are distrustful of men. Men are angry at the offenders who give masculinity a bad name; women are not sure how to proceed in terms of what to expect in dating situations. In a sexist campus culture, social power is often given to men who have status in that community (often through athletic achievement) and who can exhibit the worst aspects of traditional masculinity, such as dominance over and disrespect for women. In that culture, good men may not be listened to or valued.

In coordination with campus resources such as Title IX offices, we can help educate our clients as well as other students on our campus about the damage caused by sexual misconduct, why it happens, and how to prevent it. We can raise discussions around the gray areas of sexual misconduct that need to be better understood. We can help our clients who have experienced sexual misconduct see that there are many good men who are not offenders. Our culture has often undermined women in terms of men's respect for women, so we are fighting a system that may reinforce sexual misconduct. Ultimately the change has to start with early childhood socialization, where boys are taught respect for girls, and girls are taught to be assertive and self-confident. However, in the current work we do with students both in and out of our offices, we can strive towards the following goals:

- empower women to be more assertive
- help students understand the impact of gender roles on #MeToo behavior
- help students understand the impact of alcohol in reducing good judgment
- help men act more respectfully towards women
- encourage men to be allies in addressing and stopping sexual misconduct
- educate students about how to handle the gray areas of sexual misconduct

We believe that men can serve as allies and women can be assertive: both sexes can learn how traditional gender role norms may contribute to #MeToo behavior. Stopping sexual assault is not just about stopping sexual harm; it's about prevention and education and working together to address the problem from a non-shaming point of view. Although stopping *all* sexual misconduct, harassment and assault on our campuses is not realistic, we do what we can in our own spheres to support women and their allies in changing campus culture to one that is safer and more welcoming for women.

Chapter 10

Sexual Harassment in Work Environments
Coping With a Toxic Workplace

Sexual harassment in the workplace is widespread. Some of the most publicized #MeToo behaviors have taken place in a work setting. The June 2016 EEOC Select Task Force on the Study of Harassment in the Workplace found that 45% of the 90,000 charges received by EEOC in fiscal year 2015 included an allegation of harassment on the basis of sex.[1] One of the biggest problems with harassment lies in the victims' reluctance to report these offenses. The task force report states that "roughly three out of four individuals who experience (any kind of) harassment never even talked to a supervisor, manager or union representative about the harassment conduct. Employees who experience harassment fail to report the harassing behavior or to file a complaint because they fear disbelief of their claim, inaction on their claim, blame, or social or professional retaliation."[2]

According to a random sample in a recent poll,[3] out of 740 female respondents, 80% say they have been sexually harassed at work but 95% of those women say the male harasser went unpunished. The main feelings they report as a result of these incidents are anger, feeling intimidated, and a sense of humiliation. The Stanford Sexual Harassment Policy office (www.upcounsel.com) reports that feelings of insecurity, shame, frustration, low self-esteem, anxiety, depression, denial, fear, isolation, powerlessness, and guilt are typical. The feelings listed in the Stanford report are perhaps more destructive to a woman's sense of self. She has not only internalized the toxic environment, which can contribute to her sense of demoralization, disempowerment and increased negative feelings about herself, but also feels isolated and powerless. Isolation can serve to increase helplessness (*I can't do anything about it right now*) and hopelessness (*I will never be able to do anything about it*) as one suffers alone without the support and experience of others. With support, victims can feel more powerful and better able to address the harassment.

The #MeToo movement has been instrumental in helping victims of harassment bond together and be heard and validated. However, many women still suffer from lack of support in dealing with peers' and supervisors' micro- and macroaggressions, which can erode self-esteem and sense of agency. The good news is that counseling typically has a positive effect with victims of any kind of sexual harassment and abuse. Our job as counselors and clinicians is to help clients who have experienced these aggressions, understand their emotions, see the harassment for what it is, decrease negative feelings that can paralyze them, and mobilize their strengths and support system. Working towards these goals in therapy can increase their ability to feel and act in powerful ways. Please note that in this chapter we use the term "sexual harassment," to include sexual misconduct, but not acts of physical sexual force.

Workplace Versus Academia

Counseling clients who have experienced sexual harassment in the workplace presents special obstacles that might not apply for clinicians in academic settings. These include the following:

- fewer resources for women in the workplace compared with college students
- no ready-made community (such as dormitories) for support
- more serious consequences of career retaliation from authority figures

Given these differences, there is still common ground in how we help clients who have been harassed by peers or authority figures. This common ground includes listening to their experience, exploring and processing their feelings about the incident or work culture, and helping them find ways to gain a greater sense of personal and professional power.

Types of Sexual Harassment in the Workplace

The legal definition of sexual harassment as outlined by the U.S. Equal Employment Opportunity Commission is "unwelcome sexual advances, requests for sexual favors, and other verbal or physical contact of a sexual nature when this conduct explicitly or implicitly affects an individual's employment, unreasonably interferes with an individual's work performance, or creates an intimidating, hostile or offensive work environment."[4] Sexual harassment in the workplace is typically divided into two categories: (1) peers who create or foster a hostile workplace and (2) bosses who demand a quid pro quo for promotions, job offers, or career advancement.

Sexual harassment occurs on a continuum, with many gray areas. To meet the legal definition of harassment, the act must be unwelcome. Unless it is egregious behavior that a reasonable person would find unwelcome, how does a man know what is welcome and what is not? And how does a woman effectively communicate that the behavior is unwelcome? What might seem welcome to one woman might not be welcome to another. The confusion about what is and isn't sexual harassment can result in men being uncomfortable around women and therefore limit socializing with them inside or outside of the workplace. They may fear being accused of sexual harassment (not being clear what it is) and worry they might not be believed if a female peer accuses them of harassment. They might view HR as a kangaroo court where they are judged guilty until found innocent. This is the "#MeToo backlash" and serves no one, especially women who may already feel out of the loop in a male-dominated company.

Peer-to-Peer Harassment

Let's explore several examples of sexual harassment by peers. Note that some of this behavior may be deliberately hostile and some might be clueless and unintentional. Unless the woman speaks up, a man might not know that his behavior is unwanted (see examples that are underlined). Some of the interest may in fact be wanted (mutual flirting or welcomed attention), even if it is inappropriate for a professional setting. But what is clear is that no woman wants to be treated in a demeaning, disrespectful way or to be seen solely as a sex object in the workplace. Sexual harassment behaviors by peers may include the following:

- discussing women's bodies or sexuality in a disrespectful way
- making unwanted, sexually suggestive remarks or jokes
- making verbal or physical unwanted advances
- teasing a woman about her physical attributes or love life in a demeaning way

- continuing to pursue a woman <u>who does not want to be pursued</u>
- writing <u>unwanted</u> sexually explicit emails or ones with sexual innuendos
- touching women in ways <u>that make her feel uncomfortable</u>
- showing pornography or posting pornographic images—this can include cartoons, photographs, and having sexual objects such as condoms or dildos visible in the workplace
- addressing women in a sexually objectifying way
- using sexually crude terms

To complicate matters, the harassment may be the act of a group of men in a culture that demeans or dismisses women; or it can be undertaken by just one man. Are the offenders unaware of the negative impact their behavior has on the woman, or are they knowingly being disrespectful? Do the perpetrators understand why they act as they do toward women in the workplace? Unfortunately, supervisors may be part of this abusive environment and personnel in HR may or may not be able to change the culture.

We offer several vignettes to help explore peer-to-peer sexual harassment. The first depicts a hostile culture for women; the second portrays an individual man acting inappropriately, rather than being hostile. In both cases, the woman's physical and verbal boundaries are being ignored. For a variety of reasons she is having a difficult time speaking up and stating clearly, "This behavior is unwanted," which is key part of determining whether sexual harassment has occurred.

For the sake of simplification, we will not include variables such as race, sexual orientation, religion, or socioeconomic status. But for your therapy practice, you need to consider how intersectionality (as covered in Chapter 5) informs your treatment. What if our client is African American or Latina and her peers are all white men? What if she is lesbian? Transfemale? A Muslim woman who wears a hijab? How might these considerations affect how she views the situation and how she is being treated? How she views therapy? Think about how these issues might change what you do in therapy.

Typically, we hope that therapists can do the following when working with clients who have experienced harassment in their work environments:

1. Help the client communicate her boundaries more clearly, both in the current situation and in future ones.

2. Help the client feel more empowered to confront the behavior and report egregious and/or repeated violations if she determines that the cost of this is in her best interests personally and professionally.
3. Help her not internalize the blame for what happened or doubt her own perception of reality.

The following vignettes are a guide to help you identify pathways to achieving these therapy goals as well as confronting inevitable roadblocks.

1. Peer-to-Peer Group Sexual Harassment: *Women Are Sexual Objects, Not Workmates, This Is a Boys Club and Girls Don't Belong*

Jane is a 26-year-old college graduate who works in the high tech industry. She has experienced hostility and disrespect by her peers at work, which makes her feel ashamed and confused. In college she felt like a fish out of water because most of her classmates in her computer science classes were males. Occasionally one of them would say that she got into the program only because she was female, or that although she got better grades than them, *they* were really the smart ones who would do better in the workplace. Men in her classes made jokes about women and how they were only good for one thing—sex.

Upon graduation, Jane took a job in high tech, which offered her the opportunity to advance in her field. She was initially excited about the position. However, once she started her new job, she was disappointed to notice that some of the same harassment patterns she was subjected to at college were occurring in her workplace. Her office was dominated by young men and very few women worked there. Men in her workgroup indicated in a variety of ways that they saw her as a sexual object more than a colleague. They would tease her about the clothes she wore ("Are those *fuck me* pumps?"), make comments about her body ("You have sexy legs"), ask her questions about her love life, and make sexual suggestions to her. Some of them would hang around her work cubicle and ask if she wanted to date them. Several would put their arms around her shoulders, asking if she would like a massage. One of them had a pinup on his cubicle wall which she could easily view from her own cubicle.

The last straw was when one of her male workmates left a packet of condoms on her desk with a suggestion that she use them with her coworkers. She became increasingly uncomfortable, feeling disrespected and isolated. She started to shy away from spending time with her colleagues, and would eat lunch alone at her desk. At this point, Jane considered looking for another job but decided to see a therapist before she took that final step. She was cautious about seeing a therapist, unsure if she would be believed or, even if she were, whether the therapist would make light of what happened to her, given that she wasn't suffering from a major mental illness or severe PTSD.

In the first session with the therapist, Jane wasn't sure that she needed therapy, saying, "Maybe I'm just too sensitive." The therapist suggested that Jane put that belief on hold, and that together they could explore what had happened instead of labeling her issues as minor. The therapist acknowledged that her clients often came in saying the same things, but that she felt that her clients were practicing good self-care by addressing the problem directly. She asked Jane to tell her story at her own pace, raising questions only to clarify what Jane said. In addition, the therapist asked her how she felt about how her male colleagues had been treating her.

Jane replied that she was confused about whether she was being too sensitive. Because of that, her strategy had been to play along with the jokes and comments, as uncomfortable as that made her. She said she didn't want to make waves or be singled out. She felt she had to be "nice" and accept the sexualized behavior, because if she didn't, disrespectful behavior by her male peers might increase.

The therapist explored with Jane why she felt this way. Together they looked not only at her background and her experience with harassment but also how traditional female gender roles might have influenced Jane's behavior and attitude. The therapist legitimized Jane's right to what she felt and said that from what Jane had told her, her peers' behavior would be defined as sexual harassment. She also inquired about any past experiences Jane might have had in being told by men that she was too sensitive, or times when she felt she was being devalued and treated like a sexual object. Jane remembered situations when men had told her she was being too sensitive when she tried to speak up for what she needed or didn't like. The therapist asked her what that was like for her, and what she would say to a friend who was being dismissed in that way.

Through exploration of her background and the messages she had been given early on about needing to be quiet and accepting of men's misbehavior, Jane became more aware of why she was having a difficult time confronting the harassers. They also explored why men might act like this, and how male gender norms might be playing out in her workplace. As she thought about these questions, she realized that she had been adopting men's views of women rather than standing up for herself and confronting their behavior. She said, "Wow, I can't believe I did this—and so many of my friends do the same thing." Jane began to get angry at being demeaned as a woman, and of having her sexual boundaries violated by her male peers both verbally and physically.

Once Jane realized that not only was she angry but that she had a right to be, she and the therapist looked at her options about how to proceed, as well as possible outcomes she would like from therapy. She said she wanted men to treat her more respectfully and professionally and not sexualize her or other women in the office. She wanted to find allies, male and female, as well as get help from HR personnel to deal with this issue in a way that would not result in her being ignored, or create a backlash where the men might "up the ante" in terms of being more disrespectful of her boundaries.

Together they looked at her options in terms of what Jane felt would be in her best interests. What if she did nothing? Could she talk to her boss? Would he be sympathetic to her situation? Was there an HR department at her job—and if so, what are the pros and cons of making an appointment with personnel there? Did she want to talk directly to the offenders? What other resources might be available in her company? Were there other women who might be allies, or men who could act as good role models and "active bystanders"?

They explored what she felt comfortable with and what she imagined would be the consequences of speaking up. They did some role-playing simulating how she might talk to the offenders, her supervisor, or HR personnel. The therapist suggested a list of resources about handling sexual harassment in the workplace. As they went through various options, the therapist asked her how she felt about each one and was supportive of how Jane wanted to approach the situation. She knew she had the right to do nothing, although this option felt like defeat to her. She also knew that the outcome no longer rested on her fear of speaking up but rather on finding her voice and having access to available resources to be able to confront the men's disrespectful behavior.

After several sessions, Jane finally felt ready to talk to her supervisor about her male peers' behavior. To her surprise, he was sympathetic to her concerns and said he would talk to HR about establishing an ongoing training in reducing harassment and increasing respectful relationships. In spite of this, Jane eventually decided to leave the workplace for a variety of reasons (in particular the negative feelings she still had about the harassers). However, she took with her the ability to stand up for herself if a similar situation presented itself in her new job. She also knew that the culture of harassment would not continue to exist in its same form if confronted on a regular basis by authority figures, and that future female employees were likely to benefit from what Jane had gone through.

2. Peer-to-Peer Individual Sexual Harassment:
I Don't Take No for an Answer

Susan is a 35-year-old receptionist at a local advertising agency. She decides to see a therapist because she doesn't know how to handle the unwanted attention of a coworker. She was popular in high school and received the attention of many boys, but she never knew how to say *no* to them gracefully. Her main role model was her mother, who was known in her community for being helpful in many volunteer capacities. Her mother told her when she was young that the most important thing in communicating with others was to not hurt their feelings, even if one had to tell a white lie. Susan learned that being feminine meant being kind to others even at cost to herself. She also learned from popular culture that she could be sexy but not act too sexual, a message which left her confused. What did it mean to be sexy and attractive yet not sexual? Where was her own sexuality, her sense of control in a dating situation? She liked to dress up, to wear the latest styles. She liked having attention from men but only from men she liked and to whom she was attracted.

Although she liked her job and her workmates, her fellow coworker, Tom, had a crush on her. He followed her around and tried to make conversation wherever and whenever possible. She wasn't at all attracted to Tom, but didn't know how to tell him in a way that she felt wouldn't make him feel bad. As she tried to be nice and respond to him politely, he didn't take the hint. He began to spend increasingly more time with her, leaning over her desk, making comments to her about how attractive she was and asking why she didn't have a boyfriend. When he saw her in the lunchroom, he would come over and put his arm over her shoulder, asking her if she wanted to go out with him. He did this regularly, behavior which she felt was inappropriate in a professional environment.

However, she went out with him on a few occasions because she didn't want to hurt his feelings. She felt uncomfortable around him but she couldn't say *no* to him. She wanted to continue to work with Tom, didn't want there to be any hard feelings, and hoped his behavior would just stop. It didn't. She began to feel frustrated that he didn't get the hint and became increasingly anxious about how to handle his unwanted behavior. She decided to see a therapist to help her deal with Tom's behavior in a manner that she hoped wouldn't leave bad feelings in the workplace.

In the first session, Susan said that it was all her fault, that she led Tom on by going out with him. She felt guilty and responsible for the situation but didn't know how to stop his behavior. The therapist explored whether Susan thought that what Tom was doing was acceptable in the workplace. She asked how Susan would feel seeing this happen to another female coworker. They explored her feelings about saying *no* to him, what it brought up in her, and how she learned from her mother the importance of being nice. They examined the main problems that stopped her from saying *no* to someone who was pursuing her in an inappropriate and unwanted way, and was not picking up on her clues that his behavior was unwanted.

The therapist and Susan explored the definition of sexual harassment: Susan agreed this is what was happening. Susan was unsure about how to tell Tom to stop, so they role-played how she might do this and what might come up for her if she decided on this course of action. The therapist also educated Susan about the socialization of men, and how Tom might be subject to male norms of dominance over and sexualization of women of which he was unaware.

After several sessions in which the therapist supported her feelings and explored possible strategies for Susan in handling the situation, Susan felt better prepared to talk to Tom and tell him that his behavior, however well-meaning it might be, was not wanted by her and to ask him to stop. She now knew she had a right to do this. She realized that part of her problem in not doing so lay in unconscious adherence to traditional female gender norms, which can make it difficult for women to confront unwanted behavior by men. In one session they explored the possible outcomes of her intended behavior. If he stopped, she has done her work. If he retaliated or continued to harass her, she could go to her supervisor or HR if necessary. The therapist prepared her for these possible outcomes with proactive responses. They discussed the fact that she was now in a better position to stop the behavior without self-blame or guilt, or feeling that she was being unfriendly or unfeminine for saying *no*.

Susan eventually talked to Tom in a firm, clear and non-apologetic manner, and asked him to stop pursuing her. She made it clear that she wasn't interested in him romantically. Tom looked hurt but agreed that he had misinterpreted her behavior towards him and that he would like to continue to be colleagues only. The therapist commended Susan on her assertive behavior, asked her how she felt about it, and said that Susan was welcome to come back into therapy if Tom reverted to his old behavior.

Sexual Harassment by Bosses: *Quid pro Quo*

This is the most problematic of all sexual misconduct in the workplace because the consequences can be severe and successful recourse difficult. A woman often has limited ability to stand up to authority figures. This may be for a variety of reasons including fears of retribution, a possible loss of position or job, or a black mark on her work record. She may feel powerlessness, not knowing where to turn to for help, and have the concern that no one will believe her. Jobs and careers may be on the line, and the distinction between being a mentor and being a seducer may be blurred. As in the Weinstein case, some men in power ostensibly say they are trying to help young women move ahead in their careers. But their ulterior motives almost always involve power over women with whom they feel they can "help themselves to"—because they see these women as vulnerable, and lacking the power to confront them or to be believed by others.

Male authority figures can feel privileged and entitled to sexual interaction with subordinate females. The more powerful the male and the more the culture of the workplace supports him, the more difficult it can be for women to speak up about sexual misconduct. This is particularly true for older white male bosses and younger women from marginalized populations. It took complaints by 100+ women and 3 women who went to trial to get Harvey Weinstein convicted of rape, and even then the outcome of the trial was in doubt until the jury decided to convict him on two lesser accounts (rape) and acquit him on more serious charges of serial sexual assault.

Part of the lesson from the Weinstein case is that no man, no matter how powerful or important, should be implicitly or explicitly supported by his colleagues and the power structure around him for his sexual acting out. The Hollywood industry protected Harvey Weinstein and the U.S. Gymnastics Association protected Larry Nassar. The more important and powerful the perpetrator is to an organization or industry—and the less important and less powerful the victims are—the more this cycle will continue without institutional intervention unless the sexual assault is made public and has support from a variety of people and institutions.

But who do we typically deal with in our offices? Are they women who have experienced sexual assault by famous men? Or are they more often women who have experienced a range of sexual boundary violations in a wide variety of workplaces from bosses who aren't famous? In her book *#MeToo in the Workplace*,[5] Sylvia Hewlett says that the typical victim is not a current or future Hollywood movie star or an elite gymnastics figure. She is more often a woman who works in less public environments where authority male figures can act out sexually, but where challenging them can result in negative results for she who speaks up.

A culture of acceptance and silence around sexual acting out by male supervisors in many environments makes it difficult for women to challenge their harassers. What about a woman who doesn't feel she has the resources emotionally or practically to confront a boss who might fire her if she doesn't go along with his requests for sexual favors? What is the reality of her situation in terms of her job or career? What emotions has the harassment brought up and what are her options?

Therapists try to help their clients identify and work to heal the emotional costs that have been incurred by the harassment and to confront internal and external barriers to help them deal effectively with a bad situation. But as we have consistently stressed, looking at internal barriers does not "blame the victim." Indeed, examining internal barriers and how to overcome them is a crucial part of both the prevention and the recovery process. It serves to educate the victim about how women learn to act in ways that disempower them, including traditional gender role norms and societal expectations that women should be nice, go along with what men want, and not make waves or stand up for themselves. Knowing what her rights are will help her deal with harassment in ways where she can see herself not as a victim, but instead a woman with power and good self-esteem. Although she has been victimized by sexual acting out, she does not have to own the label of being a victim. Her abuser may be a predator and see her as prey, but she is not necessarily helpless. Her vulnerability and his power create a negative feedback loop that disempowers women and empowers men. It is this feedback loop that we try to change in our therapy with clients who have experienced sexual harassment by supervisors or other authority figures. While men who harass are 100% responsible for their behavior (as are the institutions that turn a blind eye to harassment), our clients have to work within that framework, which unfortunately often changes slowly. Given this reality, we need to help our clients take charge and confront bad behavior where and when they can.

3. Microaggression/Supervisor to Supervisee: *I Think You Are Sexy*

Jill is a 22-year-old college grad who has just started a new job in a market-
ing agency. She has had excellent experiences in college in terms of helpful
male advisors. Her background with men in authority has always been positive, starting with interactions with her father whom she adored, and continuing with school teachers and counselors, and university professors and
advisors. Her faculty thesis advisor supported her work, treating her as a valuable colleague.

Jill really liked her boss John, at first. He was helpful and fatherly, treating
her with respect and kindness, much like what she was used to with men who
had some kind of authority over her. However, over the past six months, John's
behavior began to have sexual overtones that made her increasingly uncomfortable. On one occasion he patted her on her butt and said, "Nice dress; you
wear it well." On another occasion, while she was working late, he came in, put
his arm around her shoulders and suggested that they grab drinks at a local
bar, saying, "What's a pretty girl like you doing alone on a Friday night?"

She didn't want to be unfriendly, but her attempts to put him off were
ignored and he persisted. She finally made up an excuse about needing to go
home to take care of a sick roommate. John said he would walk her to her car
and put his arm around her again, pulling her close and giving her a kiss on
the mouth. She was very confused by the change in his behavior. She liked
and trusted him. He had been appreciative of her work, so she didn't want to
confront him, especially since he seemed nice on the surface. Maybe she was
misreading his signals; maybe he was just being friendly.

Jill's discomfort got to the point where she started avoiding John and
stopped working late. Her work performance started to decline and she felt
depressed and powerless. In addition, her anxiety and confusion about the situation and what to do about it was interfering with her ability to sleep, so she
was tired all the time. Feeling she was at a breaking point, she decided to see a
therapist to sort out what she should do.

The therapist explored what was happening with Jill at work, why it might
be happening, and discussed her current feelings about the situation. Jill said
that her main feeling was confusion, followed by anxiety and some depression. She said that these feelings were difficult to handle since she didn't really
know what behavior on his part was appropriate and what was not. What was

particularly difficult for her was that she liked her boss. He had been support-ive of her since she began work at the office.

In session, they looked at the fact that someone can be nice *and* inappro-priate, supportive *but* with poor sexual boundaries. They examined how her boss's situation had changed (he was recently divorced and now lived alone) and how this might play a part in why his behavior had shifted inappropriately toward her in the year she had been at the company.

They explored whether her boss's behavior was sexual harassment and, if so, what she could do about it. She was reluctant to call it sexual harassment, but when she read the term's definitions and saw examples, she agreed that this is exactly what his actions were. She became angry at what she saw as his betrayal of her trust, yet she still felt bad for him because of his divorce. Could she hold these two feelings together at the same time? Was it possible that she had a right to be angry and to stand up to him, yet also feel some empathy? They looked at whether empathy was helpful, or whether it got in the way of doing what she needed to do to have the behavior stop.

After a number of sessions, Jill felt herself move from helplessness and self-blame to anger and greater self-worth. She explored possible courses of action for herself. These included talking directly to John, doing nothing and avoid-ing contact with him as much as possible, talking to HR about his behavior, or looking for a new job. She decided that the best way to approach this was to talk to her boss in private, stating that his behavior made her feel uncomfortable, and requesting that in the future he work with her only on a professional basis, as he had done previously. She role-played the scenario several times with her therapist, sometimes as herself, sometimes as her boss.

Once she felt comfortable enough to speak with her boss, she made an appointment to meet. She told him that she really liked working with him and that he had been supportive and helpful, but that his current behavior (she specified what) was making her uncomfortable and created a working environ-ment that was difficult for her. Her boss was at first defensive and denied that what he was doing was inappropriate, but Jill kept repeating what she wanted to have stopped. Finally she said, "If someone in a supervisor position behaved toward your daughter the way you have done to me, do you think this would be okay?"

At this point John said, "No, of course not," and began to understand that his behavior was not only inappropriate but that it caused negative consequences for Jill. Although he backed off from her and said he would be careful to keep his distance from her from now on, he eventually began to resume a "normal" professional relationship with her. Jill felt vindicated and relieved that she had navigated tricky waters without lasting damage.

However, she had a friend (Charlotte) who had faced a similar situation with a boss who did not understand. Charlotte took her complaint to the HR manager, who didn't take her complaint seriously and suggested she just move to another office within the company. Although this didn't seem fair to Charlotte or Jill, the harassment stopped because Charlotte and her boss were no longer in contact with each other on a daily basis. Jill and Charlotte agreed this was not the best outcome, but that other courses of action might be more harmful than helpful.

4. Macroaggression/Authority Figure to Subordinate:
I Can Help You Professionally If You Provide Me With Sexual Favors

Mary is a 40-year-old upper-level administrator in the healthcare industry. Her goal is to move up the corporate ladder, and she has the skills to work in a managerial setting. Mary is a woman who is used to standing up for herself and considers herself a feminist—she's there for herself and for other women who experience devaluation by men in either personal or professional relationships.

Mary had recently attended a health conference where she was excited to meet people who could help her advance her career. After dinner, a group of colleagues sat in the hotel bar and chatted about new models for the healthcare industry. Her supervisor Bill sat next to her, and over a few drinks they discussed where the industry was headed. It was noisy in the bar, so he suggested that the two of them meet in his room to discuss her professional growth. She was uncomfortable with this offer but went along with it since she didn't want to cause a scene or antagonize him in any way. Once in his room, she remembers that he sat on the sofa with her and as he talked about her career, he put his arm around her and proceeded to touch her breasts, telling her how sexy she was. She said *no* several times to his behavior and got up to leave. He stopped her at the door and said he really couldn't help her professionally and might not be able to give her a good review unless she agreed to have sex with him. Again, she said *no*, and left his room feeling ashamed, confused, scared, and in shock. The next day he was cold to her and ignored her requests for a meeting.

Mary began to experience a sense of fear, that her career was on the line, that she had done something to annoy him, that she couldn't trust him. She felt powerless to speak up and began to feel like it was her fault, that maybe she had led him on by drinking with him and by going to his room. She felt that if she complained about his behavior to HR or to his boss, no one would believe her. In fact, she was worried that on hearing her story, they might even imply she was somehow responsible for what happened, and that having drinks with him was clearly an invitation for more intimate physical contact. Adding to her doubts, she recalled that she had also worn one of her sexiest outfits that evening; she enjoyed dressing up and rarely got the opportunity because most of the time she had to wear suits to work. She was worried that she would be labeled as provocative because of her clothing. One of her friends noticed Mary's increasing depression and helplessness and suggested she see a therapist to sort out what to do next.

The therapist explored and validated her feelings, focusing on the ones that Mary said were most disabling for her emotionally. She confessed that she was confused about why it happened and felt a sense of powerlessness: how could she confront someone who held her future in his hands? Would there be retribution if she didn't go along with future sexual favors? The therapist gently explored any past experiences of sexual harassment by authority figures she may have had that might be triggered by the current event. How did she resolve these? Were unresolved feelings of powerlessness and shame making things harder for her?

As Mary felt more heard and validated, the therapist helped her reframe her situation and her feelings. The sessions helped her better understand that, although she had clearly been sexually harassed by her supervisor, she did not have to be a victim and that she did have power to explore options for further steps. They looked at her ability to say *no* to him despite pressure to do so and possible retribution from her supervisor. They explored her feelings of shame, guilt, and helplessness that women often feel when they have been sexually harassed by an authority figure. Most of all, Mary began to feel anger at her perpetrator—and compassion for herself for doing the best she could under difficult circumstances. The therapist asked her, "What would you advise a friend to do?" as a way to appeal to her sense of caring for others in a similar situation.

They explored what her resources might be, including going to HR, finding allies, talking directly to her boss, talking to her boss's boss, telling her story to others she trusts, and getting help from local or online groups that deal with

#MeToo issues. They looked at which options seemed most helpful to her, as well as the pros and cons of each option. The therapist suggested that she look at the #MeToo website to see the value of strength in numbers and who else might be experiencing this. Mary was given a copy of the EEOC guidelines as well as some reading to do that the therapist felt might be helpful to her in terms of understanding she is not alone and that there were ways to confront offenders that are effective.

They also explored the reality that it might be seen as a "he said, she said" situation by others and that she might be revictimized by people not believing her or not doing anything to help. When Mary felt ready to deal with possible fallout from speaking up, she decided to go to HR personnel directly to report her boss's behavior.

She returned to therapy the next week to say that the HR personnel were sympathetic but didn't have any concrete strategies for her other than advising her to avoid being alone with him. At this point Mary felt that she had to leave her job. With the help of her therapist, she found a new job in an environment where women were respected and believed. Mary realized that she couldn't change her boss, and that the corporation she resigned from did not prioritize a culture that would confront and discourage sexual harassment. However, she knew she had a right to remove herself from a toxic environment. This was a great relief for her to know she had taken active steps to redress the situation.

A Special Kind of Workplace: Dealing With Doctors and Other Trusted Authority Figures

Although noncriminal sexual misconduct is the focus of this book, it is worth starting this section with an infamous case of serial rape by a medical professional that galvanized the public. As noted in Chapter 3, Larry Nassar was the worst kind of predator because he raped girls under the guise of helping them improve their gymnastics skills. The girls and their parents had given him their trust. The organization for which he worked chose to ignore the abuse for their own ends (producing world class athletes at all costs). The young athletes were true prey, unable to defend themselves against the power of his profession and his organization, which protected him, not his victims. Nassar abused girls over a long period of time because his victims stayed silenced by their belief that a "nice" doctor would not abuse them, or that the doctor knew better than they how to help them; the victims rationalized his actions by assuming that parents and other staff did not seem concerned about what he was doing so it must be okay. Rape victims and victims of noncriminal sexual assault share similar emotions and reactions to their abuse by trusted authority figures—fear, helplessness, shame, and a great deal of confusion about how someone who they thought was helping them could harm them. Fortunately, in the Nassar case, a number of courageous girls spoke out; he was found guilty and sentenced to life in prison.

Doctor Harassment: *I'm Your Doctor and I Know Best*

We rely on doctors to care for us and to help us get better. Often the work they do involves touching our bodies in some way such as when they check our breathing, heart rate, blood pressure, or examine painful or "private" places on our body that are giving us discomfort. We assume a normal physician–patient relationship when we trust our bodies to our doctors. In the case of OB/GYN doctors, this often involves vaginal exams such as pap smears, or breast exams checking for lumps. These health checks are necessary and done on a regular basis to ensure a woman's physical well-being. However, it can be confusing to a woman if a male doctor's behavior appears to violate boundaries that make her uncomfortable. She may think that being uncomfortable is a normal part of medical exams done by a male doctor. She is not an expert in medical care, and he is. She may find it hard to challenge him because of this discrepancy in knowledge, plus she does not want to annoy or anger him for fear she will not get good care in the future.

In one of the *That's Harassment* videos,[6] a doctor (whom we will call Dr. Kelly) is shown treating a woman for her complaints of sinus pain and headaches. This is not her known and familiar physician, who is on vacation. She has never met this man before. But, after all, he is a doctor, so there should be nothing to worry about.

Dr. Kelly starts off engaging in what looks like standard assessment practice to assess her symptoms. So all appears safe at first. However, he does rest his hand on her inner thigh while he is tapping her forehead. He asks her if she's had a mammogram lately and then says, "You have a lovely chest—it would be a shame not to have it checked." He insists that he teach her how to give herself a breast exam. This is standard practice for an annual physical for women but has nothing to do with sinus pain and headaches. He asks her to lie down on the examining table and unbutton a couple of buttons of her blouse. He moves the stethoscope to her chest, then puts his hand on the edge of her breast, then a little bit more on her breast, then a little bit more. All in little baby steps. Except the way he does it includes taking both of his hands and covering most of her breast and lightly squeezing her nipples for an excruciatingly long moment. We see the look on her face: stricken, confused, frozen, betrayed. Dr. Kelly pats her hand and tells her that everything is fine. His parting line is that she has a classic case of sinusitis.

We are all left wondering why he had to do all these other procedures for a case of sinusitis. Her face tells us that she is thinking the same thing. He has successfully altered her reality to the point where she can't quite clearly grasp how much she has just been violated and how "off" this is. This is gaslighting— where a person (in this case, a patient) has been told by an authority figure that her version of reality is wrong.

Let's imagine the continuation of this vignette once the woman leaves his office. She decides not to see this doctor again and just wants the whole episode to go away because it is so upsetting. She does nothing for a while. However, she can't stop thinking about what happened. She continually second guesses herself about why she hadn't stopped him but wonders if the exam really was necessary (although her gut says it wasn't). Her self-esteem plummets and her anxiety and sense of helplessness increases. She feels isolated. She is too ashamed to talk to anyone about it. She doesn't bring up the incident with her regular doctor for fear of offending him by criticizing a colleague. Finally, she confides in a friend who suggests she should make an appointment to see a psychotherapist.

Picture yourself as this therapist. You start by listening to her recounting of the scenario, asking her periodically what she was thinking and feeling. She says she didn't want to "cause a scene" because she was afraid Dr. Kelly might retaliate by impeding access to specialists or badmouth her to her regular doctor as a "difficult" patient. She says she wasn't sure that what he was doing wasn't in fact part of a standard protocol for sinus pain and headaches since she had no medical training. But she is experiencing a lot of guilt, confusion, depression, and anxiety, and wants help handling these feelings.

You explore why she had a hard time trusting her gut that "something isn't right." You validate her feelings and thoughts, saying that her sense that something was "off" sounds correct. You discuss her attitudes toward male doctors who are highly regarded and why they might not be trustworthy despite their accolades. You also help her see that a male doctor would be highly unlikely to do this kind of exam for sinus pain and headaches—and if he did, a female nurse should be in the examining room.

She continues in therapy while she works through her shame, fear, distrust, and overall sense of helplessness. Once she feels less triggered by the incident and more in control of her sense of self, she says she wants to consider what she might want to do.

You discuss different options for action. Should she confront Dr. Kelly directly? Not discuss it but remain as a patient? Talk to her regular doctor about the incident? Talk to the office manager about Dr. Kelly's behavior? Report his behavior to the Ethics Commission of the American Medical Association? Change her regular doctor but not report the behavior of Dr. Kelly? Change her regular doctor but report Dr. Kelly's behavior? Talk with friends in the medical profession about his behavior?

With each option, you ask her what she feels about taking that action. What are the pros and cons to each one? What are her fears? What does she feel strongly about? What if she took no action? And if so, how would it be helpful? What resources does she need? What outcome would she like to have? What would make her feel the safest and best about herself? You reassure her that there is no one right answer, nor an answer that everyone in her situation would take. The outcome then depends on what she decides to do, and it depends on what she feels best about doing in the short and long run.

Therapists, Priests, Teachers, Mentors, Gurus, and Coaches: *Breaking Trust*

The doctor-patient relationship is only one of many settings where there is a betrayal of trust. Over the past decades, we have learned all too well about doctors sexually abusing both boys and girls. And we know about coaches and teachers who have exploited their trusted positions to abuse the athletes and students who trust them and depend on them. Therapists can do this too. So can workplace mentors. The common theme of all of these situations is that the girl or woman has placed her trust in this important figure, and she has assumed that what he is telling her or asking her to do is both appropriate and helpful. The lag time between his boundary-crossing behavior and her recognition of the violation is delayed, sometimes to the point where it never registers at all.

There is a cognitive dissonance problem here: She trusts him, he starts to act inappropriately, and this feels profoundly dissonant to her. She then resolves the dissonance—*not* by recognizing the truth and acting, but rather by changing her narrative about what he is doing so that it does not seem wrong. This way, the dissonance between her belief in him and her distress about his actions is no longer so misaligned.

A recent example of cognitive dissonance is shown in the 2020 documentary on Bikram Choudhury.[7] The film explores how the founder of hot yoga built an empire for himself by offering expensive training programs mostly to women. He made it clear to them that they could not start their own yoga studios without his training. After many years, a few women in his programs came forward to tell their stories about how he sexually abused and raped them. When asked why it took so long for them to speak up, they said that that the abuse started very slowly, that they couldn't see it as abuse because they regarded him as a beloved father figure, and because they felt they needed him to further their careers. In addition, it was hard for them to believe that someone who presented himself as a spiritual teacher (similar to a priest) would betray not only their trust in him but also in an environment that many of them felt was sacred.

This is perhaps a classic example of what can happen intrapsychically when women trust an authority figure who slowly and through small but steady steps proves to be a predator. The red flags are there, but it becomes hard for her to see them, as they conflict with her image of this man as someone she admires and could help her professionally.

These are situations where, for any of us in a counseling role, it is usually helpful to patiently ask our clients to pay attention to their gut feeling. If it walks and quacks like a duck, it usually is. If it feels creepy, it usually is. Even though gut feelings may sometimes mislead us, we want our clients to trust their gut feelings as much as possible. Once the damage is done, we have much repair work to do in helping them regain their sense of autonomy, and trust us to help them work through their feelings of shame, betrayal, disbelief, and anger. We are, after all, also authority figures who may be untrustworthy as far as they know.

Helping Women Take Charge

In her book *#MeToo in the Corporate World*,[8] Sylvia Hewlett makes some suggestions about what women can do to limit sexual misconduct. The following list appears in her chapter entitled "Individual Action Steps."

- Don't dress provocatively
- Don't meet in bars, hotel rooms, or apartments
- Don't flirt or sleep with someone very junior or senior to you, or married to someone else

Although well-intended to help women stay out of harm's way, these suggestions offer up what women shouldn't do, but not what they *should* do. The list offers no explanation as to what women could do to handle sexual misconduct, what stops them, what could help them, or what the core issues are (personal as well as cultural) that might lead them into potentially difficult situations. Does a woman have a right to dress "provocatively?" Yes. Will she get sexual comments if she does? Maybe. If she goes to a boss's apartment, does she bear responsibility for any sexual misconduct that might happen? No. Would it better if she stayed away from potentially unwanted sexual situations? Yes. If she chooses to flirt with someone junior or senior to her, is that her right? Yes. Is she likely to get into trouble if she does? Possibly. What is her responsibility in all of these situations, how does she protect herself, and what do we do once the damage has happened? As therapists working with women who have suffered sexual misconduct, we walk a tightrope between acknowledging that misconduct has happened and empowering a woman to take control of the situation once it has happened, or to stop it from happening if they can. How do we help women in the workplace without seeming like we are blaming the victim?

One powerful way is to help our clients understand what gets in the way of being assertive. Helping our clients see how to challenge these beliefs is good therapy because it allows them to confront some of the cultural expectations that make sexual harassment more prevalent, and lets them consider ways to act and think that are in their best interests. Listed below are some of these beliefs: you could probably add more.

- I don't want to hurt anyone so I can't "out" the offender.
- I'm afraid of retaliation.
- It's my fault this happened.
- I don't want to cause a scene because it will get in the way of my professional advancement.
- If I ignore the unwanted behavior, it will go away.
- If I do speak up, the misconduct will continue.
- I don't have a right to speak up.

- It was my fault it happened.
- I won't be believed by others such as my boss or HR.
- HR won't do anything to stop unwanted sexual behavior.
- I'm not sure anything bad really happened.
- I'm just too sensitive.
- I want to be a team player and speaking up will ruin that.
- I won't get any support from my colleagues.
- I won't get promoted, will get fired, or will get a poor recommendation for a future job if I speak up.

Resources for Clinicians

As clinicians dealing with clients who have experienced sexual misconduct in the workplace, we may need some help in dealing effectively with #MeToo cases. A list of suggestions for college clinicians are covered in the previous chapter; the ones we provide here are more specific for clients experiencing harassment in the workplace.

Appropriate referrals: If your client has a trauma history that has been triggered by current sexual harassment, you might consider referring her to a trauma specialist, or perhaps a trauma group for ongoing support. Knowing who in your community to refer her to is important; have those names and phone numbers readily available to you.

Peer consultation: Having a group of fellow therapists with whom you consult regularly is always useful; bringing #MeToo cases to that group could help you decide on your best course of action with a client.

Information about dealing with sexual assault in the workplace: There are many resources that describe the impact of sexual harassment on victims. It would be useful to have them available in your office. Some of these resources are listed in the Resources section.

Knowing the legal definition of harassment: The EEOC[9] has specific legal information about sexual harassment and there are numerous training programs available. Although these are pitched to HR personnel, it is useful information to know as a potential resource for your clients.

Understand how HR offices work: You might consider contacting anyone you know who works in HR to get their take on how they handle victims of sexual harassment in the workplace, or go online to find various companies' HR policies on sexual harassment.

Education about gender role norms: It is important to know how traditional gender role norms might contribute to sexual misconduct, as described in Chapter 2. This knowledge can help inform your work with both men and women as they understand how their behavior may be strongly influenced by these norms in ways they aren't necessarily aware of.

Supervision: Getting supervision from a clinician with a background in sexual harassment treatment might be helpful in thinking through your cases.

Therapy: If you have experienced sexual misconduct in your own workplace or in your personal life, you may have strong reactions to cases of sexual misconduct. To maintain a more neutral stance, you may need to examine what these cases bring up in you, and how your own background may negatively or positively impact the work you do with victims of sexual harassment.

Getting Out of the Office

Counselors and clinicians can stay within their offices, dealing with patients on an individual or group basis. Most probably will not be able to work directly with the company for which their client works, but they can offer their services in facilitating sexual harassment trainings for companies in general. In running these trainings, scenarios similar to ones their clients experienced can be offered. The EEOC offers some guidelines for effective training formats,[10] which include the following:

- Interactive and experiential, not just lectures
- Run by a male and female
- Opportunity for participant feedback
- Opportunity for small group discussions
- Ongoing training, not one-shot offerings

If you are comfortable thinking about expanding your practice to include consultation and trainings, these trainings are needed in the workplace. If you can find a colleague of a different gender than your own, your training will be more effective. You might not be able to directly help your client with her harassment case, but running these kinds of trainings will help detoxify workplaces in general. You could also gain a reputation for being an expert on handling sexual harassment so that women experiencing this in the workplace may seek you out.

The Bigger Picture: Gender Inequality in the Workplace

In American culture, key positions of power in academic, politics and business are overwhelmingly held by men. Consider the following statistics:

- Academia: As of 2016, 69.9% of American college presidents are male.[11]
- Politics: As of January 2019, 76.3% of the House of Representatives and 75% of senators are male, and only 9 out of 50 state governors are female.
- Business: As of 2019, 93.4% of *Fortune* 500 CEOs are male.[12]

In a male-dominated system of power, it is probably more likely that harassment will occur, that women's complaints will not be taken as seriously, and that men will want to keep the status quo, which benefits them in terms of status and power. Given that system, our female clients have to deal within that system to change it as they can on both a micro and macro level. Our main job is to help them work through the specific issues they present in our offices and are related to peer-to-peer or authority-figure perpetrated sexual harassment. We can also work in our communities toward placing more women in positions of power. Although this is not the role of a therapist, it would help change institutions that currently allow (or even encourage) sexual harassment to continue without consequences for men who harass.

Chapter 11

Working With Couples
Using Lessons From #MeToo to Bridge the Gender Gap

All of us who are counselors of one sort of another know that most men do not harass women, most men do not assault women, and most men take women's concerns about their treatment by men very seriously.

A lot of men show up in our offices as part of a couple, along with their wife or partner. And, while most of these men have never committed any #MeToo violation, the profound issues from the #MeToo movement still reverberate in the intricate details of their intimate relationships. At the core of these issues are the importance of women speaking up about the trauma of their experiences with sexual misconduct, men believing them, and men learning to respect a woman's sexual boundaries.

When we work with couples, we have a golden opportunity to utilize lessons learned from the #MeToo movement to help good men become even better men, to help self-respecting women find even stronger voices, and to further bridge some of the inevitable gaps between men's and women's experience. Or for that matter, between the members of any couple, gay or straight, where one individual has experienced more trauma or threat than the other.

The cases we discuss here and the principal lessons we extract from them do *not* apply if someone in this relationship has been overtly abusive—physically, sexually, or emotionally. The cases in this chapter are, by definition, for couples where the inevitable and normal and imperfect relationship issues have been activated in some way by #MeToo behavior.

We want to focus here on helping couples therapists generate empathic accuracy between women and men about gender roles and behaviors—and not just when someone has been accused of or has experienced #MeToo violations. As you read this chapter, it is important to keep in mind that we are presenting cases of straight couples for the reasons we explained in the preface. We are certainly aware that gay or lesbian couples suffer the consequences of previous sexual harm in terms of the health of their relationships in perhaps similar ways to heterosexual couples. But since the book is oriented toward the most common forms of #MeToo behavior (men abusing women), we have chosen to focus on that demographic for the cases presented here. We have also not included intersectional factors such as race or ethnic background. However, it is certainly worth thinking about those aspects as you consider the cases and how you might handle them differently if intersectionality is taken into account.

The Extra Door

In 2018, Dr. Christine Blasey Ford accused Judge Brett Kavanaugh, then a nominee for Supreme Court Justice, of committing an act of sexual assault against her at a drunken high school party in the 1980s. Despite widespread public protests, Judge Kavanaugh was confirmed by the Senate.

But it is the backstory of Dr. Ford that is relevant for this chapter—because of the way it illustrates the emotional, psychological, and sexual impact of #MeToo experiences on the lives of so many couples.

According to extensive interviews of Ford,[1] she and her husband of 10 years went into marital therapy in the summer of 2012. This was relevant in the Kavanaugh hearings because it provided evidence that she described the alleged assault six years earlier, to both her husband and her therapist. As Ford tells the story, she and her husband Russell Ford were in conflict prior to entering marital therapy, when they were in the process of remodeling their home in Palo Alto. One of the points of contention revolved around her insistence on building a *second* front door to their home, which made no sense to him. She tried to explain to him that she would feel trapped without it.

We can imagine how this must have looked and sounded to her husband. The plan made no sense. Who needs two front doors? It added extra expense, and it probably seemed like an unnecessary addition to the entrance to their home. Most of us, upon hearing this kind of insistence from our partner without further explanation than "I will feel trapped without it," would likely get impatient and irritated by something that seems so irrational.

Apparently, even several years after this argument, there was fallout from this episode. They entered the marital therapy in 2012 to deal with "communication issues," which included resolving some fights that dated back to the remodeling a few years back.

Ford had told the therapist about the ways in which she continued to be haunted by her memories of the Kavanaugh assault. The therapist urged her to tell her husband more fully what she had only revealed to him in very general terms before. She proceeded to tell him the events in detail, that in high school she had been trapped in a room and pinned down by a drunken boy while his friend watched. This drunken boy had grabbed at her clothes and tried to pull her one-piece bathing suit off. She divulged that the boy had put his hand over her mouth to keep her from screaming. She was terrified that, in his drunken state, and with his dominating physical strength, and in the frenzy of his teenage hormones, that he was going to kill her.

She told her husband that she was eventually able to escape before she was raped, but that the experience was traumatic because she felt like she had no control and was physically dominated. She admitted that this was the real and previously secret reason that she needed two doors on their house and multiple exit routes.

Her husband recalls that she told him that the attacker's name was Brett Kavanaugh. That, of course, was very relevant for the Senate hearings, but completely irrelevant for the issues we are highlighting here. Her attacker could have been anyone.

As a result of her counseling, Ford became increasingly aware of how formative this assault had been. Her long-standing fear of being confined in spaces started to make more sense. So did her pattern of wanting to remove herself from any situations that represented conflict.

None of us were in the room with this couple, and Dr. Ford has not provided more details about how the disclosure or of the attack affected their relationship. But it is extremely likely that her decision to reveal these events to her husband—and her emotional recounting about the powerful impact this had on her over decades—helped break through their marital impasse. Any normal man at this moment would smack himself in the forehead and say, "Of course! Why didn't I get this before?" And it is likely that his heart would go out to her *now that he understands what this is all about*. When a woman informs a man about the background to behavior that has previously seemed irrational or controlling or just plain annoying, a reasonable man is going to feel compassion rather than frustration. We can hope that this was the effect of revealing this information in the Fords' therapy session.

The lesson for the traumatized woman: If you can find a way to do so, speak up. The lesson for the woman's partner: Expand your awareness of the ways so many women have been traumatized and be on the lookout for the effects from this—and certainly be her ally when she lets you in the door.

We have to remember, however, that the "speak up" lesson for a traumatized woman is complicated by the fact that she sometimes can't speak up until well after the incident. And with the lapse of time, her story is likely not to be believed or she will be questioned as to why it took her so long to speak up. The power of Ford's public testimony in the Kavanaugh hearings was eroded by criticisms of her for not speaking up *earlier*. It is unrealistic, unfair, and misinformed to expect a trauma victim to speak up earlier if she isn't ready, or if she hasn't managed her trauma well enough to push through the triggers allowing her to disclose.

More of these stories are emerging for couples therapists and—distressing as these often are—the moments offer a unique opportunity to help bridge the chasm between men and women.

Speaking Up and Waking Up

One couple, Jake and Hayley, entered couples therapy because of long-standing resentments by Jake about feeling neglected and rejected. The dynamics in this marriage distinctly reflected a mismatch of attachment styles.

Jake was clearly on the spectrum of anxious (preoccupied) attachment. He needed a lot of attention and reassurance from Hayley. He reacted to perceived slights in exaggerated fashion. He was hypervigilant to any signs of her disinterest and betrayal. Although he didn't readily admit it, he was plagued with deep fears of her abandoning him—not necessarily total abandonment (as in divorce), but rather that she would pull away from him and withdraw her love and attention. He did not self-soothe well, and he often turned against her when he was feeling alone—as if she had *made* him feel this way. He was unskilled at reading her. He wasn't off the charts with any of these issues, but what confounded their dynamics is that he was inept at communicating his emotional needs clearly. He was more likely to pout, criticize, blame, and withdraw as a way to indirectly communicate what he was needing and feeling.

Hayley, as often happens, had a different attachment style, showing more traits of avoidant (dismissing) attachment style. She was conflict avoidant and often withdrew at the first sign that a conflict was coming. When Jake wanted to talk about an issue, she would typically refuse to discuss it and retreat to a safe zone, leaving the room or even the house. When she did this, he felt foolish or needy for showing frustration with their relationship, as if emotions were a sign of weakness. Long ago, Hayley learned not to create too much trouble or be too needy, because with family, as she had learned growing up, this rarely went well. She carried around a deep belief that nobody—including Jake—would ever really be there for her when she was in need or vulnerable.

One of their ongoing issues revolved around sex. All these attachment issues—which showed up in numerous forms throughout their relationship—crystallized around their issues in the bedroom. Jake wanted more sexual frequency. It is important to consider that men are socialized to want sex and may use sex as a pathway to intimacy when other ways for them are restricted. Jake consistently interpreted her sexual reluctance as rejection of him, and he brooded resentfully when his expectations were not met. He engaged in the classic anxious preoccupied attachment dance of overreacting to slights and rejections, then by acting in ways that made these slights and rejection even more likely to occur in the future.

In a couples therapy session, Jake and Hayley got down to talking about the details of their sex life and the politics that played out in the bedroom. Early in their relationship, Hayley had told Jake that she had been sexually abused by an uncle when she was a girl. But (in typical dismissing avoidant attachment style) she was always vague about it and never seemed to indicate that it affected her very much.

There was clearly trauma in the room. One of the symptoms of trauma is emotional numbing, and the interlacing of this numbing and Hayley's attachment style was becoming clearer to the therapist. But it wasn't clear yet to Jake. In this session, Jake was hurt and resentful because Hayley was so nonresponsive when he touched her genitals. He could not understand why she froze up when he tried to touch her as part of their sex play. He accused her of being cold and not being into him anymore.

And here is where the #MeToo issues came into play (or at least issues related to previous sexual misconduct). She told him, rather unemotionally (as was her way), that the main form of sexual abuse by her uncle involved using his fingers to stimulate her genitals. She said to Jake, "You can touch me there if that's a turn-on for you, but just don't expect that to do anything for me." She told him she was fine with other forms of contact and sexual arousal.

This revealed more evidence of her trauma reaction. She froze (a typical trauma reaction) when her husband's sexual touch triggered associations to the trauma in her history. And her offer to let her husband touch her this way required dissociation (another typical trauma reaction).

At first, Jake acted annoyed and put out and could not really relate to why he should be deprived of this form of contact. But soon it sunk in that this was not about him. This was about the history of the woman he loved that long predated him, and it had nothing to do with *him* other than it limited one form of sex play in his marriage. He slowly came around to a position of empathy for Hayley: "I guess I never really understood this all these years. It never occurred to me how much the abuse has affected you, and all I could see was that you were being withholding or something. Now I wish you had told me this way earlier. I'm not sure if I would have really gotten it, but maybe. I do get it now. And I'm sorry I've made you feel even worse about something that has been so hard for you."

Hayley tried to dismiss this level of understanding as no big deal, but there were tears in her eyes.

The issues raised by the public revelations in the #MeToo movement were one key factor—not the only one, but still central—that enabled Hayley to pay more attention to how her history has affected her. She also was inspired to put words to these feelings during these most intimate conversations with her husband in ways that she never could before. And he (despite his initial defensiveness and self-preoccupation) got it. His empathic accuracy rose, and together they were able to disarm this ongoing area of tension in their relationship. Because finally, in the context of this couples therapy and the pervasive impact of the #MeToo movement, she spoke up. And, to Jake's credit, he woke up.

"It's Not About You"

Here's another clinical example. Celia and Carl were both high-functioning but deeply wounded souls. They co-owned a upmarket woodworking company. They had no kids and spent most of their time—for better or for worse—together. In their conflicts, they both projected onto each other in the most negative ways and engaged in what researcher Amy Holtzworth-Munroe[2] calls "assuming greater partner negative intent" (also known as "hostile attributional bias"). When either of them felt hurt or thought they were not getting enough attention or recognition, they were quick to blame the other for making them feel this way. The hurt always seemed to mean that the other person was trying to injure; as a result, their fights were often bitter and nasty.

One of the ways Carl would try to be affectionate with Celia was to come up to her while she was in the kitchen and nuzzle her from behind, often giving her butt or breast a squeeze. For him this was a playful gesture of sex play. It felt like love.

For Celia, the experience was radically different. She had a history of being sexually assaulted (but not raped) in high school, much like Christine Blasey Ford's experience. She also had been in a previous relationship where her boyfriend groped and grabbed her, often trapping her in areas of the house and not letting her free.

Here's where her trauma history, like Hayley's in the preceding story, would show up. Although Celia was a very sexual person and very attracted to Carl, she froze whenever he approached her like this. Any sexual trauma victim will recognize this freeze response. Trying to be receptive so as to avoid offending him and starting a conflict only sometimes worked. He could feel her cold reaction—in his self-centered world, this was a narcissistic injury that she was purposefully inflicting on him. Like narcissistically injured people anywhere, he turned this into anger toward her. He yelled at her and threatened never to touch her again: "Why should I touch you if you don't even want me?"

At the height of the #MeToo movement, when daily headlines broadcast one story and then another of male boundary violations and female voices being heard, Celia became clearer and bolder. Although she had told Carl the basic story of how she was treated in her previous relationship, she became even more aware of the connections between past and present. She sat down with him and tried, calmly and with feeling, to help him understand the depth of the damage that had been done by experiences in her past. And she explained how much of a trigger his "groping" behavior was, even though he was not actually doing to her what her previous partner had.

In other words, Celia was communicating that her reaction was not really (well, maybe somewhat) about Carl. But she needed him to view her behavior as not personal to him—and to transcend his hurt and rejection so that he could be compassionate instead. She needed him to know that this didn't mean that she was rejecting him, only that she froze in reaction to this particular way he approached her.

As long as he could reframe this as a nonpersonal rejection, his nervous system could stay calmer and his better self could emerge. Since his narcissistic issues ran deep, this breakthrough for the two of them did not exactly lead to miraculous changes in their conflicts—but it helped. And it became possible directly as a result of the #MeToo issues permeating the atmosphere—again, helping Celia speak up and Carl wake up.

"Don't You Care About Me?"

At a time when reports of #MeToo offenders were blanketing the news and prominent men were getting knocked off their perches on a weekly basis, Miles and Michelle got into an argument. A young Korean-American couple with no kids, they often got into conflicts because of gender role issues. Miles came into the relationship with rigid ideas about how a husband should be taken care of by his wife: cooking, cleaning, sex, being attentive and available to him when he came home at the end of the day. He would get critical—and sometimes verbally berating—when he felt like she had let him down. Michelle was raised with a lot of the same values about gender roles, and (while she did not report any sexual or physical abuse) she remembers vividly her father's controlling message and his anger. But now, in her late 20s, she was starting to challenge the ingrained cultural expectations of being the "accommodating" female she had been raised to be. And she was growing much less tolerant of her husband's demands of her—and of her own complicity in their system.

Their #MeToo conversation actually started out fine. Despite Miles' traditional expectations about male–female roles, he was politically progressive and sensitive about women's political issues. Like many men who may have their own blind spots about the way they treat women, he was still fully on board with branding abusive male behavior as plain wrong. So the conversation focused on how outrageous and offensive some of the #MeToo offenders were.

But then the discussion hit a speed bump. Miles started thinking out loud about the continuum of #MeToo behaviors. Many intelligent people have been engaging in this same thought process (and we certainly do in this book). They recognize that all of these behaviors are damaging, but that some are worse than others. Much of this book focuses on these different levels of offense, intent, and impact.

Miles said, "I know that what Louis C. K. did was really wrong, but, wow, not as horrible as Michael Jackson or R. Kelly. They went after children. That's the worst!"

Michelle got her back up. All she heard in that was her husband minimizing Louis C. K.'s offenses. Referring to the offenses committed by Louis C. K., she shot back, "So you think that if some guy masturbated in front of me that would be OK? I can't feel safe with someone who thinks like that!"

In a court of law or on a high school debating team, the point that Miles was trying to make was legitimate and worth pondering. But intimate partner relationships are governed by more complex nuances and rules than are courts of law. Michelle was in the process of sorting out her identity and her voice as a woman, and she often felt emotionally unsafe with her husband. So all she could hear, when her husband seemed to be minimizing the behavior of a man in a power position who masturbates in front of his staff, is that her husband might be capable of mistreating her and minimizing that too.

Miles could not get that. He got defensive: "Why are you trying to control my thoughts and opinions? You're not listening to me."

In a #MeToo climate, with a woman who has been berated by her husband for not conforming to traditional female roles, this was the wrong response. With some coaching, however, Miles was able to see and hear the anxiety lurking beneath Michelle's attack on him. He stopped trying to defend himself about the Louis C. K. comment—that was not the point. He told her he understood (and wanted to understand more) how fearful she was, and he reassured her that he would never ever tolerate any man treating her that way.

This was another moment when the man's empathic accuracy became disabled because he felt like he was being misunderstood, blamed, and attacked. And once he started to think about his wife's reaction in the context of #MeToo—and in the context of his own past treatment of her—his capacity for empathic accuracy was restored. When that shift happens, it is so much easier to not take comments personally, to not get defensive, and to respond to the core feelings of the other person with the love and respect that they deserve.

When *She* Needs to Understand *Him*

This next case comes from the work of couples therapist Marianne Tamulev-ich,[3] who describes herself as passionate about using couples therapy—and the issues of the #MeToo movement specifically—to bridge rather than widen the gap between the sexes.

In all the previous couples' patterns deconstructed here, the basic sequence has been the same: Woman has history of being violated or harassed by men; man knows this but doesn't fully comprehend the impact; #MeToo issues in the stratosphere trigger an emotional reaction from her that he doesn't under-stand; he gets defensive and critical of her; she feels alone, unheard, and angry. Then it's his job to understand the roots and depth of her experience (and her job to communicate this more clearly) so they can get past the divide between them. And so on.

But this next story illuminates a slightly different pattern, or at least a dif-ferent primary intervention. Miranda and Phil had been in couples therapy, dealing with issues stemming from an emotional affair that Phil had engaged in. The repercussions of this showed up in periodic emotional outbursts from Miranda triggered by painful associations: a love song on the stereo, a blonde resembling Phil's old girlfriend walking into their favorite café, Phil retreating to another room to take calls from old college pals.

And then President Trump entered the therapy room. Many of us who work with couples found old stories, memories, and traumas reemerging for many women during Trump's rise to power, and then again after the public reve-lations about Harvey Weinstein jump-started the #MeToo movement. Many women were stirred up for reasons they couldn't exactly explain.

Just days after the election results were finalized, Miranda said she was dis-gusted that a man who had assaulted women and sexually objectified his own daughter could be elected to the highest office in the land.

Phil's response was muted. He was noticeably quiet while his wife vented. Miranda finally turned to him and asked, "Why aren't you speaking?!"

He dropped eye contact and said, "Look, I agree with you, I'm just not going to get as emotional as you. That's not me."

Miranda's anger overflowed. "'That's not me!'" she spat back at him. She called him insensitive and ignorant. She launched an attack about his privilege as a man in the world. Phil went into defensive mode, saying that he refused to accept responsibility for all the bad guys in the world: "That's not me. I'm not one of those men who harass women!"

Like all of us who work with couples, this therapist had seen this dance before. The woman expresses strong emotions about issues that have affected her and other women, the man does not seem very worked up about it, and she deeply resents his ability to treat this like it's not that big of a deal. This same breakdown takes place with issues of race or other issues of entitlement and privilege, where the person from the dominant group seems to act like the person from the disenfranchised group is overreacting and seeing all issues though one victimized lens.

Here's where Tamulevich chose the less traveled path. Most of us would have immediately validated Miranda's resentment and pushed Phil to express more emotion and compassion. But she could see how this would just lead to Miranda berating Phil, and she couldn't see the payoff in that.

So she chose to help bridge the deepening gulf in a different way: "You know I can say this because I'm a woman," Tamulevich said to Miranda, "but I hope you can see that in a way, you're doing to him what's been done to you as a woman in the world. By telling him he's not sensitive enough, not passionate enough, it's like how *we've* been told over time we're too emotional, too sensitive, too passionate."

This was not what Miranda expected to hear. The therapist pressed on: "You can help him understand what the effects of it may be on you and your marriage. Hopefully, he'll listen to you, and you'll listen to him when he tells you what he doesn't get about the way you're feeling."

In time, Tamulevich engaged in the obvious intervention of encouraging Phil to engage with Miranda rather than just shutting down. But he was afraid of what this would set off. He finally was able to tell her about what led to keeping his mouth shut: "I am so afraid of bringing up anything with you—I'm scared of being accused of representing the white male privilege class."

"Men like Phil," Tamulevich says, "may feel defensive about being lumped in with some pretty bad guys in our culture, or feel scared or confused by their partner's feelings, but they don't know how to express that, so they swallow it."

Many counselors and therapists (not to mention many women everywhere) might react to this concern as being irrelevant and distracting from the most important concerns. We have all heard the complaint: "What difference does it make *why* men treat women the way they do? They just need to figure it out and stop." But you don't change these behaviors and heal these wounds by activating even more of a gender war. Certainly not with people we love and so deeply want to trust and feel close to. Phil needs to grow and reach deep within to understand his wife's experience—even if he feels only slightly personally responsible. But if Miranda talks to Phil in a way that shuts him down, nobody wins.

The issues—both the obvious and the murky—aroused by the #MeToo movement provide a rare and golden opportunity for all us working with couples (and all of us in an intimate relationship) to take things to a new level.

More Notes About Trauma-Informed Treatment

As you read through these vignettes, there is one central theme: The woman in these relationships has experienced some degree of sexual trauma in the past and it is affecting the quality of her intimate partner relationship in the present. And the man doesn't really understand.

Sometimes, as in some of the examples, just bringing the experience to light and talking about it together can go a long way. But if a woman is having a hard time finding the best words to explain it, or if she has a strong reaction to everyday conflicts, or if it significantly impacts their sex life, or if her partner reacts poorly to what she tries to explain to him, then it makes sense to address these issues more intensively.

One option, of course, is to refer her to a clinician who specializes in PTSD. But there are also a number of interventions that have been specifically developed for use by a couple together to help understand and cope with one person's trauma reactions. These programs include couples therapy to address the impact of trauma on an intimate partner relationship, and they focus more on relieving relationship distress than on reducing an individual's PTSD symptoms.

One of the leading centers for trauma research and studies, the International Society for Traumatic Stress Studies, identifies the following couples'-based interventions.[4] For more information on all these programs, see the Resources section.

- *Emotionally focused couple therapy* offers a systematic map to understanding and treating the chaos that PTSD symptoms and attachment anxieties create in a love relationship, focusing on enhancing the perception of emotional availability from a significant other within the context of a safe, supportive, and loving relationship

- *Critical interaction therapy* identifies patterns of dyadic processes that commonly occur in families of trauma survivors and uses a series of interventions to teach about the process, point out connections to the trauma, encourage partners to offer support, and promote better problem solving and communication

- *Cognitive-behavioral couple treatment for PTSD* comprises 15 sessions in which the clinician educates the couple about PTSD and its impact on relationships, introduces communication skills, helps the couple to overcome experiential avoidance, and applies cognitive interventions to change the core beliefs related to persistent PTSD symptoms

Of special interest is a new couple-based PTSD treatment called Structured Approach Therapy (SAT). Originally developed and used with very promising results for families with returning war veterans who suffered from combat zone trauma,[5] SAT is designed to help partners decrease their avoidance of trauma-related stimuli and enhance their emotional regulation. This series of interventions involves education about how trauma impacts the processing of emotions that are crucial for maintaining intimate relationships. Couples also are trained to identify, label, and communicate about their avoidance of trauma-related stimuli, and they are provided with emotion regulation tools to cope with trauma-related emotions.

Central to this model is the encouragement of disclosure, in which the person with the trauma history is prompted to reveal and discuss trauma-related memories and emotions with her partner. Couples learn to approach and not avoid the trauma-related problems that have impaired their relationship in the past. The couple is also coached to use their empathic communication skills to identify and discuss their emotional responses to the disclosure. SAT's emphasis on disclosure is grounded in findings that trauma survivors who speak about their trauma to an intimate partner experience decreases in posttraumatic stress[6] while simultaneously improving their relationship quality.

Moving Forward

As we noted in previous chapters, it is important to keep in mind how previous sexual trauma can impact not only the individual who has experienced it, but also how it can play into the problems that couples experience. This information can be crucial in treating a couple successfully; how and when you gather this information depends on your clients and on your own clinical style. If a woman has been through sexual trauma that her partner does not know about, or if she isn't aware of how this might affect her ability to be intimate, or if both are uninformed about how important the consequences of trauma may be for impairing intimate sexual relationships, counseling without attention to trauma history can be limited in its effectiveness. Ignorance is not bliss in this case, but is instead a recipe for unsuccessful couples therapy, where both partners are left in the dark about why their attempts at intimacy fall short.

Chapter 12

Creating a Culture of Alliance

We Are All in This Together

This final chapter will examine ways that those of us who are counselors, therapists, and educators can provide effective guidelines for helping men and women confront and reduce #MeToo behavior through allying with each other. This alliance is crucial for recovery in a #MeToo culture, where so many men are socialized to be dismissive and disrespectful of women's bodies and voices.

Too often, men and women are seen as adversaries, almost as if they are from different planets. It is vital that we do not see the other gender as irrelevant or hostile as we work together to reduce #MeToo behavior. When the #MeToo movement is viewed as only a woman's issue and when men aren't invited in to join the conversation (or are shamed if they have questions about the #MeToo continuum), we shortchange men who can be valuable allies to women. When allowed to participate, these men can confront and educate the men who are acting out. Men can be instigators of cultural change for other men in challenging traditional social norms, banding together and supporting one another in stopping #MeToo behavior.

When they "wake up" to the impact of #MeToo behaviors on women, men are better positioned to become allies—to be more protective of women, to be more respectful of women's experiences, to activate intervention as bystanders, and to serve as better role models for other men. And, as we discussed in Chapter 7, men who have sincerely taken stock of their own missteps or outright misconduct with women are usually the ones who are especially motivated to act.

Although we will primarily look at ways men can confront #MeToo behavior in themselves and others, we will also look at the ways women can welcome men as allies, and how women can support other women in confronting sexual misconduct. Working together creates a culture of gender equality and respect; it heightens awareness of each other's needs and how to respect boundaries around sexual interactions. Several organizations of men supporting women have been created (see Resources section), but few include men and women together.

We offer some guidelines for therapists working with men who genuinely want to treat women respectfully, to be role models for other men, and to be more aware about how women have been impacted by #MeToo behaviors. We also offer recommendations for counseling women who want to ally with "good" men and serve as role models for other women in handling #MeToo behavior. These are only suggestions; you will probably have ideas of your own to share with colleagues.

Conversations With Other Men: Challenging Perceived Social Norms

Many men are often seeking meaningful dialogue with other men. This includes men who are questioning their own pasts but who are themselves *not* #MeToo offenders, men who genuinely want to live up to higher standards about male behavior, and men who are genuinely compassionate and concerned about the effects of #MeToo behaviors on women. They often want to compare notes with their peers about ways that they (as in the stories in Chapter 7) may have crossed some lines and what they can now do about it.

However, a lot of men are reluctant to have this conversation because they are afraid that they will be discounted or ridiculed by the men they seek out. What gets in the way is that men often guess wrong about other men, and they have a warped idea of what other men are really doing. This may not be true for all men, but if you listen to a lot of guys talk, you would think that every guy is getting laid all the time, women never say *no*, men are always in charge, and women are the enemy. A man might secretly act a lot more sensitively with his girlfriend, but never let on about this to his male friends. So sometimes, men only see the image of how other men think they *should* be seen. Then the rest of men think they are supposed to match that—or else they're not "real men." This is the downside of traditional male norms—that men must adhere to a rigid set of restrictions on their behavior, which then impedes their ability to connect intimately with other men.

We now have research studies that illuminate men's misperceptions of the norms and beliefs of their male peers. Men secretly show allegiance to certain positive and respectful values about gender relations and behavior toward women, but they think that other men do not. So they don't express themselves—and in many situations, don't take action—because they think they are more of a lone wolf than they actually are. In a series of studies about the "Social Norms Approach,"[2] it has been found that men report that they do not personally believe in many societal myths about masculinity but believe that other men do.

One study[3] asked male college students to rate, on a five-point scale, how strongly they endorse the following statements.

- I would stop sexual activity when asked to, even if I were already aroused.
- It is important to get consent before sexual intimacy.
- I believe one should stop the first time a date says no to sexual activity.
- When I hear sexist comments, I indicate my disapproval.
- When I witness a male "hitting on" a woman and I know she doesn't want it, I intervene.
- When I witness a situation in which it looks like a female will end up being taken advantage of, I intervene.

They were then asked to rate what they thought the average male student on their campus would say in response to these same questions. There was a significant gap (26% for the first three items identified as "Importance of Consent," 14% for the last three items identified as "Willingness to Intervene") between their own responses and their guesses about the responses of their male peers. They consistently believed that other men didn't care as much as they did.

The conclusion? Men underestimate the extent to which other men are uncomfortable with sexist behavior toward women—and this misperception is likely to keep men from intervening against the inappropriate behavior of other men.

In another illuminating study,[3] male college students were asked to fill out an anonymous survey with the following instruction: "Briefly describe something that bothers you which men do when there are no women present."

The survey found that that 75% said they were uncomfortable with the language men use to describe women or the way they talk about their sexual experiences. Most men don't know that other men are uncomfortable with this, so they are reluctant to share their true feelings and attitudes. Here are the rest of their comments about how they are bothered by the way other men talk about women:

- when they talk about the sexual habits of women that they know nothing about
- demands by friends to know how far sexually you've gone in a relationship
- bragging about sexual acts—giving details including names and positions, in a mocking way
- lying or exaggerating greatly the extent of sexual behavior
- speaking about women as purely a means of pleasure and that is all
- talking about "taking advantage" of women
- talking about women in crude sexual terms
- talking about female anatomy

As one man said: *Guys like to talk about fooling around with girls and often, not always, talk about it with apparently no qualms. I tend to think fooling around is special and feel guilty, as if I had just betrayed that girl, when I reveal intimate moments.*

In working with men individually, in groups, or in educational settings, we can raise consciousness by asking them the following questions:

Think of how many times, in high school, in college, at work, or just hanging out with buddies, you've been asked, "Did you score?" "Well, did you do her?" "Did you get any?" "How was she?" We are supposed *to score. This is how we prove ourselves to other men. This certainly proves we're not weak or lame. It's like there is a silent audience when we are negotiating sex with a reluctant woman: Our "boys" are in the room watching us.*

In comparison, think of how many more times you have heard, "Yeah, she deserved it," or "I wouldn't let any girl get away with that with me!" Think of how few times you may have heard a buddy say, "You know, she might have been right," or "How would you like it if you heard about some guy treating your sister like that?"

How many of you have ever heard your buddies say, after you've gone out with someone, "What was her name? Did you really like her? Do you think you'll ever see her again? What did you all talk about?"

We don't usually hear other men talking like this. But you may be surprised to find out how many other men actually welcome talking this way about women, if they're given a chance.

Actually, the news about men being receptive to these conversations is better than many men realize. When given the opportunity, men are more capable of discussing these issues in depth and, despite their armor and bravado, are often hungry for it. In *The STOP Program* groups, which treat male domestic violence offenders, one specific session is called "What's Up with Sex?"[4] Despite original concerns that this group discussion would devolve into defended, locker-room banter, group leaders have consistently found that the men in these groups (even these men, who have engaged in acts of intimate partner violence) are interested in and willing to examine the attitudes they have about sex. Sometimes leaders can't get them to shut up, because they want to talk more—in ways that they clearly do not have access to in other areas of their lives—about the experiences of sexual rejection, of empty sex, of their failures at sex, and more.

In the same way, women can sometimes see men as caricatures of who they really are inside. One study[5] showed that women saw men as less afraid of rejection than men saw themselves; they saw men as unwilling to talk about their feelings (versus unable to) or afraid of people's reactions if they did so. Women can misinterpret men's actions in a more disrespectful manner than was meant. In good psychoeducational training, women and men are better able to see men for whom they really are, rather than who the world expects them to be.

And women can be supportive of men's groups and men who are good role models. There are some ways that men can work best with men, where older, wise men can nurture younger men into respectful behavior toward women. Encouraging men to join men's groups is one way of doing this.

Bystander Issues:
How Men (and Women) Can Take Action

Tarana Burke (founder of the #MeToo movement) asks men to call out bad behavior when they see it. In the new era of #MeToo consciousness, many counselors and therapists are seeing men and hearing stories about men who are not only concerned about no longer offending women but are also ready to confront friends and coworkers that do.

Current theory and research on bystander behavior[6] indicates that there are a number of stages a man often goes through before he is willing to intervene when he sees or hears about offensive male behavior toward women.

To help a client reach the point where he will activate some sort of intervention, the therapist needs to guide the man through four steps. Please note that these steps can apply to women bystanders although there are different reasons why they might be inhibited in doing so:

- Notice the event (Step 1).
- Interpret it as a problem (Step 2).
- Feel responsible for dealing with it (Step 3).
- Find effective ways to intervene (Step 4).

As therapists, we can help men go through these stages in both individual and group therapy. We can also use our clinical skills in offering an educational and non-shaming approach.

Steps 1 and 2 involve helping men understand some of the barriers to accurately noticing and interpreting the event, in particular, having them confront their mistaken beliefs about other men. These beliefs include the following (please note the beliefs which are underlined would apply to female bystanders as well):

- *Nobody else really cares about this.*
- *I don't see anyone else taking action, so there isn't a problem.*
- *I assume that someone else will do something.*
- *I'm afraid that intervening will make me look weak or less "manly."*
- *I feel guilty about my own behaviors, so I don't want to call out another man about the same thing.*
- *I'm afraid I'll embarrass myself or somebody else.*
- *I'm afraid other men will turn against me.*

One factor that typically obstructs this process is the strong tendency for men to misperceive the attitudes of other men, as we discussed earlier. Research on "social norms theory"[7] has consistently found that men are more

likely to intervene in a situation that leads to sexual assault when they perceived that other men were *also* likely to intervene in such a situation. Unfortunately, men typically misperceive the norms of peers, believing that they are
less concerned about consent and less likely to intervene than is really the case.

Men's perceptions of norms, accurate or not, exert a strong influence on
men's own consideration of consent and willingness to intervene. Educating
men about the disparities between their beliefs about how other men think
and how they *really* think is our job as therapists. We also need to help men
recognize the pressure that traditional male norms puts on them, including the
"requirement" to be seen as masculine to avoid being seen as feminine.

Furthermore, the more men endorse traditional rape myths (*it's not really*
rape when a person changes their mind in the middle of sexual activity; if a
woman goes to her date's room on the first date, it implies she is willing to
have sex, etc.), the more inhibited they are about intervening. These patterns
highlight the importance of targeting and reducing rape myth acceptance to
encourage prosocial bystander intervention [8]

Step 3 is based on research about bystander intervention,[9] which has consistently found that, while challenging these belief systems is necessary for
successfully activating a response, it is not sufficient. Correcting misperceptions alone is not enough to get people to actually intervene. Taking responsibility for the bad actions of others involves taking risks in confronting
perceived social norms as noted earlier: *What will other men think of me? . . .*
Maybe I am just imaging this behavior is bad . . . I don't want to piss off other
guys. Our job as therapists is to help men gain courage to do the right thing,
and to develop the tools so they can intervene successfully. Women of course
can also intervene, or can support men who take the initiative to call out the
bad behavior.

This leads to **Step 4**, perhaps the most crucial step of all, because it involves
teaching men the actual skills to make a difference. Jackson Katz, a pioneer in
helping men challenge themselves and take action to protect women, has developed a series of exercises and vignettes that he uses in men's consciousness-
raising seminars. One example is an exercise from the *MVP Playbook*[10] called
"Piling On" (a football term and therefore easily understood by most men). It is
designed for educating groups of men to develop specific action plans for these
challenging situations when a bystander might be called upon to intervene:

Situation

Earlier in the evening, you saw a woman at a party who was drunk and hanging all over some of your buddies. A friend tells you that she's been taken upstairs to a bedroom, where a bunch of the guys are "doing" her. He urges you to join them.

Train of Thought:

Is this gang rape? . . . If it is, how can I stop it? . . . Or is this just guy messing with me? . . . How could a woman possibly be into this? . . . She can't really know what she is doing if she's drunk . . . What about AIDS? . . . Will they be angry with me? . . . Is there any physical risk in my breaking this thing up? . . . Am I man enough to stand up to my friends? . . . What should I do?

Options:

- Tell him no thanks and continue partying.
- Go upstairs to watch the action, even though I know I wouldn't join in.
- Explain to my friend that this could be a gang rape and the guys could be getting themselves and the whole fraternity (or squadron, or team, etc.) in serious trouble.
- Get some people together and rush up to the bedroom, and get the woman out of there.
- Join in and go for it—she must really want it.
- Call 911.

This exercise covers it all—the self-talk that either inhibits or activates an intervention, plus a review of where these beliefs might lead. Discussion with men in these settings focuses on how pursuing each of these options will make them feel in the long run. When it comes to coaching men on taking action to influence other men, rehearsal of exact wording and body language is crucial. So many hold back from these positive social responses because—even though their intentions are good—they feel inept at actually performing the task. It helps to give them specific, concrete skills in how to do this right. Working on this in a peer-group setting is the most effective format because men learn from each other's experiences and drop some of the stigma attached to not knowing how to handle these situations.

In a similar vein, the U.S. Navy developed a psychoeducational program for incoming personnel to prevent sexual assault, called "True Consent."[11] This included both male and female recruits, and one of the handouts in this program was titled "Taking Care of Shipmates":

Keeping track of our own behavior is our most important job, but it is also extremely important for us to TAKE CARE OF SHIPMATES. Some of your shipmates are men who may sexually assault. Some of your shipmates are women—or even men—who will be on the receiving end of sexual assault. As a bystander, your actions can make it appear as if you silently approve or actively disapprove. Here are some guidelines to keep in mind:

- Use peer pressure positively to help stop abusive behaviors which may lead to sexual assault (for example, put down, rather than approve, the behavior of a peer who has taken advantage of a sexual partner).
- Get involved if you believe someone is at risk. If you see a woman in trouble at a party or a male friend using force or pressuring a woman, don't be afraid to intervene.
- Be especially careful in group situations. Be prepared to resist pressure from friends to participate in violent or criminal acts. You may save the woman from the trauma of sexual assault and your friend from the ordeal of criminal prosecution.
- Do not "join in" if a friend invites you to participate in sexual behavior when there is no TRUE CONSENT.
- Women can intervene as bystanders themselves when observing destructive male behavior. Although this may not be as effective as men doing this, they can help hold men accountable for bad actions.
- Women can support men who are helpful bystanders.
- Women can support other women in avoiding situations where they may face sexual misconduct as well as speaking up against men who do.

As was pointed out in Chapter 2, if no women attended a party at a fraternity known for its sexual abuse of women and instead spoke out against that fraternity, if women were truly sisters to each other in the fight against sexual abuse, the problem would lessen. One hindrance is that women are often divided against themselves by a culture that puts men first, which values the opinions of men more than women, where campus jocks often rule the roost. If all women coalesced to fight sexism and sexual abuse where it happens, the abuse would certainly be reduced.

Men's Healthy Relationships With Women: How Counselors and Therapists Can Help

Some men come to therapy looking for help in forming romantic relationships with women. Other men come to therapy because they are worried about how to relate to women in their workplace. In the latter case, they are concerned about keeping a distance from women because they do not fully understand which actions might be considered inappropriate. In therapy, men have expressed reluctance in talking about these issues honestly due to fear of negative consequences, citing examples of men who have been treated negatively after sharing their thoughts about #MeToo. There's a great sketch from *Saturday Night Live* with three couples out to dinner, very tentatively trying to discuss #MeToo issues—with all parties terrified about making one slight verbal misstep. They actually consider switching the subject to something a little safer: race.

Even before #MeToo consciousness, men were often confused because they often read signals differently than women do. And, historically, men have not known how to ask for help when they are confused, often because it presents as unmanly or unconfident. One classic study of male and female attitudes on dates[12] concluded that "no matter who initiated the date, who paid, or where the couple went, men were always more likely than women to interpret the behavior as a sign that women wanted sex." Men who commit a sexual assault have often misinterpreted their victim's intent—because men almost always overestimate women's sexual availability and interest. Typical misreads include the following:

- When she's friendly, he thinks: *She wants me.*
- When she wears a sexy outfit, he thinks: *She's hot for me.*
- When she's a hot dancer, he thinks: *Oh, yeah, that's meant for me!*
- When she comes back to his apartment or dorm room, he thinks: *This is definitely a green light for sex.*

But, of course, these same behaviors often mean different things to different women.

Sometimes men are right, and they read the signals correctly—and that's fine. But often—very often, according to the research on sexual miscommunication—MEN GUESS WRONG. A man gets aroused and thinks he knows what *she* wants, so he falsely reads a signal of true consent. He doesn't bother to find out for sure. And sometimes this leads to sexual assault because he has misread the signals. He convinces himself that pushing hard for sex justified. He sees a green light when she is signaling yellow or even red.

Liz Plank, author of *For the Love of Men: A New Vision for Mindful Masculinity,*[13] offers modern men some valuable guidelines for treating women that do *not* mean staying away or avoiding all flirting or sexual interactions. Here are some excerpts that a therapist might share with a client who is concerned about how to interact personally or professionally with women.

1. *When trying to date a woman at work, use the rule of one.* Plenty of office romances take place, and many of these actually end up in long-term relationships and marriage. The official policy established at Facebook and Google: You only get one shot. Office romances are allowed as long as there's no conflict of interest and a coworker only asks another once. If the answer is ambiguous (*I'm busy,* or *Maybe, let me check*) or actually, *No,* the person is not allowed to ask again.
2. *Be aware that if the attraction is mutual it's not harassment (EXCEPT if there is a power imbalance in the relationship).* Men need to practice *conscious* flirting (aware of the signals and responses or lack thereof), especially in a work setting. If you pay close attention to her cues (rather than trying to just make a conquest), you will know if it is flirting or harassment.
3. *You don't have to avoid women: Just stop harassing them!* Many men are now afraid of hiring women. Women are not the problem. The men harassing them are.
4. *When it comes to chivalry in the workplace, ask if you're not able to tell.* Ask if she needs help, but never assume she does. It also helps to take on traditionally female tasks, like taking notes at a meeting, booking the conference room, or taking lunch orders.
5. *Don't do anything for a woman you wouldn't do for a man.* Pretend like people don't have genders. Treat men and women equally.

Women can also speak up and not automatically assume that men will get the clue without a clear message. This also means not automatically assuming that men are too hopeless to get the message. This is allying with men in terms of direct communication. This may be seen as women having to take on more responsibility than they should: While there may be some truth to this, we are promoting problem-solving rather than blaming. It is very helpful if women speak up clearly about what they want and need from a man; this will help him better understand how to connect with her in an open and honest way.

How a Male Ally Can Help a Woman Who Has Been Sexually Harassed or Assaulted

If a man comes in to therapy concerned about how to help a woman he knows deal with sexual assault, a therapist could use the following ideas as guidelines to help him take valuable action.

- *You can listen.* Women who have been harassed or assaulted are more likely to tell a friend than to tell a family member or professional. You are likely to feel like you need to "do something" immediately—but, for now, just listen. Having someone listen and support her is what she most needs.
- *Don't blame her.* Don't ask questions that seem to suggest she is at fault: "How much did you drink? Did you know him? Have you ever had sex with him before?" Victims often feel guilty and frightened of being blamed, so they are sensitive to any comments that suggest that the assault is their fault. If you do feel like it is important to ask these questions, make sure you repeatedly emphasize that none of these behaviors means that this was her fault in any way.
- *Let her guide you.* Ask her what she needs or how you can help. She may want you to help her think about what she needs to do: reporting, seeking medical attention, finding a place to stay for a night or two or someone to stay with her, and so forth. Help her prioritize these decisions and to consider them. Do not insist on any specific decision—she has already had enough forced upon her. Respect her decision if she chooses to do nothing.

- *Victims are often very frightened.* She may need to stay with someone or to have someone stay with her. Let her know this is okay to ask for—it doesn't make her weak or hysterical. Don't get too angry. Don't blow up in front of her. She has seen enough aggression and violence for one day.
- *Help her remember she has resources* available to her: other friends, HR at her place of employment, Rape Crisis Center, Family Service Center counselors, clergymen, and counselors and therapists.
- *If she has a boyfriend or partner* whom she has elected to tell, they are also going to need support. Support will help her partner help her.

Creating Gender-Equitable Environments

If you are counseling a man who is seeking guidelines about how to contribute to a gender-equitable world, or if you are designing education programs or education campaigns to offer men these guidelines, here are tools you may find valuable. This list was collected from multiple sources and integrated by researchers Elyssa Klann and Joel Wong.[14] These examples, identified as recommendations for men in supporting female colleagues and students, are based on academic settings, but the principles are universal. The examples provide excellent guidelines to help your male clients develop positive relationships with colleagues or students of the other gender. They are also useful prompts to stimulate a mixed-gender conversation about how both men and women can implement these actions, and how women might find ways to support men in changing as well as considering how they can act assertively in a sexist environment.

Suggestions about how a woman might respond to each topic follows each discussion. It is usually helpful to assume (until proven otherwise) that the man's behavior is unconscious or the disrespect unintended, so that he is not shamed but educated.

Male: *Be consistent when using names and title—unless otherwise advised, refer to female professors in the same way as their male colleagues. For instance, avoid using a female professor's first name if you use the title "Dr." to refer to a male professor.*

Female: *If you find yourself addressed by anyone, male or female, in a* manner which feels disrespectful, you can say "I'd prefer you to use my full title, thank you."

Male: Refer to female professors and students as "women" rather than as "girls."

Female: If you are around a man who doesn't do this, you can say "Hey, you don't say 'boys,' so don't say 'girls,' let's use 'men' and 'women' as equal terms."

Male: Avoid assigning gender-stereotyped tasks (e.g., hospitality) only to women; work to equalize workload across gender.

Female: If you find that tasks are divided according to gender stereotypes, speak up with the person who assigned them and ask that they be assigned on another basis.

Male: Offer words of praise and encouragement to female students and colleagues that address their potential for success, their leadership abilities, and their achievements. Be specific in your use of affirmations—point out specific examples that speak to their potential and accomplishments.

Female: Women, of course, should do this too. Words from a female role model or mentor are often the most important.

Male: Avoid comments on women's physical (e.g., she dresses so well) or emotional attributes (e.g., she is overly emotional). Comment on achievements and work ethic when referring to all colleagues and students.

Female: If a man says you dress well, you can say "Thank you, you look good in that outfit too" (for a sense of humor which gets the point across). He may actually be well meaning. If you are called overemotional, this is pejorative and you can say "I'm sorry you feel this way," or "That might be true sometimes, but . . . (and say what you want to say or say it again)."

Male: Include female colleagues and students in professional networking opportunities. Connect them with other scholars and researchers.

Female: Women can ask to join networking opportunities or ask their male colleagues to invite them.

Male: *Include female colleagues and students in social gatherings, which could present invaluable networking opportunities. Conduct an audit of your social groups—do you go out for lunch or hang out only with your male colleagues? And be sure that you choose social networking opportunities that will be perceived as safe and accessible for all colleagues and students. Be conscious of the insidious nature of the old boys' club, which can exclude women from important networking opportunities that could aid their careers.*

Female: *Women can ask men they trust to tell them about gatherings and then join. Women can also create gatherings of their own and invite men.*

Male: *Build your awareness of subtle cues of sexism during classes or meetings, such as how much different people speak, who they choose to sit with, and whose ideas are approved/endorsed. Actively seek to disrupt these processes.*

Female: *Speak up if you aren't called upon. Talk to the professor with a male colleague about how the class is handled.*

Male: *Disrupt a manterruption, which is men's act of interrupting women when they speak. Such acts tend to diminish the contributions of women, and research shows that men are more likely to interrupt women than to interrupt other men. When you notice a man interrupting a woman, interject and say, "I think what she's saying is important. Would you mind letting her complete her sentence?" Be aware that you could be manterrupting without realizing it. If you catch yourself manterrupting, acknowledge it and apologize: "I'm sorry that I interrupted you. Please complete what you were saying."*

Female: *When a man starts to interrupt you, say "Excuse me, please wait until I am finished." If he is interrupting a female colleague of yours, you can say "Please let her finish, I want to hear her ideas."*

Male: *Avoid mansplaining, which is an explanation by a man to a woman, or a clarification of what a woman has said (e.g., "what she really intended to say is . . ."). It is condescending and patronizing. "Mansplaining" inadvertently communicates the sexist message that women are ignorant or incapable of having authoritative knowledge and that men's opinions are more authoritative than women's.*

Female: *When a man starts to do this, you can say "Thanks for following up on what I said, it sounds like you agree with me."*

Male: *Be conscious of women's intersecting identities. Assess whether policies and customs adequately address the needs of women from diverse backgrounds and whether certain groups of women (e.g., white women) are inadvertently favored over others (e.g., women of color).*

Female: *Women need to be an inherent part of this conversation: If they start it, men should be invited in.*

Male: *Speak up if you hear (or hear about) comments, behaviors, or trends that appear to harm or may threaten women's well-being. For example, if you hear a sexist joke, you could say, "I really prefer not to speak about women in this way."*

Female: *If you hear a sexist joke, you can say "That's stupid, surely you have a better joke than that," or "Let me tell you about the joke I heard about how all men are losers (or fill in the pejorative term here)," or "You may not get what that joke does to women but it isn't great."*

Male: *Model cultural humility for others. Disclose instances in which you failed to demonstrate gender-equitable behavior. Ask questions that acknowledge your ignorance of gender issues and your willingness to learn.*

Female: *If man is willing to ask, then you must be respectful of his question, no shaming is helpful. If a man is ignorant, he needs to be educated not scorned.*

Male: *Solicit feedback from and listen to female colleagues and students about their experiences.*

Female: *Offer feedback about your own experiences and ask men about theirs—it's not just a one-way street.*

Male: *Advocate for and promote organizational policies that support the recruitment, retention, and welfare of female students and professors, such as family-leave allowances.*

Female: *Working with men on this is crucial—we need to support each other in changing policies that inhibit the best in all genders.*

Beyond a Zero-Sum Game

One of the limiting ways of thinking about #MeToo behavior is that it's just about men behaving badly, that men have to fix it, and that women don't have much of a role in changing the culture. In fact, it is a systems problem, as mentioned in Chapter 2. We all operate within a system that shapes our behavior as men or women, often in less than useful ways. When it is a sexist system, it handicaps women more than men. In our work as clinicians, it is helpful to teach men and women about the experience of the other, especially how traditional gender norms can negatively impact healthy relationships.

Some of the most effective sources for change in attitudes toward the other gender are groups, seminars, and workshops in which men and women learn how traditional gender roles can be restrictive for each gender, and the confusion these gender roles generate around healthy relationships, dating, and sex. One technique is to have a dialogue between men and women where men can express their frustration and women can express their point of view. Another technique is reverse-gender role-playing. A third technique is to have single-sex and mixed-gender breakout sessions in a training program. The Cambridge Center for Gender Relations has successfully used all of these (see Resources section), as well as many other programs, to reduce conflict and misunderstanding between the sexes.

Early intervention is the best way to prevent sexual misconduct. Training programs that are gender balanced and experiential (see EEOC guidelines in Resources section) are an effective way to do this. As clinicians, we usually work within our offices, most often with individual clients. However, we can also put our expertise in human behavior to good use by working with HR or campus programs to design constructive ways for men and women to communicate and interact with each other.

It is important to know that we are all in this together. We are part of a system that has encouraged sexual mistreatment of women in a myriad of ways. As therapists, we are in an important position to help our clients be part of a new world where men and women have equal rights, opportunities, and respect for one another. Clinicians can be at the forefront of this change.

Resources

Chapter 2

Gender Role Inquiry

Philpot, C., Brooks, G., Lusterman, D., & Nutt, R. (1997). *Bridging separate gender worlds: Why men and women clash and how therapists can bring them together.* American Psychological Association.

Chapters 8 and 9

Sexual Harassment

U.S. Equal Opportunity Commission. (2014). *Sexual harassment.* http://www.eeoc .gov/laws/types/sexual_harassment.cfm

Safe Horizon. (2020). Rape and sexual assault: It's not your fault. https://www .safehorizon.org/get-help/rape-and-sexual-assault/#overview/

Berkowitz, A. (2013). *A grassroots' guide to fostering healthy norms to reduce violence in our communities: Social Norms toolkit.* http://socialnorms.org/wp -content/uploads/2017/03/Social_Norms_Violence_Prevention_Toolkit.pdf

That's Harassment. (2018). https://www.facebook.com/pg/thatsharassment/videos /?ref=page_internal

Berkowitz, A. (2009). *Response ability: A complete guide to bystander intervention.* Beck and Company.

Sexual Assault and Trauma

International Society for Traumatic Stress Studies (ISTSS). https://istss.org/clinical -resources/assessing-trauma

Maltz, W. (2012). *The sexual healing journey: A guide for survivors of sexual abuse*(3rd ed.). William Morrow Paperbacks.

Clarke, C., & Pino, A. (2016). *We believe you: Survivors of campus sexual assault speak out.* Holt Paperbacks.

Campus Assault Programs

SARE Centre. (2020). Enhanced access, acknowledge, act (EAAA) Sexual assault resistance. https://cultureofrespect.org/program/enhanced-access-acknowledge -act-eaaa-sexual-assault-resistance/

Smith-Kimble, C. (2020). The realities of sexual assault on campus. https://www .bestcolleges.com/resources/sexual-assault-on-campus/

Green Dot for Colleges. (2020). https://alteristic.org/services/green-dot/green-dot -colleges/

Consensual sexual or romantic relationships in the workplace or academic environment. (2018). https://policies.mit.edu/policies-procedures/90-

U.S. Department of Education. Know your rights: Title IX prohibits sexual harassment and sexual violence where you go to school. https://www2.ed.gov/about/ offices/list/ocr/docs/title-ix-rights-201104.html

RAINN. Campus sexual violence: Statistics. https://www.rainn.org/statistics/cam pus-sexual-violence

Assertiveness

Paterson, R. J. (2000). *The assertiveness workbook: How to express your ideas and stand up for yourself at work and in relationships.* New Harbinger Publications.

Murphy, J. (2020). *Assertiveness: How to stand up for yourself and still win the respect of others.* Delmar Publishing

Murphy, J. (2020). Assertiveness: How to Stand Up for Yourself and Still

Chapter 10
Workplace Harassment

Hewlett, S. A. (2020). *#MeToo in the corporate world: Power, privilege, and the path forward.* HarperCollins.

RAINN. (2019, October 4). You left your job because of sexual harassment. What now? https://www.rainn.org/news/you-left-your-job-because-sexual-harassment -what-now

Enright, M. (n.d.). Identifying and preventing harassment in your workplace. www .bizfilings.com/toolkit/research-topics/office-hr/identifying-and-preventing -harassment-in-your-workplace

Howard, L. G. (2007). *The sexual harassment handbook: Everything you need to know before someone calls a lawyer.* Career Press.

Chapter 11
Emotionally Focused Couple Therapy

Johnson, S. (2008). *Hold me tight: Seven conversations for a lifetime of love.* Little, Brown and Company.

Johnson, S. (2013). *Love sense: the revolutionary new science of romantic relationships.* Little, Brown and Company.

Critical Interaction Therapy

Johnson, D. R., Feldman, S., & Lubin, H. (1995). Critical interaction therapy: Couples therapy in combat-related posttraumatic stress disorder. *Family Process, 34*(4), 401–412. https://doi.org/10.1111/j.1545-5300.1995.00401.x

Cognitive-Behavioral Couple Treatment For PTSD

Monson, C. M., & Fredman, S. J. (2012). *Cognitive-behavioral conjoint therapy for PTSD: Harnessing the healing power of relationships.* Guilford Press.

Structured Approach Therapy (SAT)

Perlick, D. A., Sautter, F. J., Becker-Cretu, J. J., Schultz, D., Grier, S. C., Libin, A. V., Schladen, M. M., & Glynn, S. M. (2017). The incorporation of emotion-regulation skills into couple- and family-based treatments for post-traumatic stress disorder. *Military Medical Research, 4,* article 21. https://doi.org/10.1186/s40779-017-0130-9

Chapter 12

Johnson, W. B., & Smith, D. G. (2018). How men can become better allies to women. https://hbr.org/2018/10/how-men-can-become-better

MenEngage Alliance. http://menengage.org

National Organization for Men Against Sexism. https://nomas.org

Cambridge Center for Gender Relations. www.drhollysweet.com/consulting.html

Notes

Chapter 1

1. Laucius, J. (2018, January 29). https://ottawacitizen.com/local-news/what-is -sexual-misconduct-exactly-depends-on-who-you-ask

2. Sheehy, G. (2018, January 29). https://ottawacitizen.com/local-news/what-is -sexual-misconduct-exactly-depends-on-who-you-ask

3. Crockford. A. (2018, January 29). https://ottawacitizen.com/local-news/what-is -sexual-misconduct-exactly-depends-on-who-you-ask

4. Cottle, M. (20 December 2017). *The Atlantic*. https://www.theatlantic .com/politics/archive/2017/12/what-does-sexual-misconduct-actually-mean /548807/

5. Massachusetts Institute of Technology. (2020–2021). *MIT mind and hand book*, Part 2, Section 23: "Sexual misconduct." Retrieved September 9, 2020, from https://handbook.mit.edu/sexual-misconduct

6. Duke University Student Affairs. *Student sexual misconduct policy and procedures: Duke's commitment to Title IX*. Retrieved on September 9, 2020 from https://studentaffairs.duke.edu/conduct/z-policies/student-sexual-misconduct -policy-dukes-commitment-title-ix

7. National Center for Victims of Crime. In *Wikipedia*. Retrieved September 9, 2020, from https://en.wikipedia.org/wiki/Sexual_misconduct

8. *Popcorn with Pete Travers*. (2017, December 12). https://abcnews.go.com/ Entertainment /matt-damon-opens-harvey-weinstein-sexual harassment-con fidentiality/story?

9. Milano, A. (2017, December 16). *Bustle*. https://www.bustle.com/p/alyssa -milanos-tweets-to-matt-damon-spread-important-message-about-sexual -assualt-7617526

10. Helmore. E. (2017, December 17). https://www.theguardian/com/film/2017/ dec/16/minnie-driver-matt-damon-men-cannot-understand-abuse

11. Miller, C. (2019). *Know my name: A memoir.* Viking Press.
12. Gessen, M. (2017). When does a watershed become a sex panic? *The New Yorker.* https://www.newyorker.com/news/our-columnists/when-does-a-watershed-become-a-sex-panic
13. Center for Talent Innovation. (2018). The pervasiveness of sexual harassment in today's white-collar workplace. https://www.prnewswire.com/news-releases/the-pervasiveness-of-sexual-harassment-in-todays-white-collar-workplace-300679484.html
14. Frankovic, K. (2017, November 17). YouGov. https://today.yougov.com/topics/politics/articles-reports/2017/11/17/sexual-harassment-reports-may-just-be-tip-iceberg
15. Lonsway, K. (1996). Preventing rape through education: What do we know? *Psychology of Women Quarterly, 20*(2), 229–265.
16. Helmore. E. (2017, December 17). *The Guardian.* https://www.theguardian/com/film/2017/dec/16/minnie-driver-matt-damon-cannot-understand-abuse
17. https://metoomvmt.org/
18. https//www.oxfordlearnersdictionary.com/us/definition/american_english/predator. Retrieved January 17, 2021.
19. https//dictionary.cambridge.org/us/dictionary/English/perpetrator. Retrieved January 17, 2021.
20. https//www.oxfordlearnersdictionary.com/us/definition/american_english/offender. Retrieved January 17, 2021.
21. https://www.merriam-webster.com/dictionary/prey. Retrieved November 30, 2020.

Chapter 2

1. Broverman, I. K., Broverman, D. M., Clarkson, F. E., Rosenkrantz, P. S., & Vogel, S. R. (1970). Sex-role stereotypes and clinical judgments of mental health. *Journal of Consulting and Clinical Psychology, 34*(1), 1–7. https://doi.org/10.1037/h0028797
2. Gray, J. (1992). *Men are from Mars, women are from Venus.* HarperCollins.
3. Philpot, C., Brooks, G., Lusterman, D., & Nutt, R. (1997). *Bridging separate gender worlds: Why men and women clash and how therapists can bring them together.* American Psychological Association.
4. Ibid., 218.
5. Ibid., 222.
6. Levant, R. (2020). *The tough standard, the hard truths about masculinity and violence.* Oxford University Press.
7. *APA guidelines for psychological practice with boys and men.* (2018). American Psychological Association.
8. Mahalik, J., Locke, B. D., Ludlow, L., Diemer, M., Scott, R. P. J., Gottfried, M.,

& Freitas, G. (2003). Development of the Conformity to Male Norms Inventory. *Psychology of Men & Masculinity, 4*(1), 3–25. https://doi.org/10.1037/1524 -9220.4.1.3

9. Levant R., & Fischer, J. (1998). Male Role Norms Inventory. In C. M. Davis, W. H. Yarber, R. Bauserman, G. Schreer, & S. L. Davis (Eds.), *Sexuality-related measures: A compendium (2nd ed.)* pp 469–472. SAGE Publications.

10. Brown, B. (2014). *The power of vulnerability.* TED Conferences. https://www .ted.com/talks/brene_brown_the_power_of_vulnerability/transcript

11. Chin, J., & Vasarhelyi, E. C. (Directors). (2018). *Free solo* [Film]. National Geographic Partners.

12. O'Neil, J. M., Egan, J., & Murry, V. (1993). The gender role journey measure: Scale development and psychometric evaluation, *Sex Roles, 28,* 167–185. https://doi .org/10.1007/BF00299279

13. Hyde, J. (2006). *Half the human experience.* (7th ed.). Cengage Learning; Matlin, M. W. (2011). *The psychology of women.* Cengage Learning.

14. Lazarus, M., Wunderlich, R., Stallone, P., & Vitagliano, J. (Directors). (1979). *Killing us softly: Advertising's images of women* [Film]. Cambridge Documentary Films.

15. Jhally, S. (Director). (2010).*Killing us softly 4: Advertising's image of women* [Film]. Media Education Foundation.

16. Graham, W & Horsfield, D. (Writers). (2015–2019). *Poldark* [Film]. BBC One.

17. James, E. L. (2011). *Fifty shades of gray.* Vintage Books.

18. Muehlenhard, C. (1988). Misinterpreted dating behaviors and the risk of date rape. *Journal of Social and Clinical Psychology, 6*(1), 20–37.

Chapter 3

1. Wright, J. (2017, November 30). The backlash to believing women has begun. *Harper's Bazaar.* https://www.harpersbazaar.com/culture/politics/a13091573/ backlash-metoo-movement/

2. Johnson, M. P. (2008). *A typology of domestic violence: Intimate terrorism, violent resistance, and situational couple violence.* Northeastern University Press. (This is part of the Northeastern Series on Gender, Crime, and Law).

   Wexler, D. B. (2020). *The STOP domestic violence program* (4th ed., revised and updated). W. W. Norton.

3. Ali, Y. (2017, October 7). TV journalist says Harvey Weinstein masturbated in front of her. *HuffPost.* https://www.huffpost.com/entry/weinstein-sexual -harassment-allegation_n_59d7ea3de4b046f5ad984211

4. LaPook, J. (2017, February 9). Former Team USA gymnasts describe doctor's alleged sexual abuse. *60 minutes.* CBSNews. https://www.cbsnews.com/news/ former-team-usa-gymnasts-describe-doctors-alleged-sexual-abuse/

5. Ibid.

6. McCandless, B. (2017, February 19). On *60 Minutes*, former gymnasts allege sexual abuse. *60 Minutes Overtime*. https://www.cbsnews.com/news/on-60 -minutes-former-gymnasts-allege-sexual-abuse/

7. Grigoriadis, V. (2019, August 26). "I collect people, I own people, I can damage people": The curious sociopathy of Jeffrey Epstein. *Vanity Fair*. https:// www.vanityfair.com/news/2019/08/curious-sociopathy-of-jeffrey-epstein-ex -girlfriends

8. Ibid.

9. Velazquez-Manooff, M. (2018, February 24). Real men get rejected, too. *The New York Times*. https://www.nytimes.com/2018/02/24/opinion/sunday/real-men -masculinity-rejected.html

10. Yoffe, E. (2018, June 26). Understanding Harvey: Power alone does not explain their abuses. *HuffPost Highline*. https://highline.huffingtonpost.com/articles/ en/harvey-weinstein-psychology-sexual-predators/

11. Transcript: Donald Trump's Taped Comments About Women. (2016). New York Times. Retrieved from https://www.nytimes.com/2016/10/08/us/donald-trump -tape-transcript.html

12. Murphy, D. (2017, April 19). Four new complaints filed against Larry Nassar, including one dating to "92. *ESPN*. https://www.espn.com/olympics/story/_/ id/19191934/new-complaints-larry-nassar-allege-sexual-abuse-dates-1992

13. Gabler, E., Twohey, M., & Kantor, J. (2017, October 30). New accusers expand Harvey Weinstein sexual assault claims back to '70s. *The New York Times*. https://www.nytimes.com/2017/10/30/us/harvey-weinstein-sexual-assault -allegations.html

14. Fiorillo, V. (2014, November 21). Kristina Ruehli says Bill Cosby drugged and tried to sexually assault her in 1965. *Philadelphia Magazine*. https://www .phillymag.com/news/2014/11/21/kristina-ruehli-says-bill-cosby-drugged -tried-sexually-assault-1965/

15. Ibid.

16. Yoffe, E. (2018, June 28). Understanding Harvey: Power alone does not explain their abuses. *HuffPost Highline*. https://highline.huffingtonpost.com/articles/ en/harvey-weinstein-psychology-sexual-predators/

17. Gabler, E., Twohey, M., & Kantor, J. (2017, October 30). New accusers expand Harvey Weinstein sexual assault claims back to '70s. *The New York Times*. https://www.nytimes.com/2017/10/30/us/harvey-weinstein-sexual-assault -allegations.html

18. Sherrill, S. (2001, December 9). The year in ideas: A to z.; Acquired situational narcissism. *The New York Times*. https://www.nytimes.com/2001/12/09/ magazine/the-year-in-ideas-a-to-z-acquired-situational-narcissism.html; Ni, P. (2017, January 8). 5 signs of a situational narcissist. *Psychology Today*. https://

www.psychologytoday.com/us/blog/communication-success/201701/5-signs
-situational-narcissist

19. Yoffe, E. (2018, June 28). Understanding Harvey: Power alone does not explain their abuses. *HuffPost Highline.* https://highline.huffingtonpost.com/articles/ en/harvey-weinstein-psychology-sexual-predators/

20. Grigoriadis, V. (2019, August 26). "I collect people, I own people, I can damage people": The curious sociopathy of Jeffrey Epstein. *Vanity Fair.* https:// www.vanityfair.com/news/2019/08/curious-sociopathy-of-jeffrey-epstein-ex -girlfriends

21. Jhally, S. (Director), Kilbourne, J. (Writer). (2010). *Killing us softly 4: Advertising's image of women* [Film]. Media Education Foundation.

22. Aviad, M. (Director). (2018). *Working woman* [Film]. Zeitgeist Films.

23. Avin, S. (Writer & Director). (2018). *#That's harassment* [Film]. https://www .facebook.com/pg/thatsharassment/videos/?ref=page_internal

24. Truong, P. (2018). David Schwimmer launches new campaign to fight sexual harassment. *Cosmopolitan.* https://www.cosmopolitan.com/entertainment/ celebs/a9215169/david-schwimmer-interview-sigal-avin-harassment/

25. LaPook, J. (2017, February 9). Former Team USA gymnasts describe doctor's alleged sexual abuse. *60 minutes.* CBSNews. https://www.cbsnews.com/news/ former-team-usa-gymnasts-describe-doctors-alleged-sexual-abuse/

26. Ibid.

27. Ibid.

28. Ibid.

29. Ibid.

30. Ibid.

31. Ibid.

32. Heffernan, V. (2018, January 24). Dr. Larry Nassar was not a doctor. *The Los Angeles Times.* https://www.latimes.com/opinion/op-ed/la-oe-heffernan-larry -nassar-20180126-story.html

33. Andrews, T. M. (2017, November 22). Olympian Gabby Douglas says she, too, was sexually abused by gymnastics team doctor. *The Washington Post.* https:// www.washingtonpost.com/news/morning-mix/wp/2017/11/21/olympian-gabby -douglas-says-she-too-was-sexually-abused-by-gymnastics-team-doctor/

34. Yoffe, E. (2018, June 26). Understanding Harvey: Power alone does not explain their abuses. *HuffPost Highline.* https://highline.huffingtonpost.com/articles/ en/harvey-weinstein-psychology-sexual-predators/

35. Ryzik, M., Buckley, C., & Kantor, J. (2017, November 9). Louis C. K. is accused by 5 women of sexual misconduct. *The New York Times.* https://www.nytimes .com/2017/11/09/arts/television/louis-ck-sexual-misconduct.html?smid=tw -nytimesarts&smtyp=cur

36. Meyers, S. (Writer & Producer). (2017, November 21). *Late night with Seth Meyers.* "Trump backs Roy Moore; Charlie Rose fired for sexual harassment: A closer look." https://www.youtube.com/watch?v=mewW_pRSgEc&ab_channel =LateNightwithSethMeyers

37. Yoffe, E. (2018, June 26). Understanding Harvey: Power alone does not explain their abuses. *HuffPost Highline.* https://highline.huffingtonpost.com/articles/ en/harvey-weinstein-psychology-sexual-predators/

38. CNN Staff. (2018, January 24). Read prosecutor's statement at Larry Nassar sentencing. https://edition.cnn.com/2018/01/24/us/nassar-sentencing-prosecutor -full-statement/index.html

Chapter 4

1. Mayer, J. (2019, July 29). The case of Al Franken. *The New Yorker.* https://www .newyorker.com/magazine/2019/07/29/the-case-of-al-franken

2. Oluo, I. (2017, December 7). Al Franken harassed women and should resign. But it's OK to admit his loss hurts. https://www.nbcnews.com/think/opinion/al -franken-abused-women-should-resign-it-s-ok-admit-ncna827556

3. Wright, J. (2017, November 30). The backlash to believing women has begun. *Harper's Bazaar.* https://www.harpersbazaar.com/culture/politics/a13091573/ backlash-metoo-movement/

4. Anderson, J. (2018). The #MeToo movement gets a movie about everyday harassment with Israel's 'Working Woman'. Retrieved from https://www.latimes.com/ entertainment/movies/la-et-mn-working-woman-20190412-story.html

5. Renwick, F. (2017, September 5). Why can't men stop sending dick pics? *Esquire.* https://www.esquire.com/uk/life/sex-relationships/a14152/why-cant-men-stop -sending-dic-pics/

6. Ibid.

7. Payne, A. (Director). (2002). *About Schmidt* [Film]. New Line Cinema.

8. Renwick, F. (2017, September 5). Why can't men stop sending dick pics? *Esquire.* https://www.esquire.com/uk/life/sex-relationships/a14152/why-cant-men-stop -sending-dic-pics/

9. Moran, G. (2019). The five cases of sexual harassment the district attorney didn't want you to see. *San Diego Union Tribune.* https://www.sandiegouniontribune .com/news/courts/story/2019-10-23/the-five-cases-of-sexual-harassment-the -district-attorney-didnt-want-you-to-see

10. Fisher, H., & Garcia, J. R. (2016). *Singles in America.* https://www.singles inamerica.com/2017/#singlesesex

11. Lehmiller, J. (2017). Why so many guys send unsolicited photos of their manhood to women. https://www.lehmiller.com/blog/2017/2/17/why-so-many-guys -send-unsolicited-photos-of-their-manhood-to-women

12. Glass, I. (Host). (2016, December 2). Once more, with feeling No. 603) [Podcast episode]. In *This American life*. Chicago Public Media. WEBZ Chicago. https://www.thisamericanlife.org/603/once-more-with-feeling

13. Quinn, K. (2015). Here's what happens when you send 40 unsuspecting guys a preemptive v-pic. https://www.thrillist.com/sex-dating/los-angeles/we-sent-a-preemptive-v-pic-before-dudes-could-send-dick-pics-heres-what-happened

14. Renwick, F. (2017, September 5). Why can't men stop sending dick pics? *Esquire*. https://www.esquire.com/uk/life/sex-relationships/a14152/why-cant-men-stop-sending-dic-pics/

15. Lehmiller, J. (2017). Why so many guys send unsolicited photos of their manhood to women. https://www.lehmiller.com/blog/2017/2/17/why-so-many-guys-send-unsolicited-photos-of-their-manhood-to-women

16. Mayer, J. (2019). The case of Al Franken. *The New Yorker*. https://www.newyorker.com/magazine/2019/07/29/the-case-of-al-franken

17. Ibid.

18. Jenkins, A. (2017). Woman says George H. W. Bush groped her when she was 16: 'I was a child.' *Time*. https://time.com/5019182/george-hw-bush-groping-allegation/

19. Jackson, D. (2017). President George H. W. Bush apologizes for sometimes patting women on the rear. *USA Today*. https://www.usatoday.com/story/news/politics/onpolitics/2017/10/25/president-george-h-w-bush-apologizes-actress-who-alleged-improper-touching/797846001/

20. Lanktree, G. (2017). George H. W. Bush 'Patted women's rears in good-natured manner,' office says. *Newsweek*. https://www.newsweek.com/george-hw-bush-patted-multiple-womens-rears-good-natured-manner-693457

21. Moran, G. (2019). The five cases of sexual harassment the district attorney didn't want you to see. *San Diego Union Tribune*. https://www.sandiegouniontribune.com/news/courts/story/2019-10-23/the-five-cases-of-sexual-harassment-the-district-attorney-didnt-want-you-to-see

22. Aviad, M. (Director). (2018). *Working woman* [Film]. Zeitgeist Films.

23. Avin, S. (Writer & Director). (2018). *#That's harassment* [Film]. https://www.facebook.com/pg/thatsharassment/videos/?ref=page_internal

24. Miller, C. C. (2018, January 26). David Schwimmer made six short films about sexual harassment. We annotate one of them. *The New York Times*. https://www.nytimes.com/interactive/2018/01/26/upshot/sexual-harassment-script-react.html

25. Way, K. (2018, January 13). I went on a date with Aziz Ansari. It turned into the worst night of my life. https://babe.net/2018/01/13/aziz-ansari-28355

26. Shih, C. (2018, January 18). How 18 women responded to 'Grace' and the Aziz Ansari allegation. https://www.thelily.com/how-18-women-responded-to-grace-and-the-aziz-ansari-allegation/

Chapter 5

1. Crenshaw, K. (1996). Mapping the margins: Intersectionality, Identity politics, and violence against women of color. In D. Weisberg (Ed.), *Applications of feminist legal theory* (pp. 363–377). Temple University Press; Brown, T. (2003). Critical race theory speaks to the sociology of mental health: Mental health problems produced by racial stratification. *Journal of Health and Social Behavior, 44*(3), 292–301.

2. Gómez, J. M., Gobin, R. L. (2020). Black women and girls & #MeToo: Rape, cultural betrayal, & healing. *Sex Roles 82*, 1–12.

3. Phipps, Alison. (2019). "Every woman knows a Weinstein": Political whiteness and white woundedness in #MeToo and public feminisms around sexual violence. *Feminist Formations, 31*(2), 1–25; Gómez, J. M., Gobin, R. L. (2020). Black women and girls & #MeToo: Rape, cultural betrayal, & healing. *Sex Roles, 82,* 1–12.

4. Phipps, Alison. (2019). "Every woman knows a Weinstein": Political whiteness and white woundedness in #MeToo and public feminisms around sexual violence. *Feminist Formations, 31*(2), 1–25.

5. Miller, J., & Garran, A. M. (2017). Background: Social identity and situating ourselves. In *Racism in the United States: Implications for the helping professions* (Chapter 1).. Springer Publishing.

6. Crenshaw, K. (1996). Mapping the margins: Intersectionality, identity politics, and violence against women of color. In D. Weisberg (Ed.), Applications of feminist legal Theory (pp. 363–377). Temple University Press.; Miller, J., & Garran, A. M. (2017). A brief history of racism in the U.S. and implications for helping professions. In *Racism in the United States: Implications for the helping professions* (Chapter 3, pp. 39–57). Springer Publishing.

7. Miller, J., & Garran, A. M. (2017). Background: Social identity and situating ourselves. In *Racism in the United States: Implications for the helping professions* (Chapter 1). Springer Publishing.

8. Miller, J., & Garran, A. M. (2017). A brief history of racism in the U.S. and implications for helping professions. In *Racism in the United States: Implications for the helping professions* (Chapter 3, pp. 39–57). Springer Publishing; DeGruy, J. (2005). Whole to three-fifths: Dehumanization. In *Post traumatic slave syndrome: America's legacy of enduring injury and healing,* pp. 46-66. Uptone Press.

9. Hill Collins, P., & Bilge, S. (2016). Intersectionality. (Key concepts). Wiley.

10. Suárez, Z., Newman, P., & Glover Reed, B. (2008). Critical consciousness and cross-cultural/intersectional social work practice: A case analysis. *Families in Society: Journal of Contemporary Social Services, 89*(3), 407–417.

11. Hardy, K. V., & Laszloffy, T. A. (1994). Deconstructing race in family therapy. *Journal of Feminist Family Therapy, 5*(3/4), 5–33.

12. Ibid.
13. Suárez, Z., Newman, P., & Glover Reed, B. (2008). Critical consciousness and cross-cultural/intersectional social work practice: A case analysis. *Families in Society: Journal of Contemporary Social Services, 89*(3), 407–417; Miller, J., & Garran, A. M. (2017). Background: Social identity and situating ourselves. In *Racism in the United States: Implications for the helping professions* (Chapter 1). Springer Publishing.
14. Miller, J., & Garran, A. M. (2017b). A brief history of racism in the U.S. and Implications for helping professions. In *Racism in the United States: Implications for the helping professions* (Chapter 3, pp. 39–57). Springer Publishing.
15. Smith, S. G., Zhang, X., Basile, K. C., Merrick, M. T., Wang, J., Kresnow, M., & Chen, J. (2018). The National Intimate Partner and Sexual Violence Survey (NISVS): 2015 Data Brief—Updated release. Atlanta, GA: National Center for Injury Prevention and Control, Centers for Disease Control and Prevention.
16. Bachman, R., Zaykowski, H., Lanier, C., Poteyeva, M., & Kallmyer, R. (2010). Estimating the magnitude of rape and sexual assault against American Indian and Alaska Native (AIAN) women. *Australian & New Zealand Journal of Criminology, 43*(2), 199–222.
17. Walters, M. L., Chen J., & Breiding, M. J. (2013). The National Intimate Partner and Sexual Violence Survey (NISVS): 2010 Findings on victimization by sexual orientation. Atlanta, GA: National Center for Injury Prevention and Control, Centers for Disease Control and Prevention.
18. Briere, J., & Scott, C. (2015). Principles of trauma therapy: A guide to symptoms, evaluation, and treatment (*DSM-5* update), 2nd edition. Sage Publications.
19. Crenshaw, K. (1996). Mapping the margins: Intersectionality, identity politics, and violence against women of color. In D. Weisberg (Ed.), *Applications of feminist legal theory* (pp. 363–377). Temple University Press.
20. West, C., & Johnson, K. (2013, March). Sexual violence in the lives of African American Women. Harrisburg, PA: VAWnet, a project of the National Resource Center on Domestic Violence.
21. Basile, K. C., Breiding, M. J., & Smith, S. G. (2016). Disability and risk of recent sexual violence in the United States. *American Journal of Public Health, 106*(5), 928–933.
22. Harvey, V., & Housel, T. (2014). *Health care disparities and the LGBT population.* Lexington Books.
23. Wesley, Y. (2009). *Black women's health: Challenges and opportunities.* Nova Science.
24. Brown, T. (2003). Critical race theory speaks to the sociology of mental health: Mental health problems produced by racial stratification. *Journal of Health and Social Behavior, 44*(3), 292–301.
25. National Association of Social Workers. (2015). Standards and indicators for

cultural competence in social work practice https://www.socialworkers.org/
LinkClick.aspx?fileticket=7dVckZAYUmk%3D&portalid=0

Sue, D. W., Capodilupo, C. M., Torino, G. C., Jennifer M. Bucceri, Holder, A. M. B., Nadal, K. L., & Esquilin, M. (2007). Racial microaggressions in everyday life: Implications for clinical practice. *American Psychologist, 62*(4), 271–286; Pedersen, P. B. (1988). *A handbook of developing multicultural awareness.* American Association for Counseling and Development.

Chapter 6

1. Hare, R. (1993). *Without conscience.* Pocket Books.
2. American Psychiatric Association. (2013). *Diagnostic and statistical manual of mental disorders* (5th ed., p. 762). American Psychiatric Association.
3. Ibid.
4. Wendy Behary, from Dockett, L. (2018). Silent and confused: Opening conversations with men in the wake of #MeToo. *Psychotherapy Networker, May/June.* https://www.psychotherapynetworker.org/magazine/article/1159/silent-and -confused
5. Dutton, D. (1998). *The treatment of assaultiveness.* New York: Basic Books.
6. Levant, R. F., Good, G. E., Cook, S. W., O'Neil, J. M., Smalley, K. B., Owen, K., & Richmond, K. (2006). The Normative Male Alexithymia Scale: Measurement of a gender-linked syndrome. *Psychology of Men & Masculinity, 7*(4), 212–224. Retrieved from Levant@uakron.edu; http://search.ebscohost.com/login.aspx?di rect=true&db=psyh&AN=2006-20658-004&site=ehost-live
7. Real, T. (1997). *I don't want to talk about it: Overcoming the secret legacy of male depression* Scribner.
8. Erickson, M. H., & Rossi, E. L. (1979). *Hypnotherapy: An exploratory casebook.* Irvington Publishers; Gilligan, S. G. (1984). *Therapeutic trances: The cooperation principle in Ericksonian hypnotherapy.* Brunner/Mazel Publishers.
9. Miller, W. R., & Rollnick, S. (1991). *Motivational interviewing: Preparing people to change addictive behavior.* Guilford Press.
10. Real, T. (2019, July/August). Working with difficult men: Where's the leverage for change? *Psychotherapy Networker.*https://psychotherapynetworker .org/magazine/article/2385/working-with-difficult-men?utm_source=Silver pop&utm_medium=email&utm_campaign=072019_pn_i_rt_WIR_noon throttled
11. Yoffe, E. (2018). Understanding Harvey: Power alone does not explain their abuses. *HuffPost Highline.* https://highline.huffingtonpost.com/articles/en/ harvey-weinstein-psychology-sexual-predators/
12. Linehan, M. (1993). *Skills training manual for treating borderline personality disorder.* Guilford Press.

13. *APA Guidelines for Psychological Practice with Boys and Men.* (2018). https://www.apa.org/about/policy/boys-men-practice-guidelines.pdf

14. Philpot, C. L., Brooks, G. R., Lusterman, D.-D., & Nutt, R. L. (1997). *Bridging separate gender worlds: Why men and women clash and how therapists can bring them together.* Washington, DC, US: American Psychological Association.

15. Avin, S. (Writer & Director). (2018). *#That's harassment* [Film]. https://www.facebook.com/pg/thatsharassment/videos/?ref=page_internal

16. Harvey Weinstein's full statement following sexual harassment allegations. (2017, October 5). https://money.cnn.com/2017/10/05/media/harvey-weinsteins-full-statement/index.html

17. Miller, C. C. (2018). David Schwimmer made six short films about sexual harassment. we annotate one of them. *The New York Times.* https://www.nytimes.com/interactive/2018/01/26/upshot/sexual-harassment-script-react.html

18. Ickes, W. (2003). *Everyday mind reading: Understanding what other people think and feel.* Amherst, NY: Prometheus Books.

19. Ira Glass. (Host). (2016, December 2). Once more, with feeling (No. 603) [Audio podcast episode]. In *This American life.* Chicago Public Media. WEBZ Chicago. https://www.thisamericanlife.org/603/once-more-with-feeling

20. Mayer, J. (2019). The case of Al Franken. *The New Yorker.* https://www.newyorker.com/magazine/2019/07/29/the-case-of-al-franken

21. Harvey Weinstein's full statement following sexual harassment allegations. (2017, October 5). https://money.cnn.com/2017/10/05/media/harvey-weinsteins-full-statement/index.html

22. Swift, A. (2017, November 20). Charlie Rose suspended by PBS, CBS after 8 women accuse him of sexual harassment—Read his apology. https://tvline.com/2017/11/20/charlie-rose-sexual-harassment-allegations-apology-statement/

23. CNN. (2017, November 17). Read Al Franken's apology following accusation of groping and kissing without consent. https://www.cnn.com/2017/11/16/politics/al-franken-apology/index.html

24. Rau, S. (2018, January 11). He harassed her. She called him out. He broadcast his apology. She accepted. *The Washington Post.* https://www.washingtonpost.com/news/arts-and-entertainment/wp/2018/01/11/he-harassed-her-she-called-him-out-he-broadcast-his-apology-she-accepted/

25. Klein, A. (2017, November 21). The recent tide of apologies by famous men has been 'awful.' Here's what the men should have said. The Washington Post. https://www.washingtonpost.com/news/inspired-life/wp/2017/11/21/the-recent-tide-of-apologies-by-famous-men-have-been-awful-heres-what-the-men-should-have-said/

26. Wexler, D. B. (2020). *The STOP domestic violence program* (4th ed., revised and updated). W. W. Norton.

27. Hazelden Betty Ford Foundation. (2020). Making amends in addiction recovery. https://www.hazeldenbettyford.org/articles/making-amends-addiction-recovery

Chapter 7

1. Truong, P. (2018). David Schwimmer launches new campaign to fight sexual harassment. https://www.cosmopolitan.com/entertainment/celebs/a9215169/david-schwimmer-interview-sigal-avin-harassment/
2. Wittmeyer, A. P. Q. (2018, October 18). Eight stories of men's regret. *The New York Times*. https://www.nytimes.com/interactive/2018/10/18/opinion/men-metoo-high-school.html

Chapter 8

1. https://dictionary.cambridge.org/us/dictionary/english/empowerment
2. Rudall, N. (translator) (1991). *Aristophanes: Lysistrata*. Elephant Books.
3. Black, M. C., Basile, K. C., Breiding, M. J., Smith, S. G., Walters, M. L., Merrick, M. T., Chen, J., & Stevens, M. R. (2011). The National Intimate Partner and Sexual Violence Survey: (NISVS) Retrieved from https://www.cdc.gov/violenceprevention/datasources/nisvs.html
4. Bedard-Gilligan, M., Jaeger, J., Echiverri-Cohen, A., & Zoellner, L. A. (2012). Individual differences in trauma disclosure. *Journal of Behavior Therapy and Experimental Psychiatry, 43*(2), 716–723
5. Weathers, F. W., Litz, B. T., Keane, T. M., Palmieri, P. A., Marx, B. P., & Schnurr, P. P. (2013). PTSD CheckList: Civilian version (PCL-C). https://www.mirecc.va.gov/docs/visn6/3_PTSD_CheckList_and_Scoring.pdf
6. International Society for Traumatic Stress Studies. (n.d.). https://istss.org/home
7. Kubany, E. S., Hill, E. E., Owens, J. A., McCaig, M. A., Iannce-Spencer, C., Craig, M. A., Tremayne, K. J., & Williams, P. L. (2004). Cognitive trauma therapy for battered women with PTSD (CTT-BW). *Journal of Consulting and Clinical Psychology, 72*(1), 3–18.
8. Johnson, M. (2011). Gender and types of intimate partner violence: A response to an anti-feminist literature review. *Aggression and Violent Behavior, 16,* 289–296.
9. Sullivan, C. M., & Bybee, D. I. (1999). Reducing violence using community-based advocacy for women with abusive partners. *Journal of Consulting and Clinical Psychology, 67*(1), 43–53.
   Reed, G. L., & Enright, R. D. (2006). The effects of forgiveness therapy on depression, anxiety, and posttraumatic stress for women after spousal emotional abuse. *Journal of Consulting and Clinical Psychology, 74*(5), 920–929; Kaslow, N. J., Leiner, A. S., Reviere, S., Emily, J., Bethea, K., Bhaju, J., Rhodes, M., Gantt, M., Senter, H., Thompson, M. (2010). Suicidal, abused African American women's response to a culturally informed intervention. *Journal of Consulting and*

Clinical Psychology, 78(4), 449–458; Constantino, R., Kim, Y., & Crane, P. A. (2005). Effects of a social support intervention on health outcomes in residents of a domestic violence shelter: A pilot study. *Issues in Mental Health Nursing, 26*(6), 575–590. https://doi.10.1080/01612840590959416

10. International Society for Traumatic Stress Studies. (n.d.). https://istss.org/home
11. Philpot, C., Brooks, G., Lusterman, D., Nutt, R. (1997). *Bridging separate gender worlds: Why women and men clash and how therapists can bring them together.* APA Publications.
12. http://metoomvmt.org
13. Pino, A., & Clark. A. (2016), *We believe you: Survivors of campus sexual assault speak out.* Holt Paperbacks.
14. Paterson, R. J. (2000). *The assertiveness workbook: How to express your ideas and stand up for yourself at work and in relationships.* New Harbinger Publications. Murphy, J. (2020). A*ssertiveness: How to stand up for yourself and still win the respect of others.* Delmar Publishing.
15. Prochaska, J. O., & DiClemente, C. C. (1992). The transtheoretical approach. In J. C. Norcross & M. R. Goldfried (Eds.), *Handbook of psychotherapy integration* (pp. 300–334). Basic Books.

Chapter 9

1. Miller, C. (2019). *Know my name: A memoir.* Viking Press.
2. Krebs, C. P., Lindquist, C. H., Warner, T. D., Fisher, B. S., & Martin, S. L.(2007). *The Campus Sexual Assault (CSA) Study.* National Institute of Justice. https://www.ncjrs.gov/pdffiles1/nij/grants/221153.pdf
3. Cantor, D., Fisher, B., Chibnall, S., Harps, S., Townsend, R., Thomas, G., Lee, H., Kranz, V., Herbison, R., & Madden, K. (2020). report on the aau campus climate survey on sexual assault and misconduct. https://www.aau.edu/sites/default/files/AAU-Files/Key-Issues/Campus-Safety/Revised%20Aggregate%20report%20%20and%20appendices%201-7_(01-16-2020_FINAL).pdf)
4. Ibid.
5. American Academy of Child and Adolescent Psychology (September 2016, Issue 95). https://www.aacap.org
6. It's Fall Semester: A time for parents to discuss the risks of college drinking. https://collegedrinkingprevention.gov
7. Rich, B. (2020, March 23). Sexual assault on campus: Awareness and prevention. https://thebestschools.org.
8. Corey, G. (2012). *Theory and practice of counseling and psychotherapy* (9th ed). Brooks/Cole.
9. Winerman, L. (2018 October). Making campuses safer. *Monitor on Psychology,* p. 58–59.
10. Ibid., 59

11. Ibid., 59
12. Rape, Abuse & Incest National Network. https://www.rainn.org)
13. Santos-Longhurst, A. (2019). Your guide to sexual consent. https://www.health
    line.com/health/guide-to-consent
14. Krebs, C. P., Lindquist, C. H., Warner, T. D., Fisher, B. S., & Martin, S. L. (2007).
    The Campus Sexual Assault (CSA) Study. National Institute of Justice https://
    www.ncjrs.gov/pdffiles1/nij/grants/221153.pdf; Cantor, D., Fisher, B., Chib-
    nall, S., Harps, S., Townsend, R., Thomas, G., Lee, H., Kranz, V., Herbison, R.,
    & Madden, K. (2020). Report on the AAU Campus Climate Survey on Sexual
    Assault and Misconduct. https://www.aau.edu/sites/default/files/AAU-Files/
    Key-Issues/Campus-Safety/Revised%20Aggregate%20report%20%20and%20
    appendices%201-7_(01-16-2020_FINAL).pdf)

Chapter 10

1. Feldman, C., & Lipnic, V. (2016) EEOC Select Task Force on the Study of Harassment in the Workplace, Executive summary, Item 2: Workplace harassment too
   often goes unreported. http://www.eeoc.gov/select-task-force-study-harassment
   -workplace
2. Feldman, C., & Lipnic, V. (2016) EEOC Select Task Force on the Study of Harassment in the Workplace, Executive summary. http://www.eeoc.gov/select-task
   -force-study-harassment-workplace
3. Gibson, C., & Guskin, E. (2017, October 16). A majority of Americans now say that
   sexual harassment is a 'serious problem.' https://www.washingtonpost.com/
   lifestyle/style/a-majority-of-americans-now-say-that-sexual-harassment-is-a
   -serious-problem/2017/10/16/707e6b74-b290-11e7-9e58-e6288544af98_story
   .html
4. U.S. Equal Employment Opportunity Commission. *Sexual harassment.* Retrieved
   from http://eeoc.gov/publications/factors-about-sexual-harassment
5. Hewlett, S. A. (2020). *#MeToo in the corporate world: Power, privilege, and the
   path forward.* HarperCollins.
6. Avin, S. (Writer & Director). (2018). *#That's harassment* [Film]. https://www
   .facebook.com/pg/thatsharassment/videos/?ref=page_internal
7. Orner, E. (Writer). (2019). Bikram: Yogi, Guru, Predator. In Netflix (Producer).
8. Hewlett, S. A. (2020). *#MeToo in the corporate world: Power, privilege, and the
   path forward.* HarperCollins.
9. U.S. Equal Employment Opportunity Commission. *Sexual harassment.*
   Retrieved from http://eeoc.gov/publications/factors-about-sexual-harassment
10. Feldblum, C., & Lipnic, V. (2016) EEOC Select Task Force on the Study of Harass-
    ment in the Workplace. Executive summary, item 2: Workplace harassment
    remains a persistent problem. http://www.eeoc.gov/select-task-force-study
    -harassment-workplace

11. American Council of Education (2017, June 20). *2017 overview: Women presidents*. https://www.aceacps.org/women-presidents/
12. Connelly, C. (2019) The number of women running Fortune 500 companies is at a record high. https://www.cnbc/2019/05/16/the-number-of-women-running -fortune-500-companies-is-at-a-record-high.html

Chapter 11

1. Kantor, J., & Twohey, M. (2019). *She said: Breaking the sexual harassment story that helped ignite a movement*. Penguin Press; Brown, E. (2018, September 16). California professor, writer of confidential Brett Kavanaugh letter, speaks out about her allegation of sexual assault. *The Washington Post*. https://www.washingtonpost.com/investigations/california-professor-writer-of -confidential-brett-kavanaugh-letter-speaks-out-about-her-allegation-of-sexual -assault/2018/09/16/46982194-b846-11e8-94eb-3bd52dfe917b_story.html
2. Holtzworth-Munroe, A., & Hutchinson, G. (1993). Attributing negative intent to wife behavior: The attributions of maritally violent versus nonviolent men. *Journal of Abnormal Psychology, 102*(2), 206–211.
3. Tamulevich, M. (2020). Personal communication.
4. Foa, E. (2009). *Effective treatments for PTSD* (2nd ed.). Guilford Press.
5. Sautter, F. J., Glynn, S. M., Cretu, J. B., Senturk, D., & Vaught, A. S. (2015). Efficacy of structured approach therapy in reducing PTSD in returning veterans: A randomized clinical trial. *Psychological Services, 12*(3), 199–212; Sautter, F. J., Glynn, S. M., Becker-Cretu, J. J., Senturk, D, Armelie, A. P., & Wielt, D. B. (2016). Structured approach therapy for combat-related PTSD in returning U.S. veterans: Complementary mediation by changes in emotion functioning. *Journal of Traumatic Stress, 29*(4), 384–387; Perlick, D. A., Sautter, F. J., Becker-Cretu, J. J., Schultz, D., Grier, S. C., Libin, A. V., Schladen, M. M., & Glynn, S. M. (2017). The incorporation of emotion-regulation skills into couple- and family-based treatments for post-traumatic stress disorder. *Military Medical Research, 4*(21). https://doi.10.1186/s40779-017-0130-9
6. Balderrama-Durbin, C., Snyder, D. K., Cigrang, J., Talcott, G. W., Tatum, J., Baker, M., Cassidy, D., Sonnek, S., Heyman, R. E., & Smith Slep, A. M. (2013). Combat disclosure in intimate relationships: Mediating the impact of partner support on posttraumatic stress. *Journal of Family Psychology, 7*(4), 560.
7. Monk, J., & Nelson, G. (2013). Military couples' trauma disclosure: Moderating between trauma symptoms and relationship quality. *Psychological Trauma, 6*(5), 537–545.

Chapter 12

1. Fabiano, P., Perkins, H. W., Berkowitz, A. D., Linkenbach, J., & Stark, C. (2003). Engaging men as social justice allies in ending violence against women: Evidence

for a Social Norms Approach. *Journal of American College Health, 52*(3), 105–112.

2. Fabiano, P., Perkins, H. W., Berkowitz, A. D., Linkenbach, J., & Stark, C. (2003). Engaging men as social justice allies in ending violence against women: Evidence for a Social Norms Approach. *Journal of American College Health, 52*(3), 105–112.

   Berkowitz, A. (2013). A grassroots' guide to fostering healthy norms to reduce violence in our communities: Social Norms toolkit. http://socialnorms.org/wp-content/uploads/2017/03/Social_Norms_Violence_Prevention_Toolkit.pdf3

   Fabiano, P., Perkins, H. W., Berkowitz, A. D., Linkenbach, J., & Stark, C. (2003). Engaging men as social justice allies in ending violence against women: Evidence for a Social Norms Approach. *Journal of American College Health, 52*(3), 105–112.

3. Berkowitz, A. (1994). The role of coaches in rape prevention programs for athletes. In A. Parrot, N. Cummings, & T. Marchell (Eds.), *Rape 101: Sexual assault prevention for college athletes* (pp. 61–65). Learning Publications.

   Fabiano, P., Perkins, H. W., Berkowitz, A. D., Linkenbach, J., & Stark, C. (2003). engaging men as social justice allies in ending violence against women: Evidence for a Social Norms Approach. *Journal of American College Health, 52*(3), 105–112.

4. Wexler, D. B. (2020). *The STOP domestic violence program* (4th ed., revised and updated). W. W. Norton.

5. Sweet, H. (1995). *Perceptions of undergraduate male experiences in heterosexual romantic relationships: A sex role norms analysis.*

6. Berkowitz, A. (2009). *Response ability: A complete guide to bystander intervention.* Beck and Company.

   Berkowitz, A. (2011). Using how college men feel about being men and "doing the right thing" to promote men's development. In D. T & J. Laker (Eds.), *Masculinities in Higher Education: Theoretical and Practical Implications* (pp. 161–176). New York: Routledge, Kegan & Paul Publishers.

7. Fabiano, P., Perkins, H. W., Berkowitz, A. D., Linkenbach, J., & Stark, C. (2003). Engaging men as social justice allies in ending violence against women: Evidence for a Social Norms Approach. *Journal of American College Health, 52*(3), 105–112.

   Dempsey, R. C., McAlaney, J., & Bewick, B. M. (2018). A critical appraisal of the Social Norms Approach as an interventional strategy for health-related behavior and attitude change. *Frontiers in Psychology, 9*(2180). https://doi.10.3389/fpsyg.2018.02180.

   Martens, M., Page, J., Mowry, E., Damann, K., Taylor, K., T., & Cimini, M. D. (2006). Differences between actual and perceived student norms: An examination of alcohol use, drug use, and sexual behavior. *Journal of American College Health, 54*(5), 295–300.

8. Leone, R. M., Oyler, K. N., & Parrott, D. J. (2020). Empathy is not enough: The inhibiting effects of rape myth acceptance on the relation between empathy and bystander intervention. *Journal of Interpersonal Violence*, 886260519900328. https://doi.10.1177/0886260519900328

9. Berkowitz, A. (2013). A Grassroots' guide to fostering healthy norms to reduce violence in our communities: Social Norms toolkit. http://socialnorms.org/wp-content/uploads/2017/03/Social_Norms_Violence_Prevention_Toolkit.pdf3

10. Katz, J. (2000). *MVP playbook for male college students*: MVP strategies.

11. Wexler, D. B. (1997). *True consent: Sexual Assault Awareness Project*. Relationship Training Institute.

12. Muehlenhard, C., & Hollabaugh, L. (1988). Do women sometimes say no when they mean yes? The prevalence and correlates of women's token resistance to sex. *Journal of Personality and Social Psychology, 54*(5), 872–879.

13. Plank, L. (2019). *For the love of men: A new vision for mindful masculinity*. St. Martin's Press.

14. Klann, E., & Wong, J. (2019). [Personal communication].

Index

About the Authors

David B. Wexler, Ph.D., is a clinical psychologist and the Executive Director of the non-profit Relationship Training Institute in San Diego. He is the author of many books and articles on men's issues, including *When Good Men Behave Badly*, *The STOP Domestic Violence Program*, and *Men in Therapy*. Dr. Wexler may be contacted through his institute website at rtiprojects.org.

Holly B. Sweet, Ph.D., is a licensed psychologist in private practice in the Boston area. She is the co-founder of the Cambridge Center for Gender Relations, a consulting company which offers experiential workshops on ways to increase gender empathy in both personal and professional settings. Dr. Sweet is editor of *Gender in the Therapy Hour* and the first female president of the American Psychological Association's Division of the Psychological Study of Men and Masculinities.